Sunset

COMPLETE
HOME
PLUMBING

SUNSET BOOKS ❦ MENLO PARK, CALIFORNIA

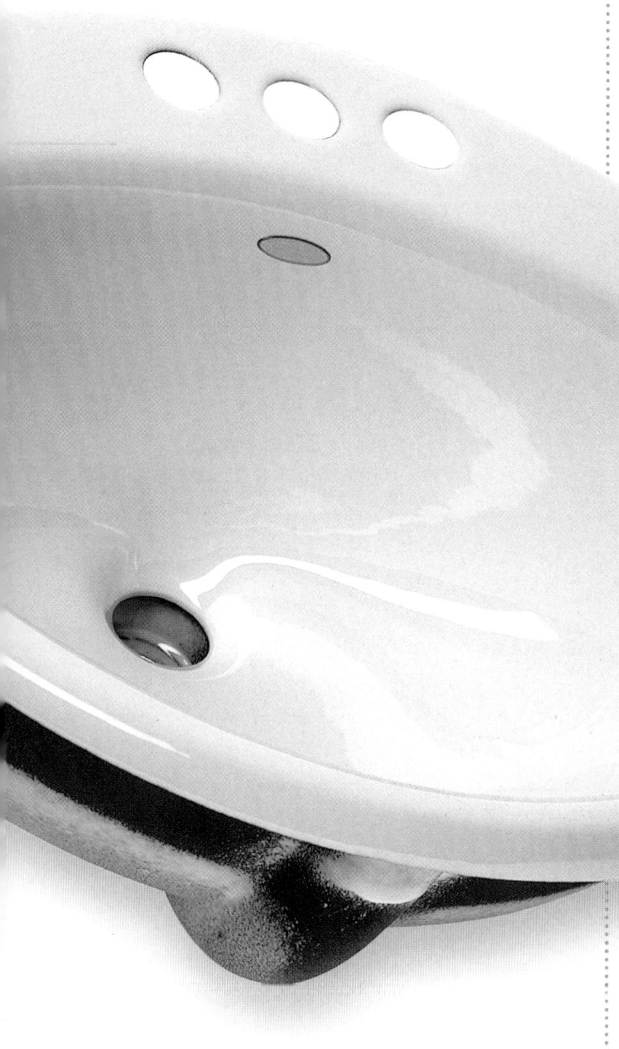

SUNSET BOOKS
Vice President, General Manager: Richard A. Smeby
Vice President, Editorial Director: Bob Doyle
Production Director: Lory Day
Director of Operations: Rosann Sutherland
Art Director: Vasken Guiragossian

Staff for this book:
Book Editor: Scott Atkinson

Managing Editor: Sally Lauten
Sunset Books Senior Editor: Marianne Lipanovich
Art Director: Elisa Tanaka
Photographer: Mark Rutherford
Illustrator: Anthony Davis
Photo Stylist: JoAnn Masaoka Van Atta
Technical Consultants: Donald E. Johnson, Chuck Crawford
Copy Editor: Julie Harris
Indexer: Barbara J. Braasch

Computer Production: Linda Bouchard, Suzanne Normand Eyre
Digital Prepress Production: Rutherford Studios/Norman Gilbert
Production Coordinator: Patricia S. Williams
Special Contributor: Bridget Biscotti Bradley

Cover: Design by Vasken Guiragossian. Photography by Mark Rutherford. Photo direction by JoAnn Masaoka Van Atta.

10 9 8 7 6 5 4 3
First printing March 2001

Library of Congress Catalog Card Number: 00-109157.
ISBN 0-376-01101-7.

Printed in the United States.
For additional copies of COMPLETE HOME PLUMBING or any other Sunset book, call 1-800-526-5111 or visit our web site at www.sunsetbooks.com.

CONTENTS

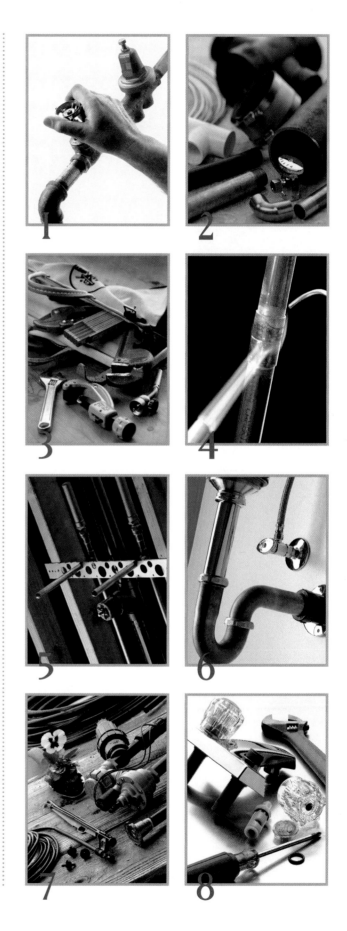

1

2

3

4

5

6

7

8

GO WITH THE FLOW

There's something so simple, yet maddening, about plumbing. You turn a faucet handle and water runs; you twist it again and the water stops. But just look at a leaky faucet with the intent to fix it and it seemingly explodes in a torrent of water. And it's always on a Saturday night, when the stores are closed.

So how do you gain the upper hand with drains, tubs, and faucets? And what if you're even threatening to install that new dishwasher or claw-foot tub yourself? Relax, we'll show you how.

HOW THIS BOOK WORKS

Complete Home Plumbing begins at the beginning—with an easy-to-follow introduction to basic plumbing concepts, including a peek at the pipe systems that run behind your walls and below your floors. When you're done with this section, you'll know where to find these pipes in your own home. The next two chapters present the specialized worlds of plumbing materials and tools, respectively. Chapter Four is a photo-filled, step-by-step primer on basic pipefitting techniques.

Got your bearings? The next two chapters head for the heart of plumbing's how-to jobs. Chapter Five, "Rough Plumbing," covers the basics you'll need to know before extending pipes to a new location. When it's time to hook up that dishwasher or claw-foot, turn directly to Chapter Six, "Finish Work." Chapter Seven visits the sunnier subjects of outdoor hose bibbs, sprinkler systems, drip components, and more.

The eighth and final chapter forms an easy access reference guide to troubleshooting and repairs. It's located at the back of the book to help you quickly find what you need—whether it's a solution for clogged or broken pipes or a fix for a faulty sprinkler. You'll even learn how to finally tame that leaky faucet. Unsure of one or more terms we're using? See the glossary on pages 190–191.

CHECK THE CODES

Faulty plumbing can cause serious health and safety hazards. Before you begin any work, be sure your plumbing plans conform to local codes and ordinances. Almost any improvement that adds pipe to the system will require approval from local building department officials before you start and inspection of the work before you close up the walls and floor.

There are six regional plumbing codes in print, but regulations regarding methods, materials, and design differ from one state, county, or municipality to the next. Local codes supersede the regional codes. A nationwide plumbing code is under consideration and could soon be in effect.

SHOULD YOU DO YOUR OWN PLUMBING?

There is a downside to working on your plumbing. It's messy. You may, on occasion, be working in places that remind you of old prison-escape movies. There will probably be spiders.

However, there's nothing inherently tricky about the basics, with the possible exception of soldering, which takes a little practice to master. But it can take a lot of sweat and stamina to pull off a major job—especially if you're extending your existing pipes below floors and through walls. Even some simple under-sink repairs can require an ascetic's patience—and flexibility—to accomplish, if you don't have easy access.

Some codes require that certain work be done only by licensed plumbers. Whether or not that's the case in your town, you should consider professional help if you're at all unsure of your abilities. Need advice? A good inspector or plumbing-supply retailer can walk you through an amazing amount of local knowledge in a short time—they've both been there before.

Two key rules for do-it-yourself plumbers are: 1) Be sure you understand the basic principles and your own home's pipe systems; and 2) learn how and where to turn off the water supply—required in many plumbing jobs—as shown on page 152. Finally, whenever you're doing your own plumbing, be sure to play it safe: read the safety guidelines on page 19 before beginning.

AN INTRODUCTION TO THE BASICS

First things first: Before you embark on any plumbing project, it's important to understand some basic terms and concepts. In this chapter you'll discover the inner workings of your plumbing system. We'll also help you assess your home's existing plumbing capacity and evaluate your options for improvements. Although everything is hidden behind walls and under floors, this network of pipes is not as complicated as you may think.

Play it safe by reading the safety guidelines on page 19. Also be sure to learn how to turn off the water supply—required in many plumbing jobs—as shown on page 152. To decipher your water meter, see page 13.

Further questions? You'll find a detailed glossary of plumbing terms on pages 190–191.

HOW DOES PLUMBING WORK?

If your plumbing experience has been limited to turning a faucet on and off, you may be pleasantly surprised at the simplicity of the system behind that faucet.

Home plumbing is largely a network of pipes and the fittings that connect them, carrying water in and out of the house by two basic forces of nature: pressure and gravity. Water fixtures—sinks, tubs, showers, and toilets—and water-using appliances like dishwashers and washing machines tap into this system, receiving fresh water from one set of pipes and discharging used water through another.

Here's a first look at the basic terms and concepts you'll need to know when evaluating, repairing, or extending your home's plumbing system. You'll find a complete glossary of plumbing terms on pages 190–191.

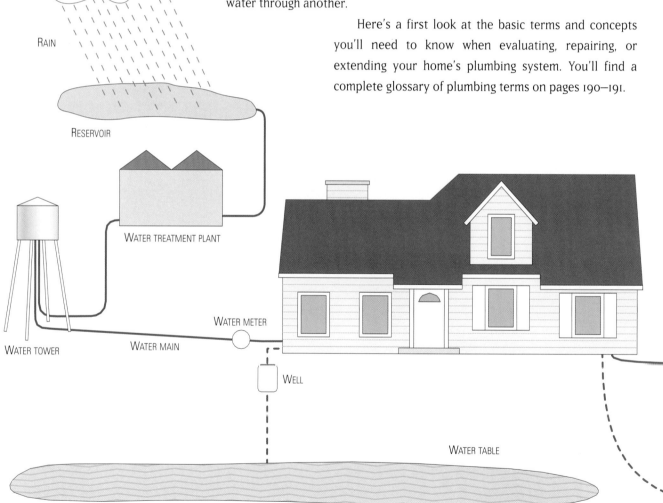

RAIN

RESERVOIR

WATER TREATMENT PLANT

WATER TOWER

WATER MAIN

WATER METER

WELL

WATER TABLE

THE WATER CYCLE

Plumbing is closely tied to both weather and geography. Water that enters your home starts way up in the sky, falling to earth as rain or snow. It flows in a stream or river to a lake or manmade reservoir, or percolates down into the water table—which is like a river or lake, only underground. The water then travels through a treatment plant, pumping station, and/or local water tower to a water main and meter or from a private well that taps into the local water table. Fresh water enters the house via a main cold-water pipe and flows, under pressure, out of whatever faucet has been turned on.

Where does used water go? So-called "gray water" and waste leave the house and head for the city sewer or a private septic system. This sewage moves by gravity—each point in the system is at a lower slope than the one preceding. From the city sewer, water goes to a treatment plant, which removes waste from water, or to a septic tank, which does the same thing. Water evaporates back to the sky, where things start all over again.

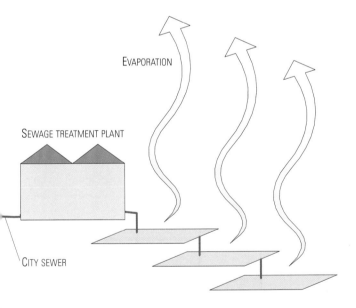

EVAPORATION

SEWAGE TREATMENT PLANT

CITY SEWER

THREE PLUMBING SYSTEMS

Now let's peek inside the house. As detailed on pages 10–15, there are really three separate but interdependent pipe systems: supply, drain-waste, and vent. (Drain-waste and vent systems are interconnected and often lumped together as the "DWV system.")

THE SUPPLY SYSTEM carries pressurized water from a utility main or private well into your house and around to all the water-using fixtures and appliances. What drives this pressure? There's either an initial "fall" (such as from a water tower) or a "push" from a pumping station; displacement does the rest. Because the water is in a closed supply-pipe system, it has nowhere to go but along the same path, pushed along by the water behind it. When you open a faucet or valve, water flows out; when you close it, the flow stops until the next time you open it.

THE DRAIN-WASTE SYSTEM transports gray water and waste out of the house into a city sewer or septic tank outside the house perimeter. Tub and sink drains flow by gravity only; toilets use a combination of pressure (falling water) and gravity. If waste needs to flow uphill at any point, such as from a basement bathroom, an electric pump helps push it up.

THE VENT SYSTEM carries away noxious sewer gases. When a drainpipe is empty, sewer gases rise up the vent pipe and out the roof. P- or S-shaped pipe bends, called traps (see page 14), below each drain remain filled with just enough water to prevent sewer gases from seeping out the drain into your home. The vent system also helps maintain atmospheric pressure in the drain system to help wastes flow downhill. It works on the same principle as the second hole on a gas can.

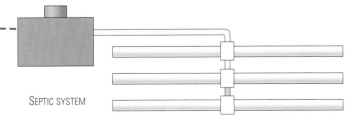

SEPTIC SYSTEM

YOUR PLUMBING SYSTEM

As shown at right and on page 15, your walls and floors hide the supply, drain-waste, and vent systems outlined on page 9. Before you begin any project, large or small, it's crucial to become familiar with these systems.

THE SUPPLY SYSTEM

If you get your water from a water utility, it's probably delivered by an underground water main regulated by a utility shutoff valve and measured by a water meter. These devices are shown at right. (In cold climates, look for valve and meter just inside the house, basement, or crawl space.) If your water is provided by a water utility but is not metered, the utility shutoff valve is likely to be at your property line; if you can't locate it, check with the water utility.

If your water is metered, look for the main shutoff valve—your "on/off switch" for water flow to the home—on the house side of the meter. It may be located on an exterior wall or, in cold climates, on an inside wall. Where water comes from a private well, the shutoff valve is usually located where the water supply line enters the house, or at the wellhead, or both.

Wherever it's located, the shutoff valve should be a full-flow type—ideally a ball valve (see page 33) so it won't restrict water flow into the house.

Once inside the house, the main supply pipe divides into two, one pipe supplying the water heater and the other remaining cold. If the system is equipped with a water softener, that device may be located either on the main supply line before it divides or on the leg supplying the water heater.

For most of their distance, hot and cold supply branches run parallel and horizontally, fastened to floor joists or buried under a concrete slab. Many supply pipes are installed with a slight pitch in their runs so that all

UTILITY SHUTOFF
VALVE

WATER METER

TURE
TOFF
ALVE

RISERS

WATER HEATER

SUPPLY BRANCHES

WATER SOFTENER

MAIN HOUSE
SHUTOFF

hot water
cold water
main supply

Fixture shutoff valve

THE GAS AND HEATING SYSTEM PIPES

If you're planning to do a plumbing job yourself, you must be able to distinguish the water supply and DWV pipes from the pipes that carry gas into your home for household appliances or a water heater. A gas pipe is usually galvanized steel (see page 30) or so-called black pipe; it runs from the gas meter directly to a gas appliance or heating system. A separate shutoff valve for emergencies is required on each gas supply pipe.

Working around heating system pipes demands equal caution. To locate your heating pipes (either hot water or steam), trace them between each heating outlet and the furnace or other heat source.

pipes can be drained through a valve or hose bibb at the lowest point. Vertical branches called risers connect the supply lines to groups of water-using fixtures and appliances. Risers are usually concealed inside walls.

Hot and cold water branches are typically ¾ inch in diameter. Risers that feed fixtures are generally ½-inch galvanized iron, copper, or plastic pipe. For sizing guidelines, see pages 64–65. Local codes and the age of your house will affect the kinds of pipe and fittings you'll find. For a closer look at pipes and fittings, see Chapter Two, "Nuts and Bolts," beginning on page 20.

Many fixtures and water-using appliances have their own shutoff valves, enabling you to work at one place without cutting off the water supply to the entire house. To be prepared for an emergency, everyone in the household should learn how to turn off the water supply, both at individual fixtures and at the main shutoff valve (see page 152).

THE DRAIN-WASTE SYSTEM

Unlike the supply system, which brings in water under pressure, the drain-waste system takes advantage of gravity to channel gray water and solid wastes to the house's main drain. Drainpipes lead away from all fixtures and appliances at a carefully calculated slope. If the slope is too steep, water will run off too fast, leaving waste particles behind; if it's not steep enough, water and waste will drain too slowly and may eventually back up into the fixtures. The normal pitch is ¼ inch for every horizontal foot of pipe.

The workhorse in the drain-waste system is the main soil stack, a vertical section of 3- or 4-inch-diameter pipe that carries waste away from toilets and other individual fixtures and appliances, as well as from branch drains, and connects with the main drain in the basement or crawl space or under the slab. From here, the wastes flow to a city sewer or septic tank.

Older main stacks probably are made of cast iron, with branch drains of galvanized steel. Newer drainpipes typically are plastic. Unlike the hard angles on supply and vent fittings, drain fittings must have smoother, curved intersections that won't restrict the flow of water and wastes. For example, compare the vent T-fitting (facing page) with the

Sanitary T-fitting

Vent T-fitting

HOW TO READ YOUR WATER METER

By learning to read your water meter, you'll easily be able to keep track of water usage in your home, as well as detect any leaks in the system.

Your home's water usage is probably measured by one of three meter types. The six-dial meter (below left) is most common. Five of its six dials (labeled 10, 100, 1000, 10,000, and 100,000 for the number of cubic feet of water they record per revolution) are divided into tenths; the needles of the 10,000 and 100 meters move clockwise, and the other three move counterclockwise. The remaining dial, usually undivided, measures a single cubic foot per revolution. To read the six-dial meter, begin with the 100,000 dial, noting the smaller of the two numbers nearest the needle. Then read the dial labeled 10,000, and so on. This meter reads 628,260 cubic feet.

The five-dial meter (below center) is read in exactly the same way as the six-dial meter, except that single cubic feet are measured by a large needle that sweeps over the entire face of the meter. The meter in this example reads 458,540 cubic feet.

The digital-readout meter (below right) looks like an automobile odometer. This type of meter may also have a small dial that measures a single cubic foot per revolution.

You can monitor the water used by a specific appliance by simply subtracting the "before" reading from the "after" reading of your meter. To track down a possible leak, turn off all the water outlets in the house and note the position of the 1-cubic-foot dial on your meter. After 30 minutes, check the dial. If the needle has moved, you have a leak. To find the leak, see page 184.

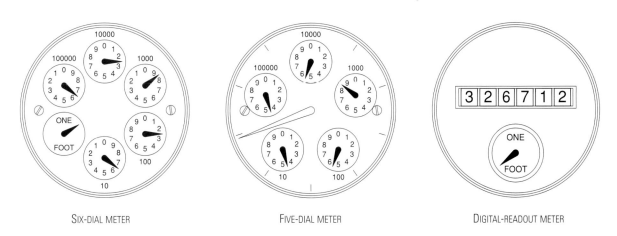

SIX-DIAL METER   FIVE-DIAL METER   DIGITAL-READOUT METER

Cleanout

sloped-shouldered sanitary T-fitting that's required for drain lines. For further details on drainage pipe materials and fittings, see Chapter Two, "Nuts and Bolts," beginning on page 20. You'll find sizing guidelines on pages 66–67.

Because any system will clog occasionally, "cleanouts" are placed in the drainpipes to provide access for removing any obstructions. Ideally, there should be one cleanout in each horizontal section of drainpipe, plus a U-shaped house trap, sometimes located outdoors, for access to sewer or septic tank connections. A cleanout is usually a 45° Y-fitting or 90° T-fitting (shown at left) with a removable cap on one end.

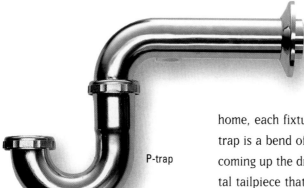

P-trap

THE VENT SYSTEM

To prevent dangerous sewer gases from entering the home, each fixture must have a trap in its drainpipe and must be vented. A trap is a bend of pipe that's filled with water at all times to keep gases from coming up the drains. The two main types are P-traps (which have a horizontal tailpiece that exits the wall) and, in older homes, S-traps (which exit the floor); both types are shown at left. S-traps are no longer allowed by plumbing codes, but stores stock replacement parts. Toilets have built-in traps.

Usually, a house has a main vent stack (which is the upper part of the main soil stack) that runs up to the roof, with additional 1½- to 2-inch-diameter vent pipes connecting to it. In many homes—especially single-story ones—widely separated fixtures make a single main vent stack impractical, so some fixtures or fixture groups have their own, secondary vent stacks, which exit the roof as well.

The four basic venting options—subject to local code—are called wet venting, back venting, individual venting, and indirect venting. For details, see pages 68–69. A fifth type, called loop venting, serves sinks in freestanding kitchen islands.

S-trap
(older homes only)

Like drainpipes, vent pipes in older homes may be cast iron or, for vent sizes up to 2 inches, galvanized steel. Newer vents typically are plastic. For details on vent materials and fittings, see Chapter Two, "Nuts and Bolts," beginning on page 20.

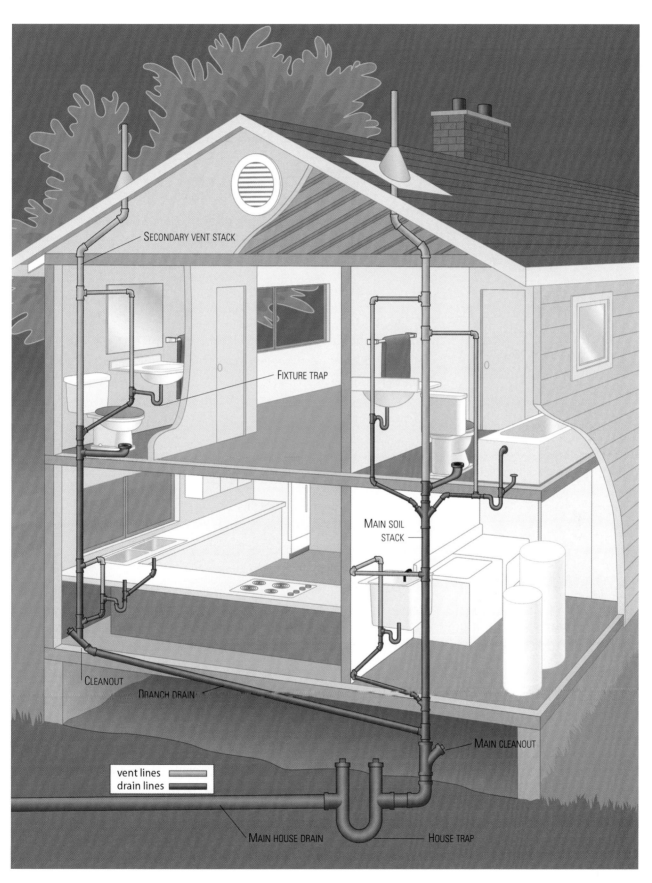

SECONDARY VENT STACK

FIXTURE TRAP

MAIN SOIL STACK

CLEANOUT

BRANCH DRAIN

MAIN CLEANOUT

vent lines
drain lines

MAIN HOUSE DRAIN

HOUSE TRAP

EVALUATING YOUR OPTIONS

When contemplating any plumbing project, start by learning the basics of supply, drain-waste, and vent systems (pages 10–15) and pipefitting (see Chapter Four, "Pipefitting Know-how," beginning on page 44). Then review the information in this section: it outlines the pipe-mapping process, raises issues you'll need to address when planning for new fixtures and water-using appliances, and offers some preliminary tips for installing new pipe runs.

MAKE A MAP

A detailed map of your present plumbing system will give you a clear picture of where it's feasible to tie into supply and drain lines for extensions, and whether the present drains and vents are adequate for your intended use.

Begin your investigation from an unfinished basement or crawl space or, as necessary, from the attic or roof. Some handy mapping tools include a folding rule or tape measure, a flashlight, a clipboard, and some graph paper.

Locate the main soil stack, branch drains, and any secondary vent stacks. Note any accessible cleanouts. Determine the materials and, if possible, the diameters of all drain and vent pipes.

Then trace the network of hot and cold supply pipes. Check the materials and sizes of all branch lines. Find the spots where vertical risers veer off from horizontal branches and head up into a wall or the floor.

Make a rough sketch of your findings as you go. Then, in cleaner, more comfortable surroundings, draw a detailed map of any area where you're considering making changes. The illustrations on the opposite page show how.

CHECK WATER PRESSURE

Water-pressure gauge

Mains deliver water to homes at pressures as high as 150 pounds per square inch (psi) and as low as 10 psi, depending on location and time of day. Most appliances, valves, and fixtures that use water are engineered to operate on 50 to 60 psi. If you're planning to add a new fixture or water-using appliance, you'll need to find out whether your existing water pressure can support it.

You can determine your water pressure by attaching a water-pressure gauge (shown at left) to an outside hose bibb or to one for a laundry hookup. To reduce high pressure or boost low pressure, see page 153.

MAPPING YOUR SYSTEM

Using some simple lines and plumbing symbols, you can make a good working drawing of your plumbing system. Such a drawing or map can save you a lot of time, whether you plan to add a fixture, plumb a house addition, or troubleshoot a problem.

The so-called "riser" drawing, a two-dimensional elevation, is adequate for sketching a small run of supply pipes. An isometric drawing (shown below), which is laid out on isometric graph paper or by using a 30°-60°-90° triangle, can render more complex DWV systems. Use a traditional plan drawing (shown at right) to help you place new or existing fixtures inside a room.

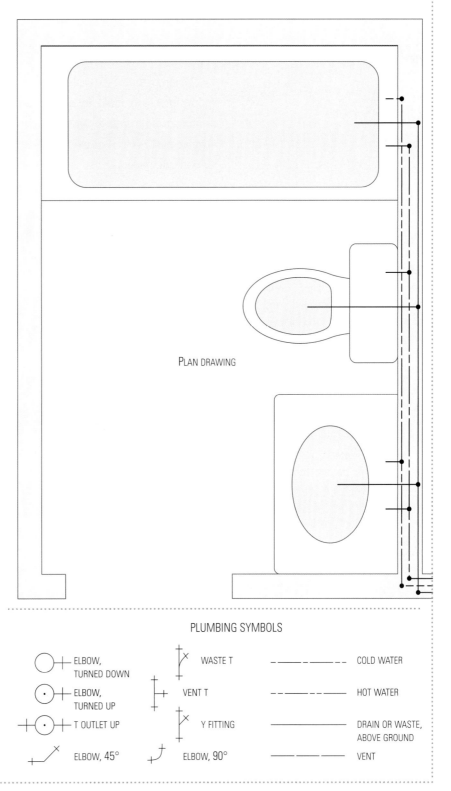

PLAN DRAWING

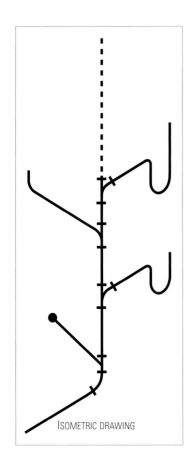

ISOMETRIC DRAWING

PLUMBING SYMBOLS

ELBOW, TURNED DOWN

ELBOW, TURNED UP

T OUTLET UP

ELBOW, 45°

WASTE T

VENT T

Y FITTING

ELBOW, 90°

— — — — — COLD WATER

– – – – – HOT WATER

———— DRAIN OR WASTE, ABOVE GROUND

– – – VENT

CHECK THE CODES

Don't buy a pipe, a fitting, or a fixture until you've checked your local plumbing and building codes. Discuss your plans in detail with a local building inspector and be sure the methods and materials you're planning to use are acceptable. Bring along a copy of your plumbing map (see page 17).

The inspector will tell you whether you need a plumbing or building permit. Projects that involve changes or additions to your plumbing pipes usually require permits. You probably won't need a permit to install a replacement fixture or appliance, or for emergency repairs, as long as the work doesn't alter the plumbing system. Learn what work is permissible to do yourself; a few codes require that certain work be done only by licensed plumbers.

PLANNING NEW PLUMBING

The feasibility of relocating or adding a fixture depends primarily on whether you can extend present drain-waste and vent pipes. You can almost always add supply pipes, as long as you have enough water pressure to serve the new outlet.

When planning new plumbing, keep in mind that while it's easy to route supply pipes to most locations, it's more difficult to put in and conceal drainage and venting pipes. To minimize cost and keep the work simple, arrange new fixtures as close as possible to the present pipes. For more information, see page 62.

EXTENDING DWV PIPES: Plumbing codes, both national and local, are quite specific about the following: the size of the drainpipe or branch drain serving a new fixture or fixture group; the distance (called the critical distance) from the traps to the main stack, secondary stack, or other vent; and the point where a new drainpipe or branch drain ties into the existing branch drain or main stack. (See pages 66–69 for specific requirements.)

If you have an old DWV system, you may want to make use of some new materials for the extension. On an old cast-iron system, you're allowed to substitute "no-hub" fittings (consisting of neoprene gaskets and stainless-steel clamps), which are simpler to install than the original "hub," or "bell-and-spigot," ends joined by molten lead and oakum (stranded hemp fiber).

Or, you may wish to switch to plastic pipe. Since plastic DWV pipe is considerably lighter than cast iron and is easily joined with solvent cement, you may want to use ABS or PVC pipe in your extension. First check the local code; some areas prohibit the use of one or both types of plastic pipes.

EXTENDING SUPPLY PIPES: Because no venting is required, extending supply pipes is a much easier task than extending the DWV system. But first determine whether both your water heater and your existing water pressure can handle the load of any additions. The selection of correctly sized pipes, as outlined by local codes, depends equally on the type of fixture to be added, the volume of water it demands, and the length of the new pipe. For details, see pages 64–65.

Your home's supply pipes most likely are either galvanized steel (referred to as galvanized or iron pipe) connected by threaded fittings, or rigid copper joined with soldered fittings. Some local codes permit the use of plastic supply lines; special adapters will enable you to convert from old, cranky galvanized to more efficient copper or easy-to-install plastic (see page 31).

WORKING SAFELY WITH PLUMBING

I t's important to play it safe at all times. Wear appropriate safety gear, shut off the water before beginning any plumbing job, and always consult your local plumbing code. Be sure you can distinguish gas and heating lines from supply and DWV pipes (see page 12).

Wear safety goggles whenever you cut or hang pipe or tubing, drive nails, work with power tools, do sweat soldering, or use drain cleaners. Leather work gloves will protect hands from abrasions while cutting or threading pipe. Wear rubber gloves when cleaning out drain clogs or using drain cleaners; there may be septic material in the water, and the caustic chemicals used in drain cleaners can burn your skin if they come into contact with it. Disposable latex gloves are great for working with adhesives and soldering compounds.

A pair of cushy knee pads can keep you comfortable and prevent possible infection from abrasions in dusty or waste-soaked surroundings.

A small headlamp instead of a flashlight will allow you to work with both hands in a dark crawl space or attic.

The work area should be well ventilated, especially when working with solvents and adhesives. When soldering copper pipe in close quarters, you'll need a metal or fiber flame protector to shield surrounding wood framing. Keep a fire extinguisher nearby.

Exercise common sense when using any hand or power tools. If you don't know how to use them, find out first. Choose double-insulated power tools and plug them into a GFCI-protected receptacle or extension cord. Better yet, use cordless power tools, which offer extra protection against electrical shock.

Remember that water and electricity don't mix. Before installing any electrical appliances, such as a dishwasher (page 105), consult an electrician. Likewise, consult a professional who's experienced with gas systems before beginning work on any gas appliance.

Fire extinguisher

NUTS AND BOLTS

Pipes and fittings are the backbone of any plumbing system. That's the subject of this chapter: a visual tour first through modern plastic and copper, then on to traditional galvanized steel and cast iron. You'll find details on more specialized hardware in later chapters.

While the basic options are easy to learn, plumbing is famous for its "local knowledge"—neighboring areas may do things differently, and plumbing suppliers only a few miles away may not have even heard of the pipe or fittings your town requires. Don't automatically assume that a material at the nearby home center is approved for use in your town.

What's the moral here? Be sure to research local codes before buying. Once you're armed with the basics found here, most building officials and plumbing suppliers will readily help with the fine points.

PLASTIC PIPE

Most homeowners who have worked with various types of pipe prefer plastic. That's because plastic pipe is lightweight, inexpensive, and easy to cut and fit. Unlike metal pipe, plastic is also resistant to damage from chemicals and corrosion. In addition, plastic's smooth interior surface provides less flow resistance than metal.

Plastic pipe comes in both rigid and flexible types. All the major plumbing codes and the Federal Housing Administration accept at least one of these types of plastic pipe, although local codes may not. For best quality, look for the American Society for Testing and Materials "ASTM" designation printed on the pipe. If the pipe is to carry potable water, it also should have the National Sanitation Foundation's "NSF" seal.

Plastic pipe has various pressure ratings—or "schedules"—stamped right on the pipe; use the schedule number prescribed by your building inspector. The pressure ratings for plastic are lower than those for metal, so it's also important to install water-hammer arresters (page 90) at all fixtures and water-using appliances (except toilets).

Take care not to store plastic pipe in direct sunlight for longer than a week or so—the accumulation of ultraviolet rays can make it brittle.

Schedule 80
PVC pipe

Schedule 40
PVC pipe

RIGID SUPPLY PIPE

Two types of rigid plastic supply pipe are used indoors: PVC (polyvinyl chloride), used for cold water supply only; and CPVC (chlorinated polyvinyl chloride), used for both hot and cold water systems. Both types are somewhat limber and can follow slight directional changes without cracking.

PVC and CPVC pipe are commonly available in both 10- and 20-foot lengths; some home centers sell shorter lengths. They can be bought by the piece or in bundles of ten. Common sizes include $1/2$-inch, $3/4$ inch, and 1-inch nominal diameters (the sizes used for matching fittings—actual diameters may be different). PVC is also available in $1^{1}/4$-, $1^{1}/2$-, and 2-inch diameters, primarily for outdoor use.

Most PVC and CPVC fittings push onto the ends of the pipes and are cemented in place with a permanent solvent cement. Couplings allow you to join two lengths of straight pipe; 45°, 90°, and T-fittings are for changes in direction. Transition fittings—those that let you link plastic pipe to pipe of a

PVC fittings

PVC primer

PVC solvent cement

CPVC fittings

CPVC pipe

different material—often have threads on one end. Reducer fittings allow you to link pipes of different diameters.

Supply fittings are smaller than DWV fittings and may have sharper turns with restricting shoulders. They are designed to work under pressurized conditions, unlike DWV fittings, which must work with the flow of gravity.

FLEXIBLE SUPPLY PIPE

Flexible plastic pipe is especially useful in cramped places because it can follow a winding course without requiring a lot of fittings. For that reason it's easier to install than rigid supply pipe, but it's much less likely to be approved for use.

Two types of flexible supply pipe are used in homes: PB (polybutylene) for hot and cold lines of pipe, and PE (polyethylene), for cold lines only. Both are sold in rolls of 25 and 100 feet and sometimes by the foot. Although PB is more versatile and less expensive than PE, it is currently in disfavor with many codes, and is not readily available.

Join lengths of flexible pipe with barbed insert fittings. Insert fittings have hollow, corrugated nipples that are held in place by stainless-steel clamps. Transition fittings have a socket on one end for joining to rigid plastic pipe.

Flexible PE pipe

Barbed insert fittings

DWV PIPE

Two types of plastic pipe are used to repair or extend DWV systems—ABS (acrylonitrile-butadiene-styrene) and PVC (polyvinyl chloride). You can tell the difference by their color: ABS is black; PVC is off-white. (Basin traps and other short connectors to DWV lines are often fabricated from a third plastic, PP—polypropylene—identifiable by its stark white color.)

Both ABS and PVC are less expensive, lighter in weight, and easier to connect and hang than sections of cast-iron pipe (see page 32). For these reasons, plastic pipe is a common choice for new work, for extending a cast-iron system, and even for replacing a leaking section of cast-iron drainpipe.

Codes often allow only ABS or PVC—rarely both. PVC is sometimes considered a better choice because it is less susceptible to mechanical and chemical damage and has a slightly greater variety of fittings available (fittings for PVC and ABS are not readily interchangeable).

Both ABS and PVC drainpipe are sold in lengths of 10 and 20 feet. Drainpipe for tubs, sinks, and lavatories normally has a $1\frac{1}{2}$- or 2-inch nominal diameter. Toilets require 3- or 4-inch-diameter drains. Vent pipe can range from $1\frac{1}{4}$ to 4 inches in nominal diameter. For pipe-sizing guidelines, see pages 66–69.

DWV fittings differ from supply fittings in that they have no interior shoulder that could catch waste. You'll find a wide assortment of change-of-direction and reducer fittings (see pages 82–83); always take care to direct the flow from the smaller to the larger pipe diameter. As with plastic supply pipe, connect plastic drainpipe to its fittings with solvent cement.

ABS fittings

ABS pipe

Copper supply fittings

Copper Pipe

Copper pipe, often called copper tubing, is lightweight, fairly easy to join (by sweat soldering or with flare, compression, or union fittings), resistant to corrosion, and rugged. Its smooth interior surface also allows water to flow easily. Compared with plastic, copper is stronger but more expensive.

Two kinds of copper tubing—hard and soft temper—are used in supply systems to carry fresh water. Another type of copper pipe—often called refrigeration tubing—is used to link supply pipes to fixtures. Yet another variety—with a larger diameter—is sometimes used in DWV systems.

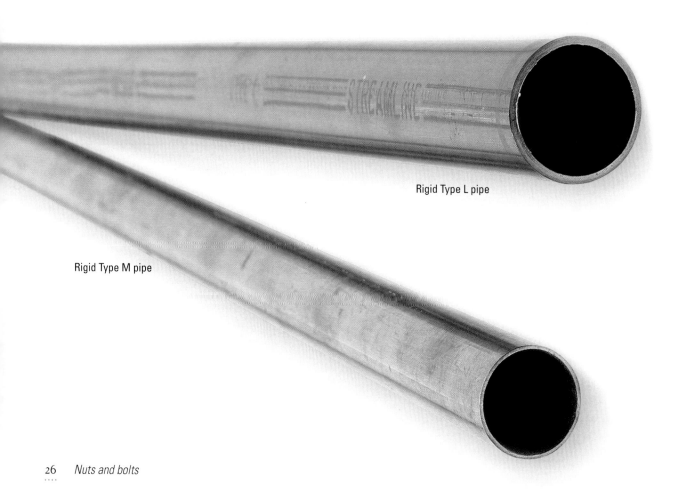

Rigid Type L pipe

Rigid Type M pipe

Copper supply fittings

HARD-TEMPER SUPPLY PIPE

Hard-temper is the most common rigid copper pipe. It's sold in lengths of 10 and 20 feet and sometimes in shorter pieces. Because it can't be bent without causing crimping, it must be cut and joined with fittings whenever there is a change in direction.

Rigid copper comes in three thicknesses: K (thick wall), L (medium wall), and M (thin wall). M is usually adequate for aboveground, interior plumbing; L is used outdoors or for burial. Standard sizes include 1/2-, 3/4-, and 1-inch nominal diameters; actual diameters are larger.

Different joining methods require different fittings. Soldering—using the necessary smooth-shouldered fittings—is the best way to keep copper pipe together. To solder a joint, you'll need a small propane torch, plus lead-free solder and some other small accessories. These items are shown at right.

In tight quarters, soldering is sometimes difficult. In these situations, you can join pipe lengths together with compression fittings (see page 28).

Reducer fittings allow you to link pipes of different diameters; transition fittings let you link copper pipe with plastic or galvanized pipe.

If you think you'll need to remove a run of copper pipe at some point—to replace a gate valve, for instance (see page 33)—you'll want to fit two short lengths of copper pipe together with a union (for information about union joints, see page 53).

SOLDERING MATERIALS

I f you're planning to work with rigid copper pipe (the most common supply pipe material), you'll need to assemble pipe and fittings with soldered joints. Soldering requires a small but specialized collection of hardware, including lead-free solder, flux, a flux brush to spread it, emery cloth or sandpaper, and perhaps a pipe brush. You'll also need a propane soldering torch (see page 39).

To learn more about these materials—and about how to solder like the pros—see pages 50–53.

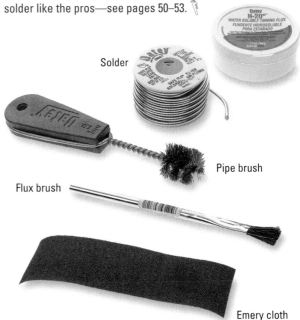

Solder

Pipe brush

Flux brush

Emery cloth

Compression fittings

Flare fittings

Copper DWV fittings

SOFT-TEMPER SUPPLY PIPE

Soft-temper copper can be bent without causing crimping, so it has the advantage of not requiring as many fittings as hard-temper supply pipe. It's also more costly.

Soft-temper is sold in 20-, 60-, and 100-foot coils and is available in K (thick wall) and L (medium wall) thicknesses; L is commonly used for buried supply lines and aboveground plumbing. Nominal diameters include 1/2, 3/4, and 1 inch; actual diameters are slightly larger.

Soldered joints make the sturdiest connections between lengths of soft copper tubing. But if you can't solder, you can choose a compression fitting (shown above left) or a flared fitting instead. A flared joint (left) is designed for soft copper only. Because it tends to weaken the end of the pipe, use a flared joint only if you can't solder or can't find the right compression fitting. You'll need a special flaring tool for assembly.

REFRIGERATION TUBING

Thin, flexible refrigeration tubing is commonly used for linking supply lines to a refrigerator's icemaker and water dispenser (hence the name), but it can also feed other fixtures and appliances. It conforms to tighter curves than soft-temper tubing and thus requires few or no fittings.

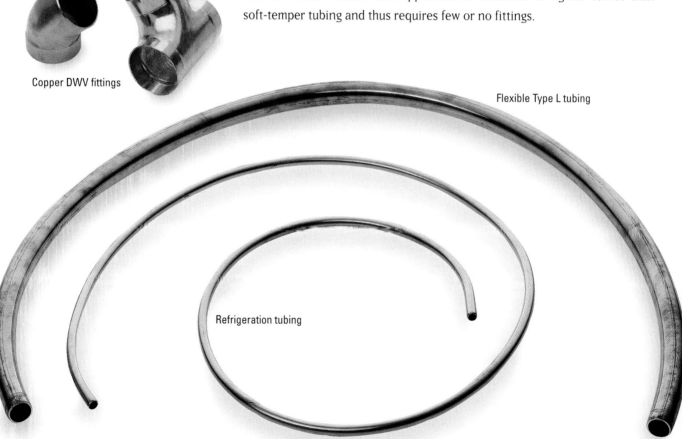

Flexible Type L tubing

Refrigeration tubing

HARDWARE HANG-UPS

If you'll be installing new runs of pipe, you'll also need to purchase the correct type of supports for the pipe you're using.

Supply-pipe hangers are made of metal or plastic and are used to hang copper or plastic supply pipe. Some have integral nails; others must be nailed or screwed to a wall stud or floor joist. Copper supply straps allow you to anchor hot- and cold-water stubouts (pages 86–91) to wall studs. Pipe bushings cushion pipes that run through drilled holes in framing members.

So-called DWV hangers are bigger than supply supports and corral large-diameter drain-waste and vent pipes. Plumber's tape works, too, and comes in both galvanized and plastic versions. Friction clamps handle heavy vertical runs of cast-iron pipe.

Note: When installing metal pipe or tubing, use hangers made of the same kind of metal or the pipe may corrode. You'll find guidelines for installing pipe supports in Chapter Five, "Rough Plumbing," beginning on page 60. See the chart on page 77 for proper support distances.

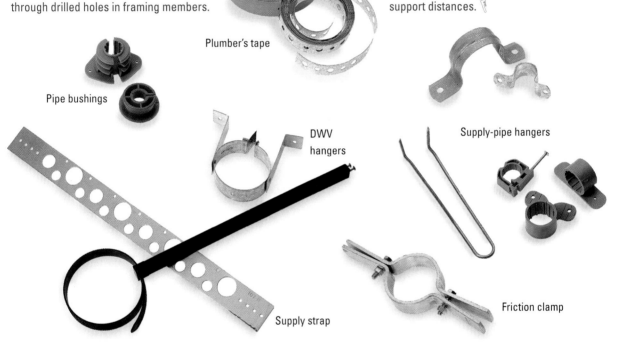

Plumber's tape

Pipe bushings

DWV hangers

Supply-pipe hangers

Friction clamp

Supply strap

Refrigeration tubing usually comes coiled in lengths of 10 to 60 feet in boxes; occasionally it's sold by the foot. Nominal diameters include ¼ inch, ⅜ inch, ½ inch, and ¾ inch. Don't confuse the larger sizes with soft-temper supply pipe; refrigeration tubing is not adequate for permanent, or "concealed," supply lines.

COPPER DWV PIPE

Why use copper instead of plastic or cast-iron DWV pipe? Actually, it's rarely done these days, but you'll sometimes see copper drainpipes in kitchen areas because their smooth interiors minimize grease buildup and corrosion. Where plastic is banned, copper DWV pipes can also save weight and bulk—especially where long vent lines run up through exterior bearing walls to the roof.

Copper DWV pipe is rigid pipe, usually sold in 20-foot lengths and in nominal diameters of 1½ and 2 inches. (Larger sizes are too expensive for most stores to carry.) Because it's not under pressure, copper DWV pipe has thinner walls than supply tubing. Join pipe and fittings with soldered copper DWV fittings shown on the facing page.

Pipe-joint compound

Galvanized Steel

If your house is more than 30 years old, chances are your supply pipe is galvanized steel; you may even have galvanized DWV pipe, although cast iron (page 32), or a combination of the two, is more common.

Galvanized pipe and its fittings are coated inside and out with zinc to resist corrosion. Despite this additional protection, galvanized steel pipe not only corrodes faster than cast iron or copper, but because of its rough interior surface it also collects mineral deposits that, over time, impede water flow.

Pipe-thread tape

It's common to replace a leaking length of galvanized steel pipe with the same type of pipe because it requires less equipment and expense than using copper, plastic, or cast iron. But when extending or replacing a supply system of galvanized pipe, use copper (pages 26–29) or, if it's permitted in your area, plastic (pages 22–25).

Galvanized steel pipe is commonly stocked in nominal diameters of 1/2, 3/4, 1, 1 1/2, and 2 inches and in lengths of 10 and 21 feet—or it can be custom-cut to length. Short threaded pieces called nipples are also available in the same diameters as the pipes, in 1/2-inch increments from 1 1/2 to 6 inches long and then in 1-inch increments up to 12 inches long. Stores often stock other commonly used lengths, such as 18, 24, 36, and 48 inches.

So-called black pipe, shown at left, is black galvanized pipe that's used for interior residential gas lines; it comes in 1/2-, 3/4-, and 1-inch diameters. "Green," or coated, pipe, available in 1/2- and 3/4-inch sizes, is designed for exterior or buried gas lines.

Galvanized fittings with interior threads are used to connect galvanized pipe. Precut lengths of pipe come threaded on both ends; if you need pipe cut to a different length, you'll have to have its new ends threaded at the store or rent pipe-threading tools (page 56) and do it yourself.

When joining lengths of galvanized pipe, cover the threads with pipe-joint compound or fluorocarbon tape (often called pipe-thread tape) to seal them against rust and to make assembly and disassembly easier. Both products are shown above. Pipe-joint compound comes both in easy-to-use tubes, as shown, and in bulk cans.

Many fittings are available for joining galvanized with more of the same pipe, with reduced sizes of galvanized pipe, or with copper or plastic. If you cut into an existing run of galvanized pipe, you'll have to reconnect the ends with a union—a special fitting that allows you to join two threaded pipes without having to turn them.

Black pipe

Galvanized pipe

Green (coated) pipe

MAKING CHANGES

No-hub coupling

When you're extending pipes or simply repairing them, you may wish to switch pipe materials while you're at it—say from galvanized to copper, or from cast iron to plastic. So-called transition fittings are available at many home centers, but for an even better selection, visit your local plumbing supplier. Be sure to double-check local codes for approved fittings.

To switch from copper to plastic or from galvanized to plastic, look for threaded adapters. They're available in both female and male versions, but some inspectors allow only male plastic threads to meet female metal threads.

Use a dielectric (nonconductive) union to connect copper supply tubing to galvanized steel. This union contains an insulating washer and an insulating sleeve to keep electrolysis from occurring between the steel and copper portions of the fittings.

To switch from cast-iron to plastic DWV pipe, use a no-hub coupling that's labeled for plastic. (This type of fitting is different from ones designed for cast-iron connections only.) No-hub couplings are also available as reducer fittings, allowing you to change pipe size while you change pipe type.

For a closer look at supply transitions, see pages 72–73. DWV changes are detailed on pages 74–75.

Dielectric union

Male adapter

Female adapter

Galvanized fittings

CAST IRON

If your home was built before 1970, it likely has a cast-iron drain system. Cast-iron pipe is strong, resists corrosion, and is dense enough to be the quietest of all piping materials. But since the weight and density of cast iron make it difficult to heft and cut, you may want to substitute plastic (see page 25) when repairing or extending a line—if your building code allows it. Plastic is also much less expensive.

There are two types of fittings for cast iron: bell-and-spigot and no-hub, or hubless. Bell-and-spigot joints are usually found in older homes and were typically joined using molten lead and oakum (stranded hemp fiber). These materials are rarely used in residences now, as most codes no longer permit lead in DWV piping. (For repairs, you can purchase oakum and a lead substitute.) The no-hub joint is now standard because it's far simpler to install and takes up little space—a 3-inch soil stack will fit into a 2x4 stud wall without "furring out," or thickening, the wall. No-hub cast iron can also be removed, reassembled, and used again.

Pipe and fitting are joined with a no-hub coupling (shown at left), which consists of a neoprene sleeve or gasket and a surrounding stainless-steel band. The band secures the joint as you tighten down on a pair of worm-drive nuts or screws. Most couplings include interior shoulders or stops; some all-rubber versions—intended for repairs or as transitions to other materials—have no stops. You can also buy reducer couplings that allow you to join different pipe diameters. Not all couplings are created equal, and some may not be approved in your area. Be sure to check local codes before shopping.

Cast-iron pipe and fittings are available in 1½-, 2-, 3-, and 4-inch diameters. Pipe is sold in 10-foot lengths and sometimes by the foot. Home centers may not stock cast iron; try a plumbing supplier or a building yard that caters to pros.

NOTE: Cast-iron pipe and fittings may crack if dropped or mishandled, which will cause leaks later. Keep an eye out for damage when shopping.

Cast-iron pipe

No-hub coupling

No-hub fittings

ALL ABOUT VALVES

Ball valve

Supply valves control the flow of water through pipes. You'll find different types of valves for different uses: some of these restrict the flow even when fully open; others allow unrestricted flow when open. The three most commonly used types are ball, gate, and globe valves. Fixture shutoff valves control the flow at each fixture.

Valves are available in a variety of materials. Those used in home plumbing are most commonly made of cast bronze, although plastic and iron valves are sold for use with plastic and iron pipe, respectively. Valves are sized to match all common supply-pipe sizes.

BALL VALVES are the cream of the crop: the straight handle twirls an interior sphere, which has a channel through it. When aligned with the pipes on either side, the channel lets water flow smoothly. To shut off the water, simply turn the handle—and the sphere—to 90°. Although a ball valve is your most expensive option, it's the best choice for a main-supply shutoff.

GATE VALVES have a tapered wedge at the end of a stem that moves up or down across the water flow. Although often used as a main supply shutoff, a gate valve is better suited to shut down branch supply lines. Because it takes a half dozen or more turns to fully open a gate valve, many people unknowingly open the valve only partially. Slightly opening a gate valve permits partial flow, but the pressure of the water moving across the wedge wears down its surface, resulting in an imperfect seal and a leaking valve. For this reason, gate valves should never be operated when only partially opened.

GLOBE VALVES, by design, reduce water pressure: when the valve is open, water is forced to flow around two partitions, which slow the water down. By turning the handle of a globe valve, you enlarge or diminish the opening for the water to pass through. Branch supply lines are sometimes equipped with globe valves, but the valves tend to break down from the constant pressure buildup. It's a good idea to replace them with ball or gate valves.

FIXTURE SHUTOFF VALVES simplify turning off the water flow to a fixture for repairs or in case of an emergency. When you shop for a shutoff valve, you'll need to choose either an angled valve or a straight one. Angled valves are used when the supply pipe, called a stub-out, comes from the wall; straight valves are used for pipes that come up from the floor. Select a shutoff valve that is compatible with the supply-pipe material: copper tubing takes brass valves; iron and plastic pipe use iron and plastic valves, respectively. You'll probably want a chrome- or brass-finished valve if it will be visible.

Gate valve

Angled shutoff valve

Straight shutoff valve

Globe valve

TOOLS OF THE TRADE

To do any job right, you need the proper tools—and plumbing is no exception. Fortunately, pipefitting is not really tool intensive. We present a complete kit for cutting and assembly tasks on pages 36–39. Plumbing repairs call for an additional set of tools; for details, see pages 40–41. Some handy remodeling tools are shown on pages 42–43. How do you corral these items? A tool bag or caddy, like the one shown on the facing page, can help.

When it comes to tool shopping, the rule of thumb is to buy the basics, then rent the more expensive power tools as you need them; if you need them again, consider purchasing your own. As in other building trades, the standard advice applies: buy the best tools you can afford.

Some simple safety gear goes hand-in-hand with tool use. For details, see page 19.

PVC scissors

These cutters make short work of cutting plastic pipe and tubing up to 1" or so in diameter. Ratcheted jaws clamp down on the pipe as you squeeze. For larger pipe sizes, use a PVC saw, shown below right.

A PLUMBER'S TOOL KIT

Pipefitting often comes down to two main tasks: gripping and cutting. You can handle virtually any job with the tools shown here. The wrenches and pliers hold pipes and fittings; the cutting tools make clean cuts in various types of pipe and tubing.

You'll find some additional pipefitting tools on pages 38–39. A hacksaw cuts metal pipe and hardware. A tubing bender allows you to smoothly curve flexible copper tubing; the flaring tool forms the broad-lipped end of a flared joint. "Sweat" copper joints with a soldering torch. Planning to work with galvanized steel pipe? The traditional pipe threader (shown on page 38) cuts new threads in pipe ends. If you need to tackle cast-iron pipe, consider renting a snap cutter and a torque wrench.

Long-nose pliers

These small, needle-nose pliers are useful for delicate work such as removing seals and springs during faucet repairs. They can get into tight spots where other gripping tools can't reach.

Tubing cutters

The two tools shown are designed to cut copper tubing. The large, ratcheted cutter (left) quickly cuts copper up to 1" in diameter; the small version (right) works slowly but fits into tight spots (such as in a cramped crawl space where you need to cut through existing pipe). There's also a larger tubing cutter made for galvanized steel pipe; rent one if you need it.

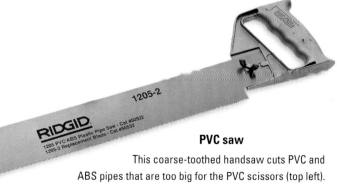

PVC saw

This coarse-toothed handsaw cuts PVC and ABS pipes that are too big for the PVC scissors (top left). For straight cuts, guide the saw with a miter box (see page 48). You can also cut plastic pipe with a power miter saw.

Adjustable wrench

This gripping tool has smooth jaws made to fit small nuts, bolts, and square and hexagonal fittings. Sizes range from 6" long on up; each size handles a range of nut sizes (depending on how far the jaws open). Consider a single 10" wrench or a set of 8" and 12" models.

Slip-joint pliers

Also known as rib-joint pliers, these adjustable grippers open wide enough to remove drain traps. You'll find both curved- and straight-jaw versions: use curved jaws for pipes, straight for nuts and fittings. You won't be able to apply much torque with these pliers, so don't expect them to double as a pipe wrench or an adjustable wrench.

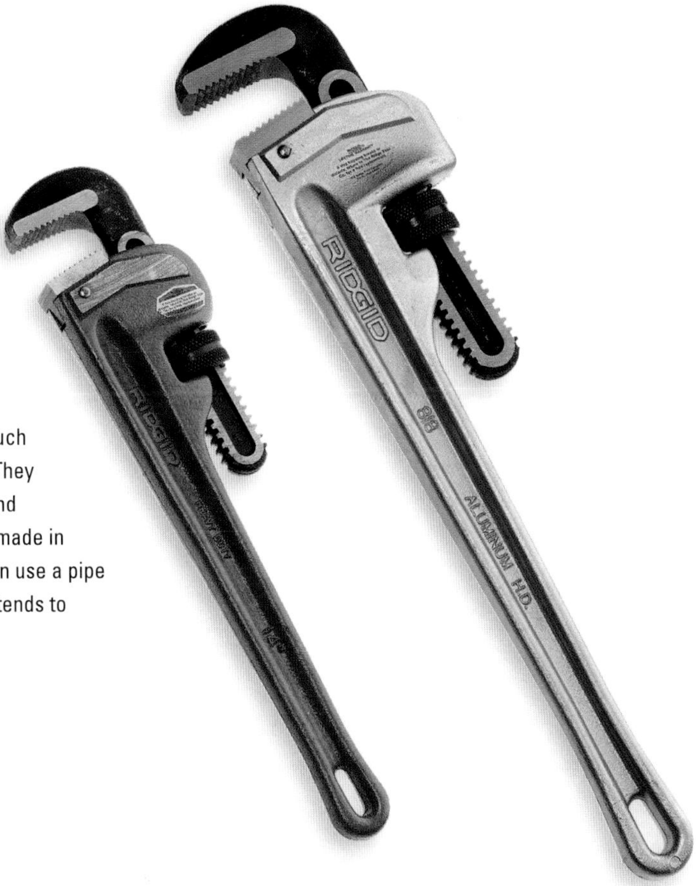

Pipe wrench

The movable, toothed jaws grip pipe and fittings; for some jobs, such as assembling galvanized pipes, you'll need two pipe wrenches. They come in sizes from 10" to 24"; a 14" wrench makes a good all-around choice. Longer wrenches, like the 18" tool shown at far right, are made in aluminum versions that lighten weight and reduce fatigue. You can use a pipe wrench on a nut when an adjustable wrench fails, but beware: it tends to damage the nut.

Flaring tool

This tool forms the lipped, or flared, end for a flared joint, which is sometimes used with flexible copper tubing. The flaring tool is probably not worth buying unless you plan to do a lot of joints—it makes more sense to rent or borrow one.

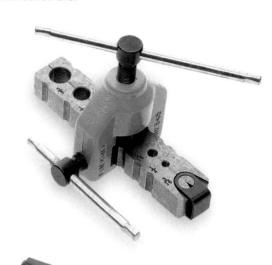

Pipe threader

What if the home center won't cut and thread your galvanized steel pipe? Rent a pipe threader, either hand-powered (as shown) or electric. Die inserts cut the threads; they match various pipe sizes and pop inside the round housing on the ratcheted handle. You'll also need a pipe vise to grip pipe while you thread it.

T-handled torque wrench

Need to tighten no-hub couplings onto cast-iron pipe? The hex-headed wrench shown here is preset to deliver the required 60 inch-pounds of torque. When you reach this pressure the handle spins freely, telling you that you're done tightening.

Tubing bender

This Slinky-like gizmo allows you to shape flexible copper tubing without crimping it. Just slide it over the pipe and bend. Different sizes are made for different pipe diameters.

Hacksaw

A tried-and-true demolition tool, the hacksaw cuts through old galvanized pipe, rusted bolts, and, if necessary, copper tubing (although not very cleanly). Interchangeable blades allow you to cut through different materials. The mini-hacksaw shown is handy where the full-size saw won't fit.

Soldering torch

You'll need a torch to sweat-solder copper pipe and fittings. Professional plumbers use acetylene tanks and hoses, but portable torches are best for home users. Disposable canisters contain either propane or Mapp gas—the latter burns hotter, but propane is safer and less expensive. A striker tool (a flint) lights the torch; a flame guard—either fiber (as shown) or metal—helps shields wood framing when soldering pipe that's in place.

Handy Household Tools

In addition to the tools shown on these pages, you may need some household items to round out your tool kit—some of which you probably own. Here's a list:

- Tape measure and/or folding wooden rule
- Felt-tip pen and grease pencil
- Claw hammer
- Pry bar
- Wood chisel
- Carpenter's level
- Miter box (for square cuts in pipe and tube)
- Ratchet-and-socket set (to drive bolts and setscrews)
- Locking pliers (an 8-inch model is best)
- Screwdrivers (both standard and Phillips versions)
- Utility knife (for deburring plastic pipe and tube)
- Putty knife
- Headlamp (page 19), flashlight, and/or worklight
- Half-round file (with one round and one flat side)
- Wire brush

Soil pipe (snap) cutter

This big, expensive bruiser cuts cast-iron pipe. Essentially, you clamp a thick chain with cutting wheels around the pipe, then work the ratcheted handle—which tightens the chain—until the pipe snaps. Most rental yards carry snap cutters; make sure the one you get handles the size pipe you're cutting.

REPAIR TOOLS

Plumbing repair sometimes calls for a different bag of tricks. Like pipefitting tools, all repair tools are not created equal: look for solid construction and a quality feel. To see these tools in action, turn to Chapter Eight, "Troubleshooting and Repairs," beginning on page 150.

Toilet (closet) auger

This 3' to 6' long clog-buster works like a snake (see facing page) but has a crank handle and a bent housing to reach into the toilet's trap. Look for a housing with rubber or plastic padding, which helps protect the toilet bowl from scratches.

Plungers

Also called plumber's helpers, plungers dislodge clogs by using alternating pressure and suction. A sink plunger (below left) has a flat face for strainers and drain openings. A toilet plunger (below right) has a special funnel-cup tip to fit the toilet bowl. Some toilet plungers fold flat to work on sinks as well.

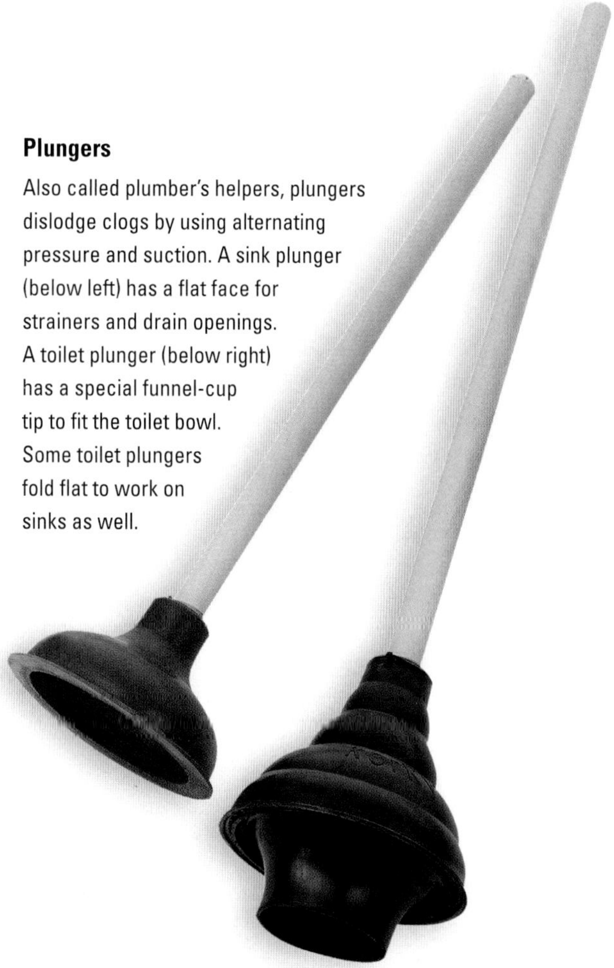

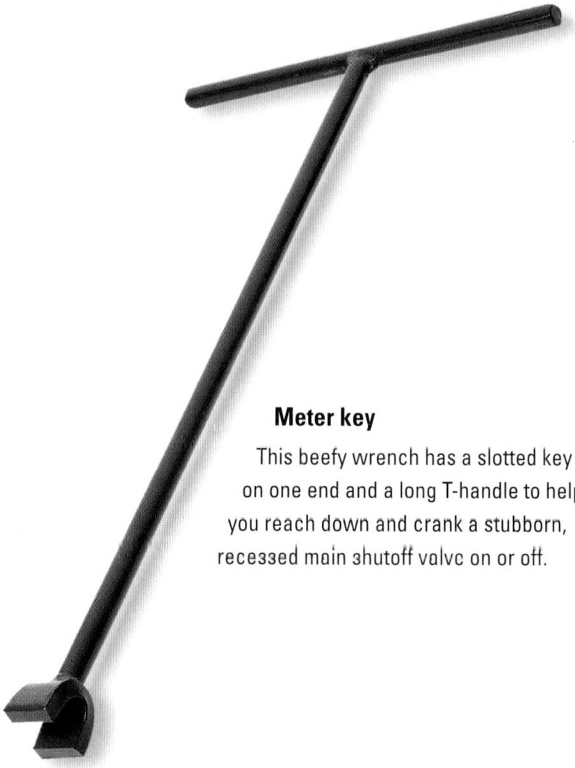

Meter key

This beefy wrench has a slotted key on one end and a long T-handle to help you reach down and crank a stubborn, recessed main shutoff valve on or off.

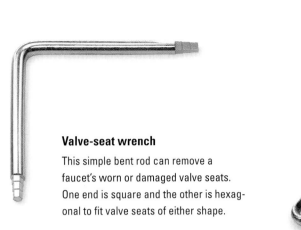

Valve-seat wrench

This simple bent rod can remove a faucet's worn or damaged valve seats. One end is square and the other is hexagonal to fit valve seats of either shape.

Spud wrench

The wide and toothless spud wrench adjusts to fit large nuts on toilets and sinks. Large slip-joint pliers might also do the trick.

Drain-and-trap auger

Also known as a snake, a drain-and-trap auger stretches 10' to 25' to remove deep drain blockages. This one includes a housing and crank; others are loose metal coils only. Some snakes are pretty cheesy—try to get a good one.

Shower socket

Ever tried to unscrew a recessed shower faucet with a wrench? A shower socket allows you to reach a valve seat from the front—without tearing out wall materials. To use the version shown, simply insert a screwdriver shaft through the side holes, then twist.

Valve-seat dresser

This specialty tool grinds and smooths faulty non-replaceable valve seats in old faucets. The one you get should come with various-size cutters.

Basin wrench

This goofy-looking wrench looks better when you need access to nuts in hard-to-reach places. The pivoting jaws and extension handle help you reach up under a sink—to tighten or loosen faucet connections, for example—without smashing a knuckle or dislocating your shoulder.

HELPFUL REMODELING TOOLS

If you're planning to run new pipe or add fixtures where there were none before, you may need a few extra tools. On these two pages, we detail some carpenter's tools that can make cutting, drilling, and other pipe-routing tasks much easier. The hand tools are generally inexpensive to buy, and some of the power tools can be rented.

³/₈" reversible drill

For most jobs, the ⅜" drill offers the best compromise between power and speed; it also handles a wide range of bits and accessories. A variable-speed drill allows you to suit the speed to the job—very handy when starting holes, drilling metals, and driving screws. Cordless drills are much more powerful and recharge more quickly than models available just a few years ago; if insulated, they offer extra protection around potentially live electrical wires.

Jab saw or drywall saw

A jab saw (shown) or drywall saw is great for cutting access holes in gypsum wallboard without making an undue mess. Both are essentially low-tech, hand-tool versions of the jigsaw (far right). Because a jab saw uses the same blades as a reciprocating saw (below right), you can use it to make controlled cuts in wood or metal as well.

½" drill

Although the ⅜" drill will handle most remodeling tasks, there are times when you may need more power, such as when you're driving long or large-diameter bits. That's where the ½" drill comes in. Some models double as hammer drills, allowing you to pound holes through masonry. If you're considering one, be sure it's a variable-speed model equipped with a pistol grip, a right-angle grip for your other hand, and a clutch. These drills develop tremendous torque and can twist your wrist and arm in a flash if something goes wrong. Learn how to use them properly.

Right-angle drill

Most drills work in a straight line, but in tight quarters (such as between two wall studs) you may not be able to get a drill body, your hand, and your line of sight into the space you need to drill in. That's where a right-angle drill shines. Be careful, though: like the ½" drill, these powerful tools require an experienced hand and extra caution. Right-angle drills now come in smaller, cordless versions, like the one shown here.

HOLE SAW

AUGER BIT

BELLRINGER
BIT

Drill bits

A collection of drill bits is shown here. Twist bits make small holes in wood and metal; spade bits are great for drilling access holes for supply pipe in wood. A hole saw makes even bigger holes—up to 2½" with a ⅜" drill. Need to drill deeper than a standard drill bit will go? So-called bellringer bits are extra-long twist bits; you can also buy several lengths of extension bits. Auger bits bore more aggressively, but may require a beefier ½" drill. Screwdriver bits, available in both standard and Phillips sizes, turn a variable-speed drill into a power screwdriver. Nutdrivers turn your drill into a power wrench.

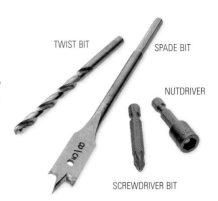

TWIST BIT   SPADE BIT

NUTDRIVER

SCREWDRIVER BIT

Portable circular saw

This workhorse cuts wood framing, subfloors, and even cast-iron pipe in a pinch (use a Carborundum blade for the latter). Get one with a depth adjustment. Traditional models handle heavy-duty jobs, but new, lightweight cordless versions, like the one shown, are convenient where power is out of reach and are safer to operate in damp areas or where live wires may be concealed.

Jigsaw

This portable power tool, sometimes called a saber saw, cuts wood, metal, drywall, and even plaster when fitted with the right blade for the job. However, you can't control the depth of cut as you can with some other saws, so be sure the blade's entire travel is free of obstructions before you go to work.

Reciprocating saw

The number one power tool for "roughing-in" or demolition work, the reciprocating saw can handle (with the right blade) old wood studs and joists, lath and plaster, steel pipe, and even nails. Use slow speeds for fine work and for cutting metal, high speeds for making cuts in wood. Saw blades are flexible, which helps when you're making tricky cuts, but they can snap if you're not careful. Have extras on hand.

Helpful remodeling tools   43

PIPEFITTING KNOW-HOW

Plastic, copper, galvanized, cast iron: Each pipe type has its own fittings and its own assembly techniques. For example, plastic pipe generally teams with solvent cement, while rigid copper requires soldering. Galvanized and cast iron have mechanical connections and are tightened with a pipe wrench or nutdriver, respectively.

All these techniques, and more, are shown step by step on the following pages, which can serve as a reference primer on pipefitting basics. Master these skills and you'll be well on your way to becoming a first-rate plumber.

When it's time to go from theory to practice and actually run some new pipe, turn to Chapter Five, "Rough Plumbing," beginning on page 60.

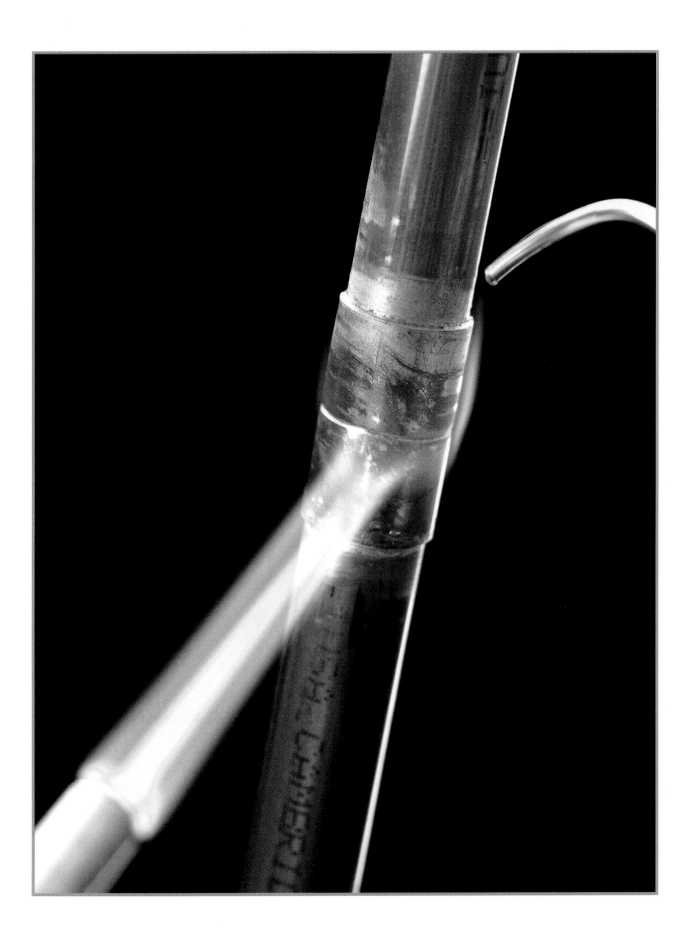

WORKING WITH PLASTIC

Rigid plastic pipes and fittings are normally joined with solvent cement; flexible PE tubing is joined with barbed insert fittings. Barbed inserts are forgiving, but solvent cement sets within seconds: if you don't get the alignment right the first time, you'll need to cut the fitting off and start over.

Before you cut any pipe, make exact measurements. Rigid pipes won't give much if they're too long or too short. Minor measuring and cutting errors are rarely a problem for flexible tubing because it usually has enough play to make up the difference.

To measure pipe or tubing, determine the distance between new fittings, then add the distance the pipe will extend into the fittings. This distance, called makeup, varies depending on the type of fittings used. In push-on fittings, such as those used with PVC or ABS, pipe ends extend all the way to the shoulder (interior stop); in threaded fittings, the pipes don't go quite as far.

The quickest, cleanest way to cut plastic pipe and tubing up to about 1 inch in diameter is with PVC scissors. You can also cut rigid pipe with a PVC saw and a miter box, or, if you have one, a power miter saw.

JOINING PVC PIPE AND FITTINGS

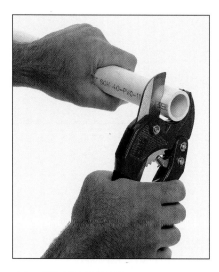

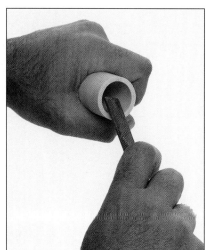

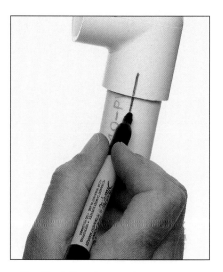

1 Cut pipe to length

For clean cuts, you can cut PVC pipe with PVC scissors (shown above), a PVC saw and a miter box, or a power miter saw. If you use a saw on an installed pipe, brace the pipe with your free hand to prevent excess motion that could affect the straightness of the cut.

2 Deburr the inside

After cutting, use a file, knife, or reaming tool to remove any burrs inside and outside the pipe end. Inspect the end for cracks, gouges, and deep abrasions. Cut a replacement piece if necessary. Then test-fit the pipe in the fitting. It should enter the fitting but stop partway in.

3 Mark the alignment

It's a good idea to put the fitting onto the pipe end temporarily and mark the pieces for proper alignment before cementing. Once the cement (which acts as a lubricant) is applied, the pipe will slip farther into the fitting, so make your marks long enough to take this into account.

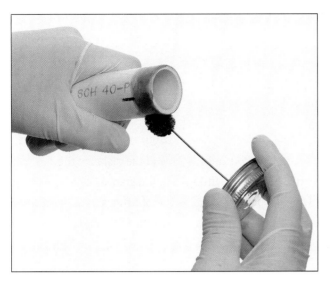

4 Apply primer

Before gluing PVC, it's best to spread a layer of PVC primer (often called purple primer) around the end of the pipe and also inside the fitting down to the shoulder. The primer should dry in a minute or so.

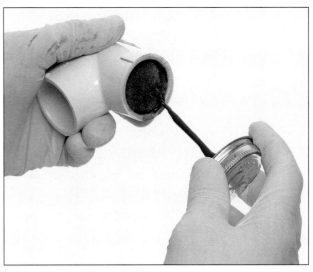

5 Apply solvent cement

Once the primer's dry, it's time for PVC solvent cement. Usually the container will have an applicator brush. If a brush isn't included, use another soft brush—for example, a ¼" brush for ½" pipe or a ⅜" brush for ¾" pipe. Work in a well-ventilated area, avoid breathing fumes, and keep lighted matches and cigarettes away from the flammable cement. Following the manufacturer's instructions, apply cement liberally to the pipe, then more lightly to the fitting socket. If the temperature is below 40°F, use a special low-temperature solvent cement.

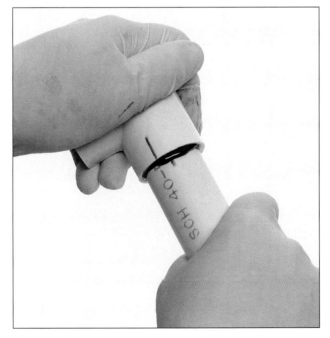

6 Secure the fitting

Slip the fitting onto the pipe so your marks are offset ¼" inch or so, then immediately twist the fitting into correct alignment. Hold for a few seconds while the cement sets. Inspect the joint between pipe and fitting. There should be a narrow band of solvent all around.

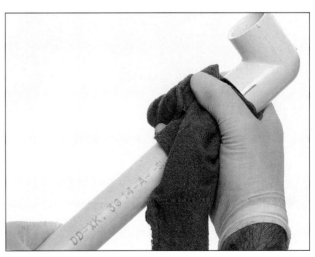

7 Clean up the excess

Wipe off excess cement with a damp rag. Solvent-welded joints can be handled gently within a minute, but wait at least 2 hours before pressurizing with water and even longer under cold, damp conditions. Then you can turn on the water and inspect for leaks.

JOINING ABS PIPE AND FITTINGS

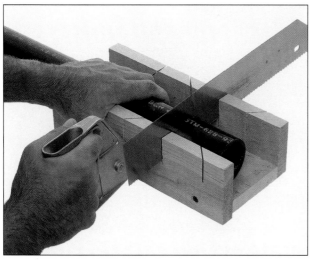

1 Cut pipe to length

For clean, straight cuts through ABS, use a PVC saw and a miter box, as shown, or a power miter saw. If you have neither tool, make the cut with a fine-tooth handsaw, being careful to make the cut as straight as possible.

2 Deburr the pipe

Use a utility knife or file to remove the rough edges around the pipe's interior that could snag waste and water. It's also a good idea to clean the outside of the pipe end with sandpaper or emery cloth.

3 Mark the alignment

Put the fitting onto the pipe end temporarily and mark the alignment for later reference. (Remember, the pipe will slip farther into the fitting once the cement is applied, so make your marks long.) A white grease pencil is easy to see on black ABS.

4 Apply solvent cement

Spread ABS solvent cement liberally around the outside of the pipe, then coat the interior of the fitting. Work in a well-ventilated area, avoid breathing fumes, and keep lighted matches and cigarettes away from the flammable cement.

5 Secure the fitting

Slip the fitting all the way onto the pipe with the alignment slightly offset, then immediately twist the fitting so that the marks line up. Hold the joint together for a few seconds. Then gently wipe away excess cement with a damp rag.

INSTALLING AN INSERT FITTING

I Push fitting into pipe

Flexible PE tubing is joined by barbed insert fittings, as shown. (The tubing needn't be cut exactly straight before the fitting is inserted.) Slide the stainless-steel ring clamp onto the PE pipe end first, then twist the barbed fitting into the pipe and position it to line up with the new pipe run.

2 Tighten the clamp

Slide the stainless-steel clamp over the fitting, then simply tighten down the screw on the clamp. If you need to make changes after insertion, usually the joint can be pulled apart by hand once the clamps have been loosened. If it can't, pour hot water over the ends of the PE pipe to soften it, then pull.

What About Threads?

You may encounter rigid plastic pipe whose ends or fittings have exterior threads (most commonly with the 1- to 12-inch-long precut pieces of Schedule 80 PVC known as nipples). Such pipe requires special plastic fittings with interior threads. To make a watertight seal, first wrap pipe-thread tape one and one-half turns clockwise around the threads of the pipe, pulling the tape so tight that the threads show through. Then screw on the fitting. Plastic threads are not tightened as much as metal threads or they may strip out—and later leak. For a proper fit, screw the fitting in by hand, then give it one turn with a wrench. Threads should still be showing outside the fitting when you finish.

Working with Copper

Cut copper tubing with a tubing cutter or, if you don't have one or don't have the space to use one, with a hacksaw. Whether the tube is hard temper or soft temper (see pages 27–28), all copper is soft metal, so you'll want to be careful not to damage it as you work. Don't use wrenches or vises, which could crush the metal.

Soldering is the standard way to join copper tubing, hard or soft. Soldered joints are made with copper fittings that have smooth interiors and, in most cases, internal shoulders, or stops. To solder, or "sweat," a joint, you'll need a small propane torch (page 39); some emery cloth, #00 steel wool, or very fine sandpaper; a can of soldering flux; and some lead-free plumber's solder (page 27). CAUTION: Use only solder that's labeled lead-free when making joints in any potable water supply or DWV system.

In tight spots where soldering would be difficult, you can use compression fittings to join lengths of copper tubing. Compression joints (page 55) work equally well on hard- and soft-temper copper tube.

A flared joint (page 54) is for soft copper tube only. Because it tends to weaken the end of the pipe and requires a special tool, use a flared joint only if you can't solder or find the right compression fitting.

If you think you'll need to take apart a run of copper tube at some point (to replace an aging water heater, for instance), fit two short lengths of the pipe together with a union (page 53). This kind of joint can be taken apart without unsoldering or cutting the run.

To determine how much new copper tubing you need, measure the distance between new fittings, then add the makeup distance the tubing will extend into the fittings. Makeup distances vary for each type of joint: soldered, flared, compression, or union.

WARNING Wear safety goggles and work gloves during the soldering process. Also be sure to keep a fire extinguisher on hand—particularly if you're soldering in place—because you'll be working with the water turned off.

SOLDERING A JOINT

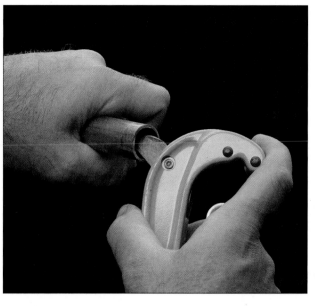

1 **Cut the pipe to length**
  Cut new lengths of copper pipe with a tubing cutter designed for copper. To use the cutter, twist the knob until the cutter wheel makes contact with the surface. Rotate the cutter around the tube, tightening after each revolution, until the pipe snaps in two.

2 **Ream the inside**
  After you've cut the tube, clean off inside burrs with a round file or with the retractable reamer often found on tubing cutters. Burrs can cause pipe friction, so reaming helps ensure a smooth-flowing joint.

3 **Polish the pipe end**
  Use emery cloth, steel wool, or sandpaper to smooth and polish the last inch of the outside end of the pipe until it's shiny. Don't overdo it: soft copper sands easily.

4 **Clean the fitting**
  Also clean the inside of the fitting from the end down to the shoulder. You can use the emery cloth or steel wool, but a pipe brush (shown above) makes cleaning easier.

continued on next page ➤

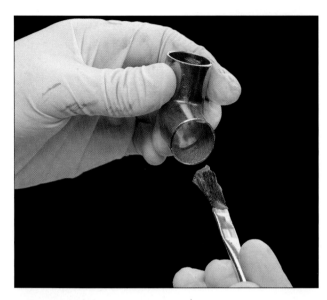

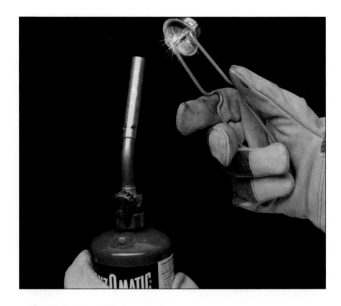

5 Apply flux

With a small, stiff brush, apply flux around the inside of the fitting and around the outside of the pipe end. Place the fitting on the end of the pipe and turn the pipe or the fitting back and forth once or twice to spread the flux evenly. Then position the fitting correctly. It's best to wear gloves when applying flux, as the chemicals in it can damage your skin.

6 Light the soldering torch

Turn the gas torch's control valve on, then light the nozzle end with a striker tool. Adjust the flame so it's steady and strong, making certain that it's not aimed at anything flammable. If necessary, shield surrounding objects with a flame guard (see page 39).

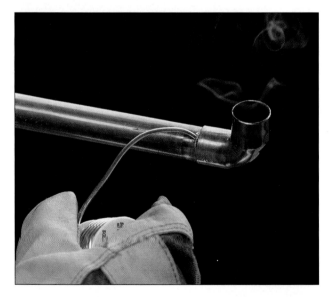

8 Test the temperature

The joint is hot enough when solder will melt on contact with it. Test the temperature by touching the solder wire to the joint occasionally as you're heating the fitting. The instant the wire melts, the joint is ready for action.

9 Apply solder

Turn off the torch and touch the solder wire to the edge of the fitting; capillary action will pull molten solder in between the fitting and the pipe. Keep applying until a line of molten solder shows all the way around the fitting.

7 Heat the fitting

Next, position the torch nozzle about 4" from the fitting and move the flame back and forth across the fitting to distribute the heat evenly. It's important to get the fitting hot but not too hot—the flux will burn and simply vanish if it's overheated.

MAKING A UNION

To install a union, first sweat-solder the male shoulder onto one pipe, then slip the nut onto the other pipe. Sweat-solder the female shoulder onto the end of the second pipe. Bring the male and female shoulders together (below), then slide the nut over the female shoulder and screw the nut onto the male shoulder. To tighten, use two wrenches—one to hold the male shoulder, the other to turn the nut.

10 Wipe off the excess

Once the solder cools (in just a few seconds), wipe off surplus flux with a damp rag. Be careful—the pipe can get quite hot as far as 1' to 2' on either side of the joint. Do not bump or move the newly soldered joint for an hour or two, until the solder hardens.

MAKING A FLARED JOINT

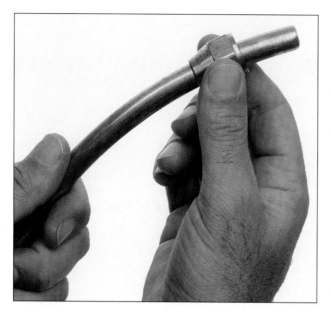

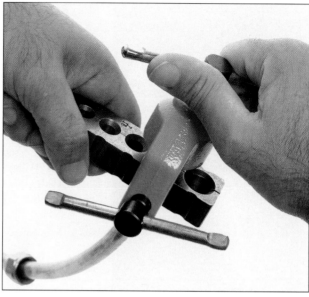

1 Slide the nut over the tubing end
To make a flared joint, first slide the flare nut onto the tube, with the nut's tapered end facing away from the end of the tubing.

2 Flare the end
Clamp the end of the tube into a flaring tool and screw the ram down hard into the opening. Remove the flared tube from the tool.

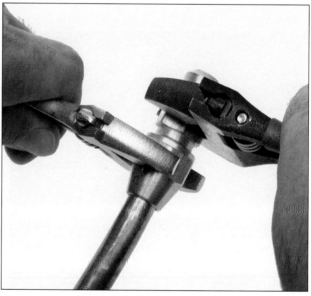

3 Add the fitting
Press the tapered end of the fitting into the flared end of the tubing, and screw the flare nut onto the fitting.

4 Tighten with two wrenches
Use two adjustable or open-end wrenches—one on the nut and one on the fitting—to secure the joint.

INSTALLING A COMPRESSION FITTING

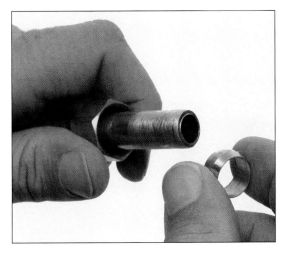

1 Slip on the nut and compression ring

To install a compression fitting, first slide the compression nut onto the tube, with the nut's broad shoulder facing away from the tubing's end. Then slip on the compression ring, as shown. Some plumbers apply a dab of pipe-joint compound (page 57) to the outside of the compression ring at this point.

2 Add the fitting

Push the threaded body of the fitting against the end of the tubing, and screw the nut down onto the fitting.

3 Tighten with two wrenches

Tighten the joint with two adjustable or open-end wrenches—one on the nut and one on the fitting. This action compresses the ring tightly around the end of the tubing and makes a water-tight seal.

BENDING BASICS

The best way to shape soft-temper copper tubing is with a tubing bender. Simply slip the bender over the pipe, then gently bend tool and tubing with both hands to the desired curve. Go slowly; if you do crimp the pipe, discard that piece and start again.

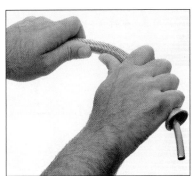

WORKING WITH GALVANIZED STEEL

Fittings are connected to galvanized pipe by means of tapered pipe threads. If you need nonstandard lengths (and you probably will), you may be able to have pieces cut and new ends threaded at the store. If that's not possible, you can rent cutting and threading tools and do it like the pros (see below).

To determine how much galvanized pipe you need, measure the distance between fittings, then add the distances the pipe will extend into the fittings. The ballpark distance allowed for each fitting is $1/2$ inch for $1/2$- and $3/4$-inch-diameter pipe and $5/8$ inch for 1- and $1 1/4$-inch-diameter pipe.

The threads on galvanized steel pipe should be covered with pipe-joint compound or pipe-thread tape to seal them against rust and to make assembly and disassembly easier. Many plumbers use both tape and compound—tape on the male pipe threads and compound on the fitting's female threads. Joining a galvanized fitting to threaded pipe requires two pipe wrenches—one to hold the pipe and the other to turn the fitting.

A PIPE-THREADING PRIMER

Pipe reamer

Pipe cutter

To thread pipe at home you'll need two pieces of equipment: a pipe vise to hold the pipe steady and a threader fitted with a die and guide of the same nominal size as the pipe (these tools can be rented). It's important to cut galvanized pipe perfectly straight so threads can be accurately started in its new end. Using a pipe cutter with a blade designed for steel pipe, follow the directions on page 51 for cutting copper tube. After you've finished cutting, use a pipe reamer or the retractable reamer in some cutter handles to remove burrs from the inside of the pipe.

Ready to thread pipe? First, fit the head of the threader die into the threading handle and slip it, guide first, over the end of the pipe.

To cut the threads (right), exert force toward the pipe while rotating the handle clockwise. When the head of the threader bites into the metal, stop pushing and simply continue the clockwise rotation. Apply generous amounts of thread-cutting oil as you turn the threader. If the threader sticks, some metal chips are probably in the way; back the tool off slightly and blow away the chips.

Continue threading until the pipe extends about one thread beyond the end of the die. Remove the threader from the pipe by rotating it counterclockwise, then clean off the newly cut threads with a stiff wire brush.

To thread steel pipe, you'll need a pipe vise and a threader.

JOINING GALVANIZED PIPE AND FITTINGS

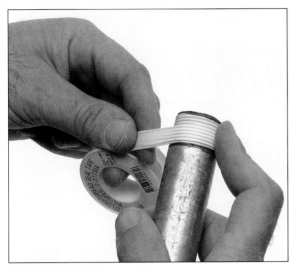

1 Wrap the pipe threads

To use pipe-thread tape, wrap it 1½ turns clockwise around the male pipe threads, pulling tape tight enough so that threads show through. Tape tears easily, which is both good and bad. If you prefer, you can use pipe-joint compound (see below) instead.

Protect Yourself

Wear work gloves to prevent cutting your fingers on newly cut pipe threads or injuring your hands while tightening fittings. Soft leather work gloves are the most comfortable. Wear eye protection while working overhead and when threading pipe or driving nails.

2 Apply pipe-joint compound

Add compound to the fitting's female threads, either by squeezing it from the tube and spreading it with a small brush or by using the brush attached to the lid of a bulk can. Use just enough compound to fill the gaps between the threads.

3 Tighten with two pipe wrenches

Screw the pipe and fitting together by hand as far as you can. Final tightening requires two pipe wrenches, as shown at left. A fitting always screws on clockwise and screws off counterclockwise. Be sure to apply force toward, rather than away from, the wrenches' jaws; otherwise, the jaws tend to come off the pipe or fitting.

WORKING WITH CAST IRON

As discussed on page 32, existing cast-iron DWV pipe comes in two versions: traditional bell-and-spigot and more modern no-hub style. To make a small repair to bell-and-spigot pipe, see below. To make your life easier, plan to use no-hub for any new work; or, if allowed by code, switch to plastic.

To determine how much new no-hub pipe you need, simply measure between the cut ends where a section of pipe has been removed. Or, if starting from scratch, just add pipe and fitting lengths together.

To cut cast-iron pipe, a snap cutter (page 39) is the tool of choice. They're available at equipment-rental stores. You can also use a portable circular saw with a Carborundum blade for the occasional cut. A hacksaw, cold chisel, and ball-peen hammer can also be used, but it's a lot of work: first chalk a cutting line all around the pipe, then score it to a depth of $1/16$ inch with the hacksaw. Deepen the cut with a ball-peen hammer and chisel, tapping all around the pipe until it breaks.

To connect a no-hub fitting or pipe to existing cast-iron pipe, use a no-hub coupling. This coupling consists of a neoprene gasket, a stainless-steel shield, and worm-drive band clamps for compressing the gasket around the pipe.

BELL-AND-SPIGOT BLUES

If you're repairing or extending an older bell-and-spigot system, it's simplest to cut out a section of existing pipe, then switch to either no-hub cast iron or plastic (if your code allows). When joining modern no-hub to older bell-and-spigot pipe, some codes require you to use a mission coupling; it's similar to the no-hub coupling shown on the facing page, except that one side of the neoprene sleeve is stepped down to accommodate the slightly smaller diameter of the older pipe.

If you do need to work with existing pipe, join spigot to bell by packing the joint with oakum (stranded hemp fiber), then hammering in cold lead wool or packing a plastic, puttylike lead substitute over the oakum with a putty knife. These materials are available at plumbing supply houses. The oakum seals the joint, so pack it tightly; the wool or plastic only keeps the oakum in place.

JOINING NO-HUB CAST IRON

1 Cut the pipe

The snap cutter uses a ratchet action to increase the pressure equally on a chain with cutting wheels that encircles the pipe, constricting the pipe until it snaps. Offcuts tend to jump, so stay clear of them. Cuts are rarely perfect; use pliers or a cold chisel and ball-peen hammer to break off any large, uneven chips.

2 Slip on a no-hub coupling

To assemble a joint, first push the stainless-steel shield and gasket assembly onto the end of the pipe or fitting; the gasket sleeve has a built-in stop to help you center the assembly at the joint. Then fold back the gasket lip, if possible.

3 Add the fitting

If you were able to fold the gasket out of the way, you're in business: simply butt the fitting against the gasket's stop and roll the gasket lip back into place. Or, if necessary, push and pull until pipe, gasket, and fitting are aligned.

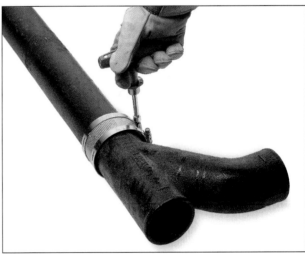

4 Tighten the band

Finally, slide the stainless-steel shield over the gasket and tighten the band screws with a socket wrench or nutdriver. Technically speaking, 60 inch-pounds of torque is required. (A T-handled wrench preset for this torque is shown.)

ROUGH PLUMBING

W e've toured the basics. Now it's time to get dirty! This chapter illustrates hands-on techniques for tying into existing pipes and routing new ones. This so-called roughing-in, or rough plumbing, leads to the locations of new fixtures or appliances; when it's time to complete the job, turn to Chapter Six, "Finish Work," beginning on page 94.

Before you can add any fixtures, you'll need to answer some questions: Are your supply pipes adequate for the additional load? Where can you place any new fixtures along your present DWV system? How will each new fixture be vented? Should you—or can you—do the work yourself? The information in this chapter will help you sort out your options; your building department can help iron out the wrinkles.

THE PLANNING PROCESS

When plotting any plumbing addition, you must consider code restrictions, the limitations of your system's layout, and, of course, your own abilities.

WHAT ARE YOUR OPTIONS?

Although it's usually straightforward to route supply lines to a new location, tying into DWV pipes is a different story. The simplest and most cost-efficient way to add a new fixture or group of fixtures is to connect them to the existing main soil stack, either directly or through a branch drain. A common strategy is to install them above or below existing fixtures on the stack, piggyback style (see below left), but check codes carefully for restrictions. Another way is to place the new fixture or fixtures back-to-back with an existing group attached to the main soil stack (below right).

If your planned addition is across the house from the existing plumbing, you'll probably need to run a new secondary vent stack up through the roof, and a new branch drain to the soil stack (see bottom right) or to the main house drain via an existing cleanout. If possible, tie a bathroom sink, tub, or shower stall (although not a toilet) directly into an existing branch drain instead, which will save on labor and demolition costs.

Once you've devised a strategy for tying into your DWV system, the next step is to study possible access routes for running pipes to the locations for new fixtures or appliances. To do that, you'll first need to bone up on some basic house anatomy.

REMODELING OPTIONS

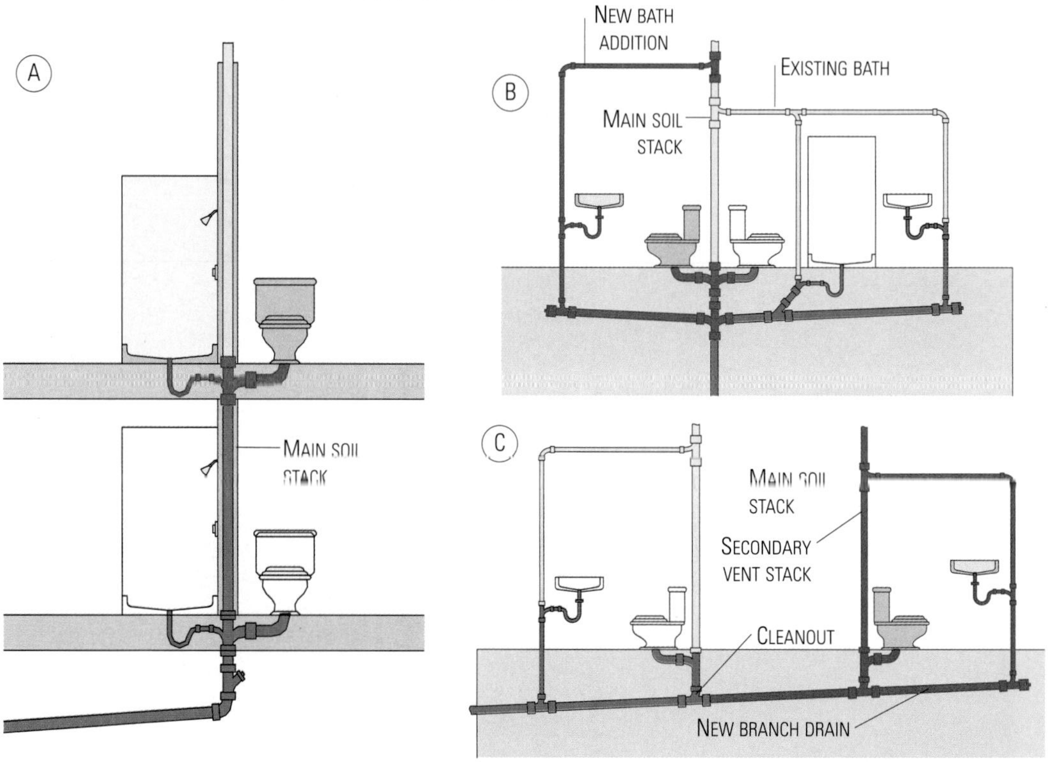

Three common ways to install new fixtures include above or below old fixtures on the soil stack (A); back-to-back with existing installations (B); and with a new vent stack and branch drain (C).

HOUSE ANATOMY

Wood-frame houses are not all built the same way, but most have 2x4 stud walls, 2x8 (or larger) floor joists, and 2x6 (or larger) ceiling joists. These wooden structural members are normally spaced 16 inches apart from center to center. In some new homes, however, the spacing is 24 inches, and in some roughly built older homes, the spacing is somewhat random. The illustration below shows the skeleton of a typical wood-frame house.

In new construction, rough plumbing is done before wall, ceiling, and floor coverings are added. Extending pipes in a finished house is a different story: you have to find ways to route pipes through existing walls, ceilings, and floors.

WHERE YOU HAVE ACCESS: In some parts of your home, installing new pipes may be pretty easy. These are areas such as attic floors and unfinished basement ceilings where wall, ceiling, or floor coverings are attached to only one side of the framing. You simply work from the uncovered side, drilling holes and threading pipes through studs or joists.

WHERE ACCESS IS LIMITED: Getting pipes into walls, floors, or ceilings that have coverings on both sides involves cutting through the coverings, installing pipes, and patching up the holes. The amount and difficulty of cutting and patching depend only partly on where the pipes go; surface material is also a factor. Gypsum wallboard, the most common wall and ceiling covering, is relatively easy to cut away and replace. But some other materials—such as ceramic tile, wood flooring, and plaster—are more difficult to cut and patch and should be left alone when possible.

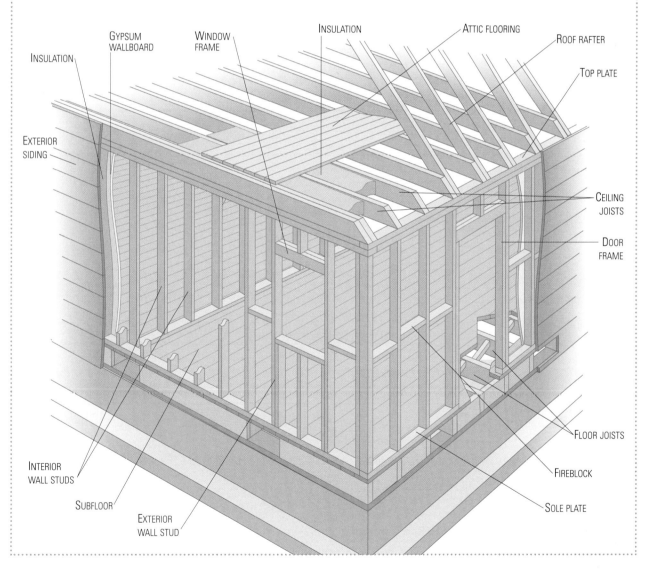

SIZING SUPPLY PIPES

Few code restrictions apply to simple extensions of hot and cold water supply pipes. You mostly just need to be sure your water pressure is adequate (page 153). The proper material and diameter for supply pipes serving a new fixture or appliance should be spelled out clearly in your local code, according to the number of "fixture units" that type of installation typically uses. (One fixture unit represents 7.5 gallons, or 1 cubic foot, of water per minute.) For some common ratings, see the facing page.

Typically, the main supply pipe leading in from the street is ¾- or 1-inch pipe, supply branches are ¾-inch pipe, and risers feeding individual fixtures are ½-inch pipe. When troubleshooting problems with your present supply system or to figure the pipe specs for a sizable remodel, you'll need to know how many total fixture units are used in your home. Add up the ratings of all the fixtures; estimate, as best you can, the length of the distribution pipes; then see the chart below to determine pipe size.

Keep in mind that ideal pipe size may vary depending on the amount of delivered water pressure and the height of a proposed addition. Water pressure drops 0.5 pounds per square inch (psi) for every foot in elevation from the source (the water main or well), so it's possible that a second- or third-story addition might require a larger pipe size than the one listed on the chart. If you have a higher or lower water pressure or a large elevation gain, consult your local code for alternative pipe sizes.

SIZING FOR WATER DISTRIBUTION PIPES

METER & STREET SERVICE	SIZE OF MAIN SUPPLY PIPE & BRANCHES	MAXIMUM LENGTH FOR TOTAL FIXTURE UNITS (46 TO 60 PSI)					
		40'	60'	80'	100'	150'	200'
¾"	½"*	7	7	6	5	4	3
¾"	¾"	20	20	19	17	14	11
¾"	1"	39	39	36	33	28	23
1"	1"	39	39	39	36	30	25
1"	1¼"	78	78	76	67	52	44

* ¾" minimum for main supply

SIZING FOR SUPPLY RISERS

	MINIMUM PIPE DIAMETER				MINIMUM PIPE DIAMETER	
	COLD WATER	HOT WATER			COLD WATER	HOT WATER
Toilet	⅜"			Bar sink	⅜"	⅜"
Bathtub	½"	½"		Dishwasher		⅜" to ½"
Lavatory	⅜"	⅜"		Washing machine	½"	½"
Shower	½"	½"		Laundry sink	½"	½"
Bar sink	⅜"	⅜"		Water heater	¾"	
Kitchen sink	½"	½"		Hose bibb	½" to ¾"	

WATER SUPPLY FIXTURE UNITS

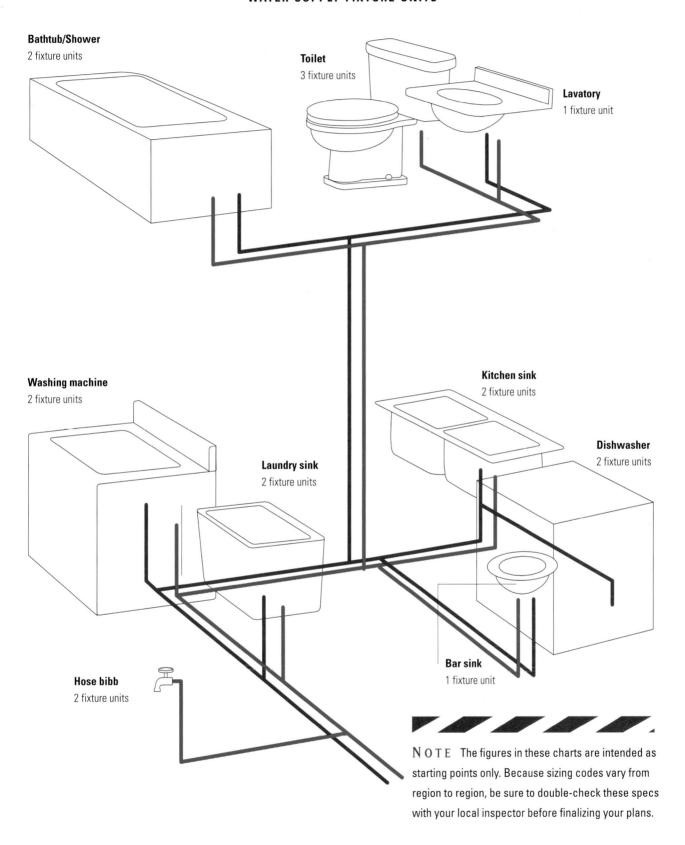

Bathtub/Shower
2 fixture units

Toilet
3 fixture units

Lavatory
1 fixture unit

Washing machine
2 fixture units

Laundry sink
2 fixture units

Kitchen sink
2 fixture units

Dishwasher
2 fixture units

Bar sink
1 fixture unit

Hose bibb
2 fixture units

NOTE The figures in these charts are intended as starting points only. Because sizing codes vary from region to region, be sure to double-check these specs with your local inspector before finalizing your plans.

SIZING DWV PIPES

The plumbing code specifies minimum diameters for drains and vents in the vertical main stack, horizontal branch drains, and separate vent systems. The diameters are related to numbers of fixture units. In the code, you will find fixture unit ratings for all plumbing fixtures in chart form.

To determine drainpipe diameter, look up the fixture or fixtures you're considering on the code's fixture unit chart (for a sampling, see the facing page). Add up the total fixture units. Then look up the drain diameter specified for that number of units, as shown at right.

The plumbing code also specifies the maximum allowable distance between fixtures and vents. This distance—from a fixture's trap to the main stack, a secondary stack, or another vent—is called the critical distance. The code lists critical distances by size of fixture drain.

The height of the fixture drain is also regulated by code: no fixture drain may be completely below the level of the trap's crown weir (see the illustration below) or the drain would act as a siphon and empty the trap. Figuring in the ideal drainpipe slope of 1/4 inch per foot, the length of that drainpipe quickly becomes limited. But if the fixture is vented properly within the critical distance,

the drainpipe's run to the actual stack or drain may be any length.

If your fixture is too far from its vent, you have several choices: increase the size of the drainpipe, move the fixture closer to the existing vent, or add a vent closer to the fixture location. For more information on planning vents, see pages 68–69.

SIZING FOR DRAINPIPES

PIPE SIZE	MAXIMUM FIXTURE UNITS FOR HORIZONTAL DRAIN	MAXIMUM FIXTURE UNITS FOR VERTICAL DRAIN
1¼"	1	1
1½"	1*	2
2"	8	16
2½"	14	32
3"	35	48
4"	216	256

* Except for sinks

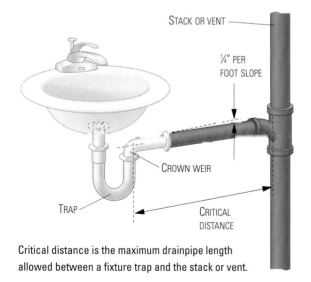

Critical distance is the maximum drainpipe length allowed between a fixture trap and the stack or vent.

STACK OR VENT

¼" PER FOOT SLOPE

CROWN WEIR

TRAP

CRITICAL DISTANCE

CRITICAL DISTANCES FOR VENT PIPES

SIZE OF FIXTURE DRAIN	MINIMUM VENT SIZE	CRITICAL DISTANCE
1¼"	1¼"	2½'
1½"	1¼"	3½'
2"	1½"	5'
3"	2"	6'
4"	3"	10'

DWV GUIDELINES

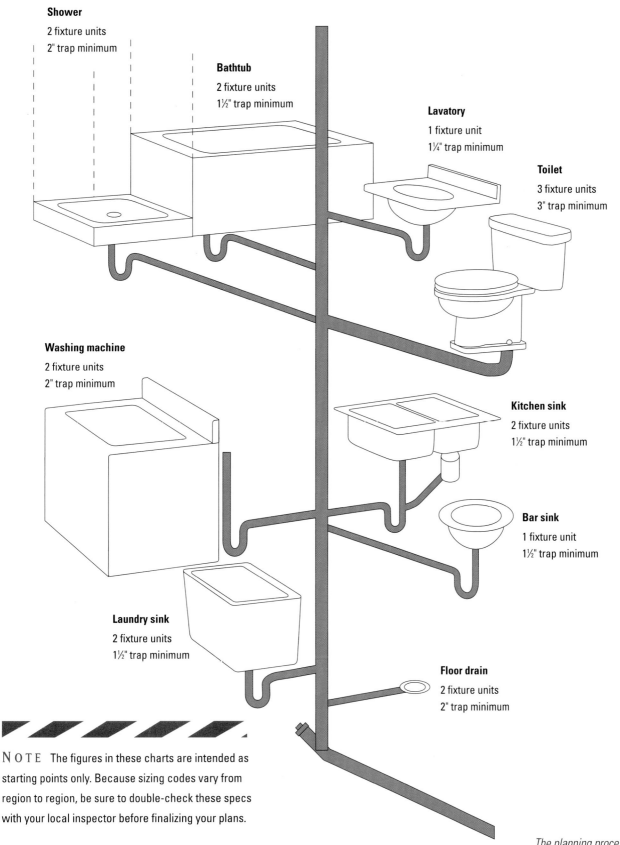

Shower

2 fixture units

2" trap minimum

Bathtub

2 fixture units

1½" trap minimum

Lavatory

1 fixture unit

1¼" trap minimum

Toilet

3 fixture units

3" trap minimum

Washing machine

2 fixture units

2" trap minimum

Kitchen sink

2 fixture units

1½" trap minimum

Bar sink

1 fixture unit

1½" trap minimum

Laundry sink

2 fixture units

1½" trap minimum

Floor drain

2 fixture units

2" trap minimum

NOTE   The figures in these charts are intended as starting points only. Because sizing codes vary from region to region, be sure to double-check these specs with your local inspector before finalizing your plans.

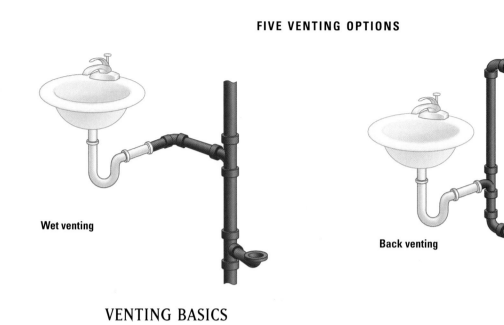

Wet venting

Back venting

VENTING BASICS

Five basic venting options—subject to local code—are wet venting, back venting, individual venting, indirect venting, and loop venting.

WET VENTING is simplest—the fixture is vented directly through the fixture drain to the soil stack.

BACK VENTING (reventing) involves running a vent loop up past the fixture to reconnect with the main stack or secondary vent above the fixture level.

INDIVIDUAL (SECONDARY) VENTING means running a secondary vent stack up through the roof for a new fixture or group of fixtures distant from the main stack.

INDIRECT VENTING allows you to vent some fixtures (such as a basement shower) into a laundry tub or into an existing floor drain without the need for further venting.

LOOP VENTING serves sinks in freestanding kitchen islands or in other spots where you can't vent within the

TWO VENTING RULES

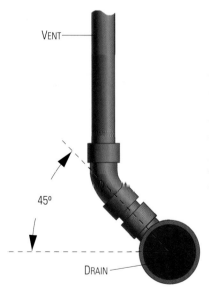

A vent pipe must meet a horizontal drain at no less than a 45° angle (left)—otherwise, waste water could back up from the drain into the vent. A horizontal vent must meet the stack or a secondary vent at a height that's at least 6 inches above the flood level of the highest fixture in the group (right).

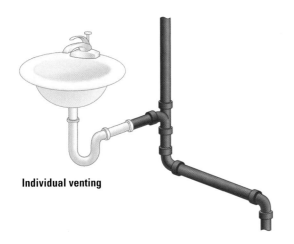

Individual venting

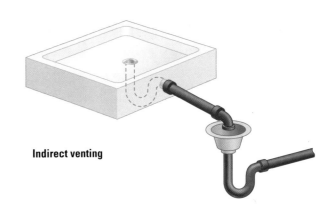

Indirect venting

critical distance. The loop, which runs up higher than the sink, allows proper air circulation for venting and drainage.

Vent runs are normally installed either plumb or level, with short diagonal sections used to traverse the occasional obstacle. Typical vent fittings have tighter bends than those allowed for drain fittings (see page 13). Some codes now require that horizontal vent pipes be slightly sloped for drainage.

Where a vent pipe meets a horizontal drain, that fitting's drain inlet must be placed at least 45° above horizontal—otherwise, waste water could back up from a clogged drain into the vent system. You'll also need to connect a back vent's horizontal arm to the stack at a height that's at least 6 inches above the rim (called the "flood level") of the highest fixture in the group. Both these venting rules are illustrated on the facing page.

Loop venting

The "No Vent" Option

If you can't access a vent stack easily or if it's awkward to run a new vent, an anti-siphon vent valve can sometimes be installed on the drainpipe. The 1½-inch-diameter PVC valve shown here automatically lets air into the drainpipe to prevent trap siphoning in wash basins, tubs, kitchen sinks, showers, and washing machine drainpipes. A larger version of the valve can serve a toilet or an entire bathroom.

The valve solvent-welds to a vertical plastic DWV pipe 6 inches or more above the fixture trap. The valve must remain accessible, and thus can double as an additional cleanout. Check local codes to find out whether these valves are allowed in your area.

PIPE CONNECTIONS

Before you can install any new fixtures or appliances, you'll need to tie into existing supply and DWV lines. Here's how to do it.

LOCATING AND EXPOSING PIPES

First, you'll need to try to pinpoint where pipes run in walls and floors. Then, to gain elbow room, you'll have to carefully remove wall, ceiling, and floor materials in the immediate area.

By now you should know roughly the location of the pipes you'll tie into. Here's where your system map

To cut into gypsum wallboard, first drill small pilot holes at the four corners of your outline, then use a drywall saw or jab saw to cut along the lines you've marked.

(page 16) comes in handy. Locate pipes as exactly as possible from above or below. You may have to drill or cut exploratory holes to find the exact locations of stacks, branch drains, or water supply risers inside a wall or ceiling. Once you find one riser, the other is normally about 6 inches away.

EXPOSING PIPES IN A WALL: To open a wall, you will need to cut a rectangle about 3 feet high between flanking studs. First, insert a steel tape measure into the exploratory hole near the pipes you're tying into. Extend the tape to the left until you hit a stud; note the measurement, then mark the distance on the outside of the wall covering. Repeat the process to the right. Then, with a carpenter's level that also shows plumb, draw vertical lines about 3 feet long through your marks to outline the edges of the flanking studs. Turn the level to the horizontal and connect the vertical lines above and below where you plan to tie into the pipes.

It's easy to cut into gypsum wallboard—just follow the steps shown at left. Be careful to avoid electrical wiring.

EXPOSING PIPES IN FLOORS AND CEILINGS: Cutting into floors can be a messier job. You have to tear out the floor covering (and repair it later), as well as the subfloor. To open up a wood subfloor, first drill pilot holes, then make the cutout with a jigsaw or handsaw, or, if you're skilled with a portable circular saw, carefully make a series of pocket cuts.

If you're tying into a branch drain, try to gain access from below—from the crawl space or basement for a first-floor drain, or through ceiling materials to reach an upper floor. To open a ceiling between joists, follow the procedure for opening walls.

PLOTTING SLOPE FOR A DRAINPIPE

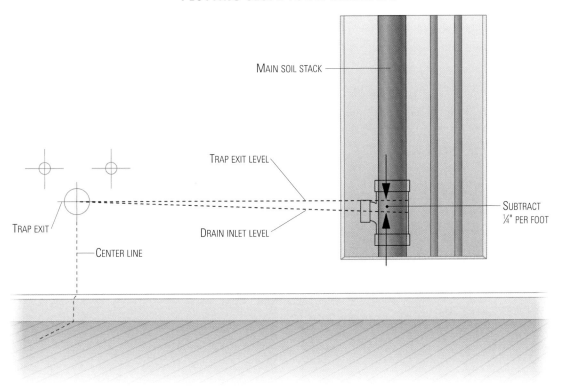

MAIN SOIL STACK

TRAP EXIT LEVEL

TRAP EXIT

DRAIN INLET LEVEL

CENTER LINE

SUBTRACT
¼" PER FOOT

Lay out a sink drainpipe by measuring from the center of the new trap exit to a point at the same height on the stack. Subtract ¼ inch per foot of distance, then mark the stack at this lower point. The new mark gives the correct slope.

PLOTTING YOUR ROUTE

Many new fixtures will include a fixture template or other roughing-in measurements for correctly positioning the supply stubouts and the trap exit (the spot where the drainpipe enters the wall or floor). Transfer these measurements carefully to the wall or floor where you want them. The combined length of the new fixture's drainpipe and the height of its trap exit on the wall or its distance below the floor will determine exactly where the connection to a stack or branch drain will be made.

For a sink, plot the ¼-inch-per-foot slope for your drainpipe by running a tape measure from the center of the trap exit mark on the wall to a point at the same height on the stack (see above), subtracting ¼ inch per foot of this distance, and lowering the mark on the stack by this amount. For a toilet, shower, or bathtub, figure the slope from a closet bend (for a toilet) or a trap (for a shower or bathtub) below the subfloor. Mark it with a chalk line snapped on a parallel joist or a string pulled taut along the proposed run.

Supply pipes are not required to slope in the same way that drainpipes are, but figuring in at least a slight downward slope allows you to drain the pipes later. Plan to run hot and cold supply pipes parallel to each other, about 6 inches apart.

TAPPING SUPPLY PIPES

Tying into existing supply lines basically entails cutting a section out of each pipe and adding new T-fittings, as shown below.

Before you begin, shut off the water supply at the main house shutoff (see page 152) and drain the pipes, if possible, by opening a faucet at a lower end. Have a pail or absorbent cloth in place to catch any spills.

If your supply pipes are soft-temper copper or flexible plastic, simply cut the lines and insert new T-fittings. With rigid plastic or hard-temper copper, you'll need to cut out a section of pipe about 8 inches long and, depending on the play available, add one or two spacers (nipples) and couplings (see below). If there's any remaining water in existing pipes, it will hinder a successful soldering job. Stuff the ends of the pipe with plain white bread to absorb any moisture, then install

CONNECTING TO COPPER

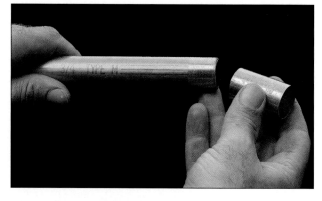

1 Cut existing pipe

First, shut off the water supply and drain the pipes, if possible. Use a tubing cutter to remove a section of the existing pipe—an 8-inch gap is usually about right.

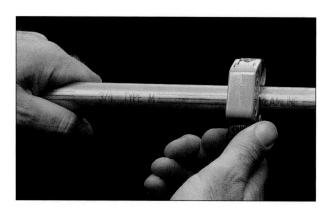

3 Add fitting and spacers

Assemble a new T-fitting and a pair of spacers to span the gap in the existing pipe. It's simplest to insert over-length spacers in the fitting, then hold them up to the gap and mark them for length, as shown. Cut spacers to fit snugly.

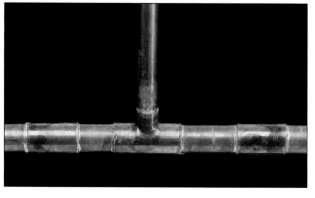

2 Slide on couplings

Ream and polish the newly cut ends, then slide a so-called slip or repair coupling over each. These fittings don't have interior shoulders, so you can push them all the way over the cut ends.

4 Assemble the pieces

Hold fitting and spacers in position, then slide the slip couplings back over the spacers so they're centered over each joint. Orient the T-fitting so that it's aimed along the line of your new extension. Finally, sweat-solder each joint.

TYING INTO GALVANIZED PIPE

1 Cut through existing pipe

To extend an existing galvanized system, you'll first need to cut through an open pipe run between threaded fittings. Make the cut with a hacksaw or with a power reciprocating saw, as shown.

2 Remove cut pieces

Next, remove the cut pipe pieces from the fittings at each end. You'll need two pipe wrenches for this job.

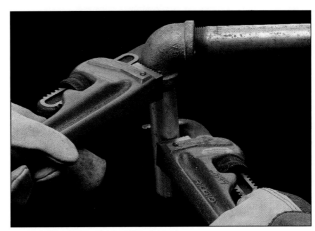

3 Add new fittings

Here we've added a short threaded nipple, a new T-fitting, a second nipple, and a union to help tie things together. Tighten these connections one at a time with the two wrenches.

4 Secure pipe to union

Finally, thread the remaining pipe length onto the existing fitting; the other end butts against the union. Slide the union's nut down across the pipe's threads, then secure the joint with two wrenches. The T-fitting is ready for its new extension.

---

the new section. The bread will disintegrate inside the pipes once the water is turned back on.

If your supply lines are threaded galvanized steel pipes, you'll have to cut the pipe (see above), then remove each cut section back to the nearest fitting. When sawing, try to brace the existing run to prevent excess motion that would strain joints and cause severed ends to sag. If the run is not supported, wrap plumber's tape once around the pipe every 3 feet and nail it to nearby joists or studs.

Using two pipe wrenches, unscrew each section of the cut pipe. One wrench twists the pipe; the other holds the nearby fitting. If the pipe won't budge, apply liberal amounts of penetrating oil to the joints; wait 5 minutes and unscrew. Install a union, the new pipe, and the T-fitting (above). If you wish to change to plastic or copper at this point, it's simplest to add a short galvanized nipple to the new T-fitting, then add a transition fitting and the new pipe type. For a look at transition fittings in action, see page 81.

WRESTLING WITH CAST IRON

1 Cut existing pipe

With pipe supported, mark and cut a section out of a cast-iron stack or branch drain with a rented snap cutter.

2 Add couplings

Slip no-hub couplings over the ends of the cut cast-iron pipe. We're switching to plastic, so we've chosen couplings sold for that purpose.

3 Secure fitting and spacers

Glue a pair of plastic spacers to your chosen fitting—the spacers should span your cut pipe section, allowing for the couplings' makeup distance. Push spacers firmly into open coupling ends and tighten down the stainless-steel bands.

TYING INTO DWV LINES

The method of tying into DWV pipes varies depending on the pipe material. Before cutting into the stack, support it by installing friction clamps or plumber's tape (see page 77) near the top and bottom of the hole you've opened in the wall. If you're cutting near an existing fitting, leave several inches of the old pipe protruding from the fitting so you'll have room to slip on the new fitting's shoulder.

To extend an existing cast-iron system, you may either add a new cast-iron fitting and pipe or switch to a plastic fitting and run plastic DWV pipe from there. The plastic option, if allowed by code, is the simplest route.

To add a plastic T-fitting to an existing cast-iron run, cut out a section of the cast-iron pipe, as shown at left; glue on spacers at both ends of the plastic fitting, using solvent cement; then join the plastic spacers to the cast-iron pipe using no-hub couplings.

All couplings are not alike; if available, opt for repair couplings that don't have interior shoulders—this allows you to slide them almost completely over the cut ends. Some codes may require you to use a Mission coupling; it's similar to the no-hub, except that one-half of the neoprene sleeve is made narrower to fit more snugly over the cast-iron pipe, which is slightly smaller than plastic pipe.

When you're required by code to stick with cast-iron pipe, use no-hub fittings and no-hub couplings. Mark the fitting's top and bottom on the pipe, then cut the pipe, slip on the no-hub couplings, and secure the fitting. For pointers, see pages 58–59.

Inserting a plastic fitting into a run of plastic pipe is similar to tying into cast iron, except that you may be able to glue one end of the plastic T- or Y-fitting directly to the cut-off end of the existing plastic pipe. It all depends on the amount of play and the coupling you use—preferably one without an interior stop or shoulder. For details, see the facing page. If you need to review plastic pipefitting basics, see page 48.

EXTENDING A PLASTIC SYSTEM

1 Cut existing pipe

Plastic is much easier to cut than cast iron: here we're using a PVC saw, but other handsaws will do the trick, too. Try to cut ends off as squarely as possible.

2 Assemble the new pieces

Depending on the amount of play and the type of couplings you have, you may need one or two spacers, plus your new fitting. Mark and cut spacers to span the pipe gap plus the fitting's shoulder and the no-hub coupling's interior shoulder (if it has one).

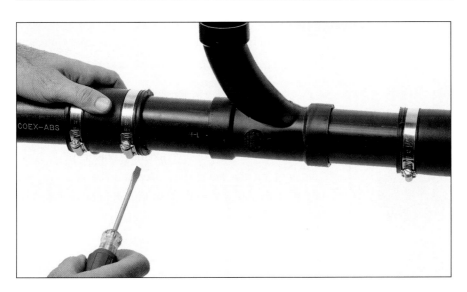

3 Tighten connections

Glue spacers to fitting, position the fitting in the gap, and slip the spacers inside the couplings. Align the new fitting in the direction of your intended extension, then tighten the coupling bands.

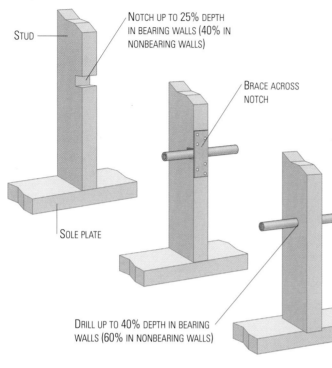

STUD

NOTCH UP TO 25% DEPTH IN BEARING WALLS (40% IN NONBEARING WALLS)

BRACE ACROSS NOTCH

SOLE PLATE

DRILL UP TO 40% DEPTH IN BEARING WALLS (60% IN NONBEARING WALLS)

1/16" STEEL PLATE

NEW PIPE RUNS

With connections made to existing supply and DWV lines, the new pipes are run to the new fixture location. Here are basic guidelines for routing and securing new pipes, plus some tricks of the trade to help make both supply and DWV jobs run smoother.

ROUTING PIPES THROUGH STUDS AND JOISTS

Ideally, pipes should always run between and parallel to framing members. At some point, though, you'll probably have to use one of the following techniques to go through studs or joists. (Note: Before cutting any framing members, check your local building code.)

CUTTING INTO WALL STUDS: Refer to the illustrations above for the best way to pass pipe through studs. You may drill a hole with a diameter up to 40 percent of the stud depth in bearing walls (those that support joists or rafters above), and up to 60 percent in nonbearing walls. You may drill a hole up to 60 percent of the stud depth in a bearing wall if you nail another stud to the first stud for strength. Holes should be centered. You may notch up to 25 percent of the stud depth in bearing walls and up to 40 percent in nonbearing walls. Notches should be braced with steel plates.

Running pipes outside the wall requires no notching and less wall patching. Use blocks of wood to temporarily support pipes, then fasten pipe supports to wall studs (see facing page). You can hide the pipes by building

At left, a cordless right-angle drill bores a string of 3/4-inch holes through a run of new wall studs. Whenever possible, drill through the centers of framing members, well away from the edges.

HANGER SPECS

Your new pipes need solid support at intervals no greater than those shown in the chart below. Four basic installations are shown here; you'll find a broader selection of hanger hardware on page 29. Remember: Don't use one type of metal hanger to support another type of metal pipe.

You'll note that most vertical intervals are listed as 10 feet. Actually, the codes state that these vertical runs should be supported at every story or every 10 feet; galvanized steel need only be supported every other story.

The 10-foot horizontal spec for cast iron is for modern no-hub pipe. If you're using traditional bell-and-spigot cast iron, it needs support every 5 feet. Any cast-iron pipe needs support within 18 inches of a joint.

Plumber's tape

Supply-pipe hanger

Pipe bushings

Friction clamp

MAXIMUM SUPPORT DISTANCES

TYPE OF PIPE	HORIZONTAL SUPPORT INTERVAL	VERTICAL SUPPORT INTERVAL
Copper	6'	10'
CPVC	3'	10'
PVC	4'	10'
ABS	4'	10'
Galvanized	12'	15'
Cast iron	10'	10'

ANATOMY OF A WET WALL

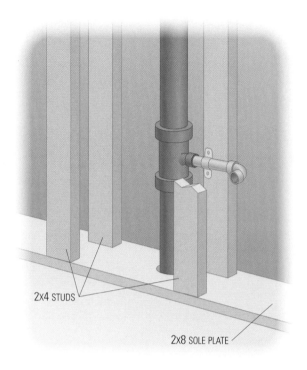

2X4 STUDS

2X8 SOLE PLATE

PIPE-JOINT JUNCTIONS

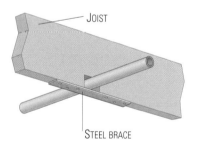

JOIST

STEEL BRACE

cabinets, a closet, a vanity, or shelves over them, or by thickening the wall to accommodate them. To thicken a wall, build out the entire wall, erecting new studs and wall coverings, or thicken only the lower portion where the pipes are, topping it off with a storage ledge or shelf. If you're building from scratch, you can also hide bulky pipes inside an oversized "wet wall," as shown at left.

CUTTING INTO FLOOR JOISTS: Refer to the illustrations below for the different types of pipe-joist junctions. If a pipe run hits a joist near its center, you may drill a hole through it as long as the diameter is no greater than one-third the depth of the joist. If a pipe run hits a joist near its top or bottom, a notch may accommodate it. The depth of the notch must be no greater than one-sixth the depth of the joist, and the notch cannot be located in the middle third of the span. Top-notched joists should have lengths of 2x2 wooden cleats nailed in place under the notch on both sides of the joist to give added support. Joists notched at the bottom should have either a steel strap or a 2x2 cleat nailed on.

You might sometimes need to cut an entire section out of a joist to accommodate a DWV section. Reinforce that section by using doubled headers on both sides of the cut (see facing page).

Building up the floor will cover a new branch drain. Either build a platform over the pipes for the fixture or appliance or raise the floor over the entire room with furring strips around the new pipes. Just remember that a raised floor will affect the fit of doors and transitions to other rooms' floors.

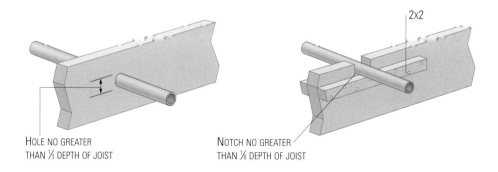

HOLE NO GREATER THAN ⅓ DEPTH OF JOIST

2X2

NOTCH NO GREATER THAN ⅙ DEPTH OF JOIST

FRAMING A FLOOR OPENING

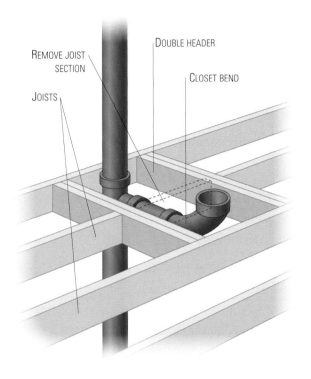

REMOVE JOIST SECTION

DOUBLE HEADER

CLOSET BEND

JOISTS

Circular saw with masonry blade

BUILDING UP A FLOOR

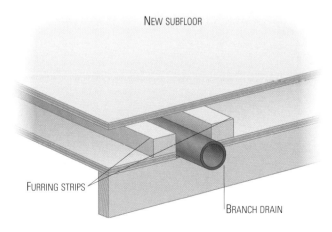

NEW SUBFLOOR

FURRING STRIPS

BRANCH DRAIN

WHAT IF THE FLOOR IS CONCRETE?

For many homeowners, a new bathroom is right at the top of their wish list for a basement conversion. Drainage is the primary puzzle: If your main drain runs above floor level, you'll probably need to pump water or waste uphill to meet it (see page 125). But if your main drain runs beneath the concrete slab, you may be able to tie into it directly with new drain lines from a toilet, sink, and/or shower. Tying in will require removing part of the slab—a messy but not particularly difficult job.

To cut through concrete, plan to use a heavy-duty circular saw with a masonry or diamond blade to score lines along the planned opening. Use chalk or tape to mark the location of the main drain and to lay out new drain lines. Then make two or more slow cuts along your lines, increasing the depth of each pass. You'll make a lot of noise and kick up a lot of dust—and even some sparks. Be sure to wear full safety gear: ear protection, a dust mask, work gloves, and safety glasses.

Break up the concrete with a sledgehammer or a rented electric jackhammer. (If you use a jackhammer, take care not to cut into the drain line!) Remove the concrete and dig out the dirt around the drainpipe.

The area around a shower drain must remain accessible after the concrete is patched so that the trap can be connected. Your local plumbing supplier may sell plastic tub boxes for this purpose; or you could build a 12-inch-square wood frame around the drain. You should also wrap the stub for a toilet drain with a cardboard sleeve, available at plumbing supply stores. This will keep concrete far enough away to allow the floor flange to fit.

After the new plumbing has been inspected, plan to return dirt and gravel to surround the pipes, then add a 3-inch layer of concrete to patch the hole.

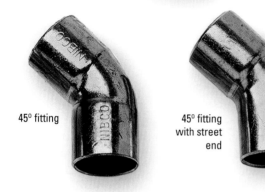

90° fitting

45° fitting

45° fitting
with street
end

T-fitting

SUPPLY STRATEGIES

Whenever possible, lay out and assemble new supply runs in large sections. If, for example, copper pipe is going in a cramped crawl space, plan to cut pipe and solder joints outside. Remember to take makeup—the distance the pipe extends inside each fitting—into account. You can often find a little slack, or room to fudge, along a run of supply pipe, but don't count on much.

Slide long pipe runs through drilled or notched holes, or use appropriate hangers to secure the runs. If possible, install the new runs with a slight pitch, and add a shutoff valve and/or drain valve (see the facing page) at the lowest point.

CHANGES OF DIRECTION: Negotiate turns and obstacles with the supply fittings shown at left. Couplings join straight lengths of pipe. Street fittings have ends that slip right into another fitting's interior shoulder, eliminating the need for a spacer (short length of pipe) to make the joint. Use 45° fittings to "leapfrog" one parallel pipe over another (see below). Remember that fittings can be rotated in opposition to each other (see below left) to create subtle directional changes.

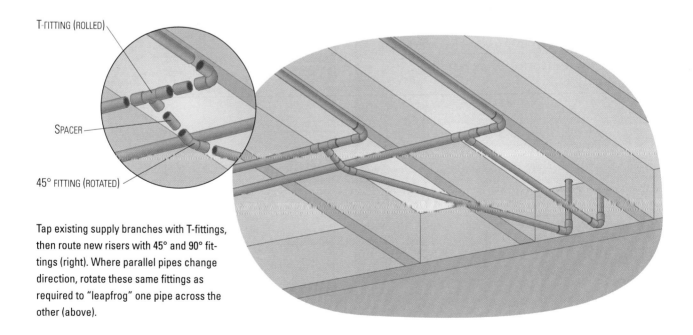

T-FITTING (ROLLED)

SPACER

45° FITTING (ROTATED)

Tap existing supply branches with T-fittings, then route new risers with 45° and 90° fittings (right). Where parallel pipes change direction, rotate these same fittings as required to "leapfrog" one pipe across the other (above).

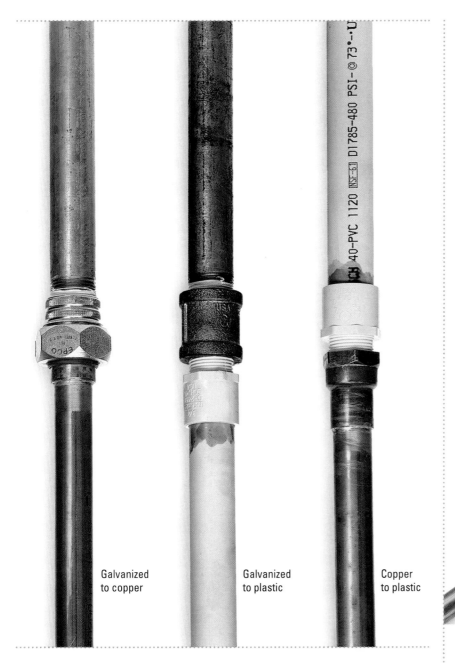

Galvanized
to copper

Galvanized
to plastic

Copper
to plastic

ADD A SHUTOFF VALVE

When extending your supply system, it's a good idea to slope each new pipe for drainage, then add a shutoff valve. The valve shown below, called a "stop-and-waste" valve, includes a bleeder screw on one side; with the valve turned off, simply open the screw to drain the pipe. 🔧

Some change of direction is good: long, straight runs lead to water hammer. However, unnecessary bends—especially 90° fittings—create friction. If your run calls for more than four 90° elbows, the rule is to replace some or all of them with gentler 45° fittings.

SWITCHING PIPE TYPE: If you wish to change pipe type—say from galvanized steel to copper or plastic—you'll need to insert the appropriate adapters at the pipe ends. Three examples are shown above: galvanized to copper, galvanized to plastic, and copper to plastic.

Long sweep 90°

Low-heel
vent 90°

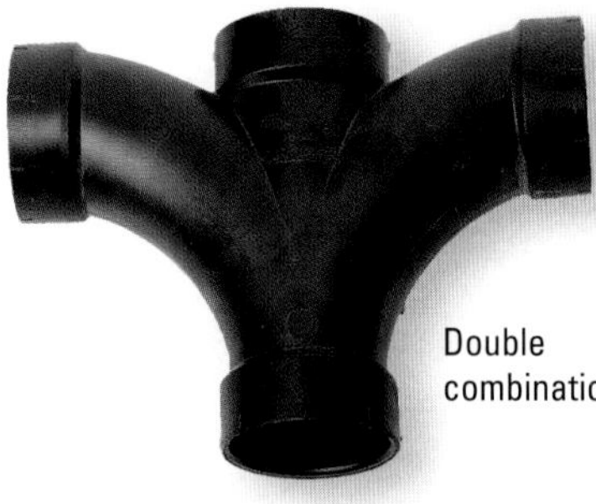

Double
combination Y

Y-fitting

45° elbow with
street end

Sanitary
cross

Combination Y

90° elbow

Sanitary T

22½° bend

DWV TRICKS

Drainpipe logistics often depend on altitude—the vertical space you have to work in. An unfinished basement may offer plenty of headroom, while a second-story drain needs to fit within the confines of the ceiling below. Because of a drain-pipe's slope requirements, available altitude also depends on how long a pipe must extend horizon-tally—the longer the run, the greater the required altitude. In addition, some fittings take up more vertical space than others. Plastic fittings tend to require less headroom than cast iron. Choose your layout and materials accordingly.

CHANGES OF DIRECTION: DWV connections are largely a game of piecing together horizontals and verticals—or changes in direction. Codes specify fittings for horizontal-to-horizontal runs, vertical-to-horizontal connections (like a fixture drain to a branch drain), and horizontal-to-vertical inter-sections (where, for example, a branch drain meets the main soil stack).

A selection of standard fittings is shown at left. Be sure to find out what's permitted in your area—for example, a sanitary T on its side is approved in some areas, but not in others (you'd need a combination Y instead). A sanitary cross may be fine for some uses, but only if the top and bottom are two pipe sizes larger than the side inlets (for example, 2-inch sides and 4-inch top). You may be required to install a cleanout wher-ever a vertical drop meets a horizontal drainpipe.

As with supply connections (see page 80), you can gain a lot of play by rotating one DWV fit-ting in opposition to another. If you have the alti-tude or horizontal headroom, use spacers (short pipe pieces) to join opposing fittings; if you're cramped for space, you can slip a street fitting inside an adjacent fitting's shoulder without using the spacer.

continued on page 84 ➤

CHANGES OF DIRECTION

LONG-SWEEP 90°   45° BEND   22½° BEND   Y-FITTING

Horizontal to Horizontal (top view)

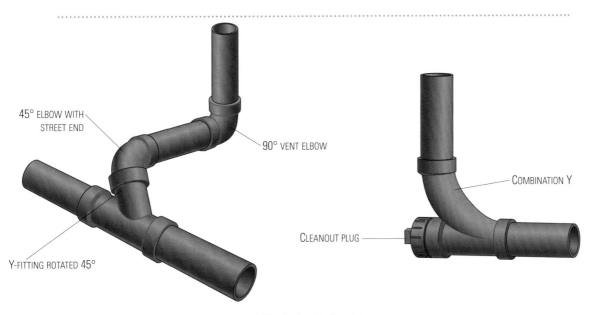

45° ELBOW WITH STREET END   90° VENT ELBOW   COMBINATION Y   CLEANOUT PLUG   Y-FITTING ROTATED 45°

Vertical to Horizontal

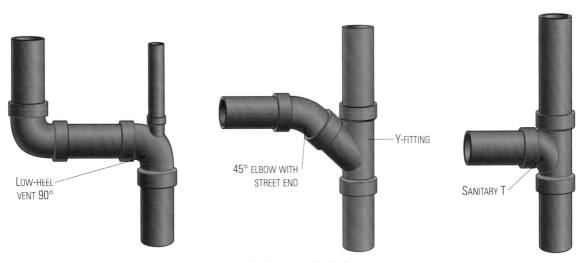

LOW-HEEL VENT 90°   45° ELBOW WITH STREET END   Y-FITTING   SANITARY T

Horizontal to Vertical

GAS SYSTEM BASICS

When you want to add or relocate a gas appliance, keep in mind a few basic requirements. There's no room for error when installing a gas system. Unless you're experienced, it's best to have a professional make the installation. You must, in any case, have the work inspected before the gas is turned on.

Materials approved for gas supply vary with the area and the type of gas. The most universally accepted indoor materials are threaded pipe of galvanized steel, and "black pipe" (threaded steel pipe without galvanizing). For outdoors and direct burial, choose "green," or coated, steel pipe. Heavier grades of copper pipe used for plumbing systems (types K and L) are also permitted in some locations.

The local plumbing code or a separate gas code will specify pipe size according to cubic-foot capacity and the length of pipe between the meter or storage tank and the appliance. All gas appliances should have a numerical rating in BTUs per hour stamped right on the nameplate. To convert BTUs to cubic feet, figure 1,000 BTUs to 1 cubic foot; for example, 65,000 BTUs equals 65 cubic feet.

Each appliance must have a code-approved shutoff valve with a straight handle to turn off the gas in an emergency. Shutoffs must be rated for your type of gas and must be located in the same room as the appliance.

An appliance is connected to the shutoff valve with either solid pipe or flexible tubing designed for gas. When using

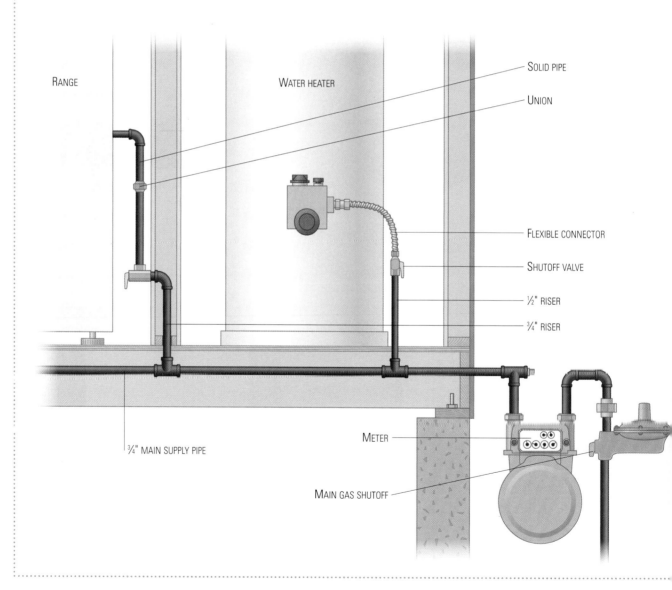

RANGE

WATER HEATER

SOLID PIPE

UNION

FLEXIBLE CONNECTOR

SHUTOFF VALVE

½" RISER

¾" RISER

¾" MAIN SUPPLY PIPE

METER

MAIN GAS SHUTOFF

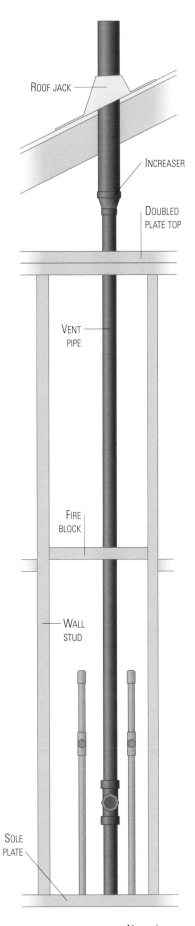

ROOF JACK

INCREASER

DOUBLED PLATE TOP

VENT PIPE

FIRE BLOCK

WALL STUD

SOLE PLATE

solid-pipe connectors, add a union fitting that will allow you to disconnect the appliance. If you use a corrugated flexible connector, join it to the shutoff valve with brass flare fittings. Some gas shutoff valves come with a built-in flare fitting for the flexible appliance connector; others require you to thread the flare fitting onto the valve or pipe.

To test extensive runs of new gas lines, cap off all the stubouts, screw on a pressure gauge, and pump up the line with 10 to 20 pounds of air pressure; maintain it for 15 minutes. Falling pressure indicates a leak. To find it, brush soapy water onto the fittings and look for telltale bubbles, as shown below. Try tightening the connection; disassemble and reconnect if necessary.

You may also use the soap suds technique to test your appliance connections and other small-scale alterations you've made to your gas lines. 🔧

continued from page 82

VENTING LOGISTICS: Fittings approved for vent use can make sharper turns than those allowed for drainage fittings. Vent elbows and vent Ts cover most vent uses. Drain fittings like 45° and 22$\frac{1}{2}$° elbows or long-sweep 90's help negotiate obstacles.

If you're running a new secondary vent out the roof, take a look at the drawing at right. You'll probably need to bore holes through wall framing as shown, then install a roof jack up top. Code may also require a switch in pipe type out in the open—plastic pipe corrodes in sunlight. In cold locales, you may need an "increaser"—a larger pipe size—as shown, to prevent the vent from icing up and freezing shut.

Test new gas fittings by brushing on soapy water; bubbles indicate a leak.

R OUGHING-IN FIXTURES

On the following pages, you'll find specific installation notes for roughing-in new fixtures and appliances that require tying into or extending your present plumbing systems.

ROUGHING-IN A BATHROOM SINK

A lavatory sink is fairly easy to install and has little effect on an existing drain's efficiency (a sink rates low in fixture units). Three common methods are back-to-back (which requires little pipe), within a vanity cabinet (which can hide pipe runs), and side-by-side. A sink can normally be wet-vented if it's within the critical distance; otherwise it's back-vented.

Pipes you'll need include 1/2-inch hot and cold water supply risers, stubouts, and shutoff valves; transition fittings, if necessary; and flexible supply tubes above the two shutoff valves. Water-hammer arresters, either prefabricated or homemade (see page 90), may be required on both hot and cold supply pipes.

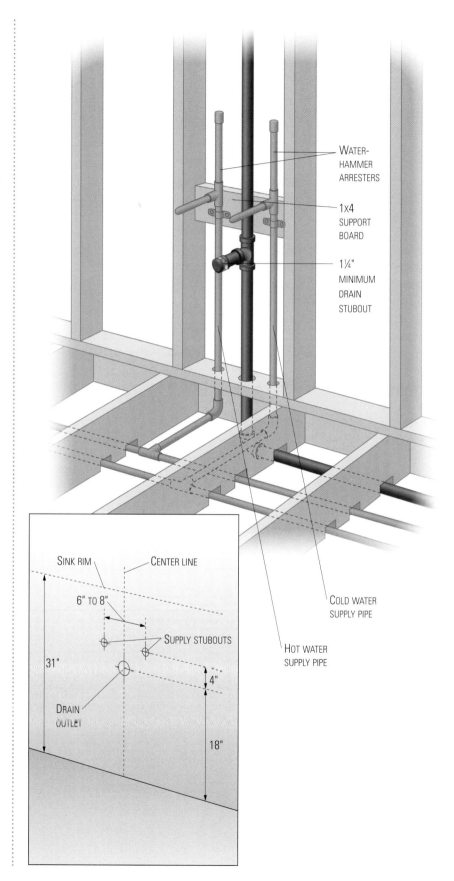

WATER-HAMMER ARRESTERS

1x4 SUPPORT BOARD

1¼" MINIMUM DRAIN STUBOUT

COLD WATER SUPPLY PIPE

HOT WATER SUPPLY PIPE

SINK RIM

CENTER LINE

6" TO 8"

SUPPLY STUBOUTS

31"

4"

DRAIN OUTLET

18"

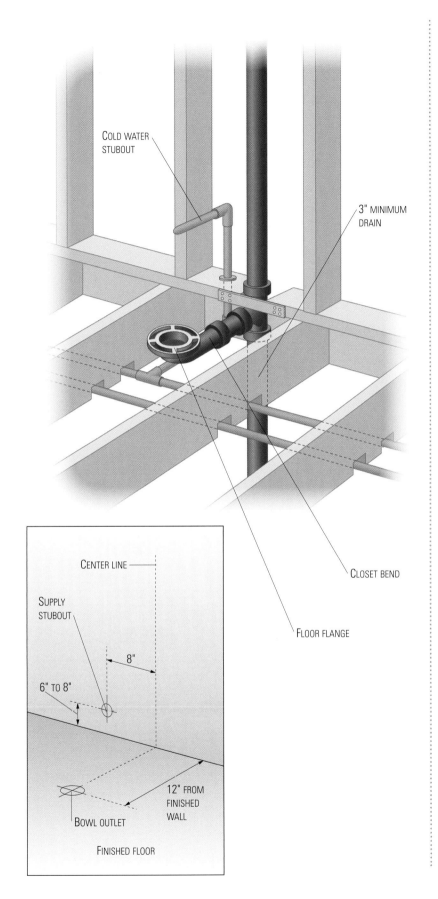

COLD WATER STUBOUT

3" MINIMUM DRAIN

CLOSET BEND

FLOOR FLANGE

CENTER LINE

SUPPLY STUBOUT

8"

6" TO 8"

12" FROM FINISHED WALL

BOWL OUTLET

FINISHED FLOOR

ROUGHING-IN A TOILET

The toilet is the single most troublesome fixture to install in a house because it requires its own vent (2 inches minimum) and a drain at least 3 inches in diameter. If the toilet is on a branch drain, it can't be upstream from a sink or shower.

The closet bend and toilet floor flange must be roughed-in first, as shown in the illustration at left; the floor flange must be positioned at the level of the eventual finished floor.

Pipes required for roughing-in a toilet include a ½-inch cold water riser; a cold water stubout with shutoff valve; and a flexible supply tube above the valve. One water-hammer arrester may be required.

Anchor Those Pipes

You'll notice that the pipes shown on these pages are secured to wall framing in one of several ways: by using 1x4 bracing boards, copper supply straps, or plastic pipe bushings where supply risers pass through the wall's sole plate. The exact method is up to you: what's important is that pipes remain rigid when pushed or pulled.

ROUGHING-IN A BATHTUB OR SHOWER

Like sinks, bathtubs and showers rate low in fixture units. They're often positioned on branch drains and are usually wet-vented or back-vented; both enter the stack at or below floor level because of their below-floor traps. A shower's faucet body and shower pipe assembly are installed while the wall is open. Tubs and showers may require support framing (see pages 116–120).

Pipes required include 1/2-inch hot and cold supply lines and 1/2-inch pipes to both shower head and tub spout. Increasingly, showers are plumbed with their own supply branches, which helps maintain both water pressure and temperature when nearby fixtures are turned on. If possible, place accessible gate or ball valves on these risers. You may be required to cut a small opening and add a door below, behind, or to the side of the tub to allow later access to both trap and drainpipe.

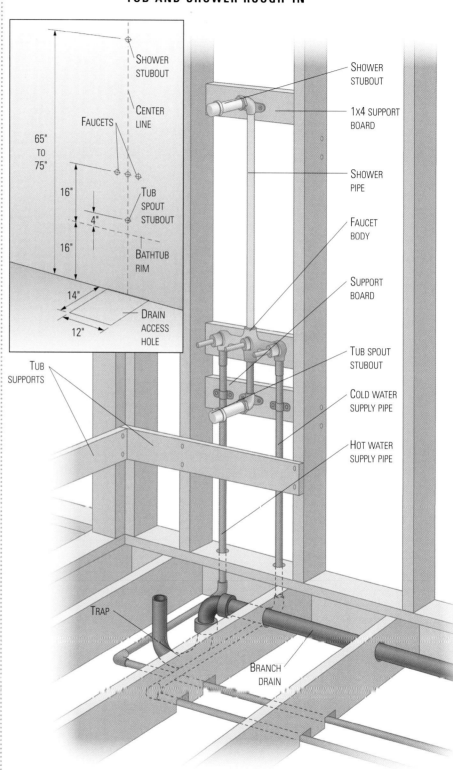

SHOWER STALL ROUGH-IN

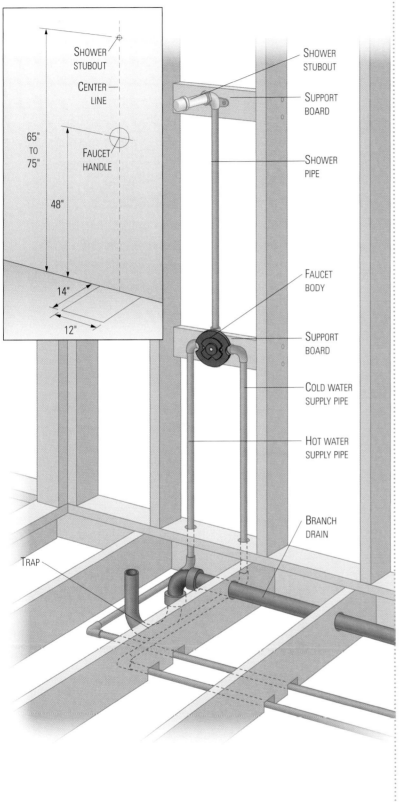

SHOWER STUBOUT

CENTER LINE

65" TO 75"

FAUCET HANDLE

48"

14"

12"

SHOWER STUBOUT

SUPPORT BOARD

SHOWER PIPE

FAUCET BODY

SUPPORT BOARD

COLD WATER SUPPLY PIPE

HOT WATER SUPPLY PIPE

BRANCH DRAIN

TRAP

BATHROOM FIXTURE CLEARANCES

Building and plumbing codes specify clearances between bathroom fixtures. These distances are minimums, and getting larger, reflecting the needs of an aging population for barrier-free design. Codes may vary somewhat, but the clearances shown here are typical. Always check your local codes before you begin to work on a layout for a new bathroom.

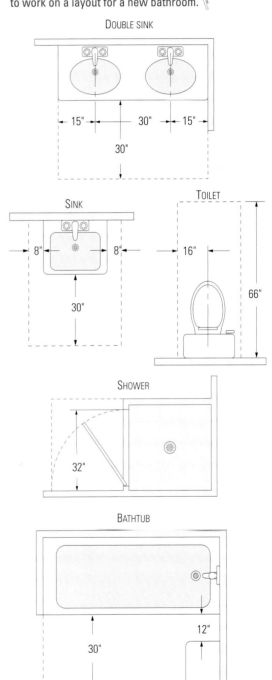

DOUBLE SINK

15" 30" 15"

30"

SINK

8" 8"

30"

TOILET

16"

66"

SHOWER

32"

BATHTUB

30"

12"

ROUGHING-IN A KITCHEN SINK

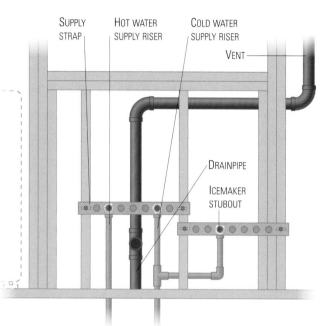

SUPPLY STRAP
HOT WATER SUPPLY RISER
COLD WATER SUPPLY RISER
VENT
DRAINPIPE
ICEMAKER STUBOUT

Generally, a single set of vertical supply pipes and one drainpipe serve the entire kitchen. For both convenience and economy, fixtures and appliances that require water are usually adjacent to the sink. Supply pipes for a dishwasher, hot water dispenser, and automatic icemaker often branch off the main hot and cold supply lines leading to the sink faucet. Similarly, the dishwasher and garbage disposer share the sink's trap and drainpipe. The hot water dispenser discharges directly into the sink. For hardware and logistics, see pages 104–107.

Pipes you'll need include ½-inch hot and cold supply risers, stubouts, and shutoff valves; transition fittings, if necessary; and flexible supply tubes above the shutoff valves. Water-hammer arresters, either prefabricated or homemade (see below), may be required on both hot and cold supply pipes.

WATER-HAMMER ARRESTERS

Water hammer occurs when you quickly turn off the water at a faucet or an appliance. The water flowing through the pipes simply slams to a stop, causing a destructive shock wave and a hammering noise. To minimize the effect, many codes require water-hammer arresters (also known as air chambers) near fixtures; they're installed at the top of a fixture's supply risers, in front of shutoff valves and supply tubes.

The arresters come in several versions—some commercial, some homemade. The photo at right shows two kinds; the homemade one is made from common copper pipe and fittings. Most installations place the arresters atop T-fittings at the tops of supply risers inside the wall. Some plumbers prefer arresters be outside the wall for easy servicing; these can be concealed inside a kitchen sink cabinet or bathroom vanity.

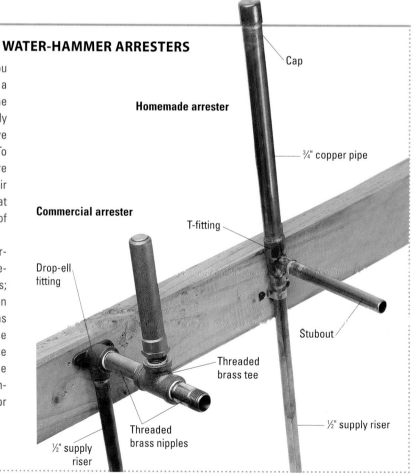

Cap
Homemade arrester
¾" copper pipe
Commercial arrester
T-fitting
Drop-ell fitting
Stubout
Threaded brass tee
½" supply riser
Threaded brass nipples
½" supply riser

ROUGHING-IN A WASHING MACHINE

You'll need to run both hot and cold water supply pipes to the desired location. Supply pipes for an automatic washer are usually ½ inch in diameter.

Plan to use either a pair of washing machine valves (they look like hose bibs), a laundry faucet (less than ideal), or a single- or twin-lever washing machine box (see pages 126–127) to make supply hookups. Space supply risers accordingly. If you're using washing machine valves or a wall faucet, plan to install T-fittings on the risers inside the wall, then add supply stubouts on the outside. A washing machine box sits inside the wall, and risers run directly to it.

If a laundry tub or sink is nearby, the drain hose can hook over the edge of it. If there is no sink or tub nearby, you'll need to drain the washer into a standpipe—a vertical 2-inch pipe that connects to a 1½-inch trap. The standpipe should be between 18 and 30 inches above the trap (some codes allow a range of 18 to 42 inches). The trap itself should be 6 to 18 inches above the floor.

Because the stop and start of washing machine cycles is particularly hard on valves, hoses, and the machines themselves, some manufacturers recommend that water-hammer arresters be one size larger than the supply pipes and as long as 24 inches.

ROUGHING-IN A WATER HEATER

To install a new water heater or to relocate one, you'll have to rough-in a cold water supply pipe, typically ¾ inch, and a hot water outlet pipe, then add either a gas line or an electrical power cable. For help with gas plumbing, see page 84. You'll also need to add a new flue if you're installing a gas heater (see pages 128–129).

Install a shutoff valve—either a ball or gate valve—on both incoming and outgoing pipes. Then plan to use flexible connectors or rigid pipe and unions to hook up the water and gas lines. Flex connectors are simpler to install, but some codes require the rigid pipes.

If you're relocating a heater, pick a location as close as possible to the main areas of hot water use in your house. Keep in mind that you must provide adequate clearance between a gas heater and any combustible materials, and you must have vents near the top and bottom of any water heater enclosure. Some codes require a floor drain within 6 inches of your heater's pressure-relief valve. A heater in a garage may have to be elevated.

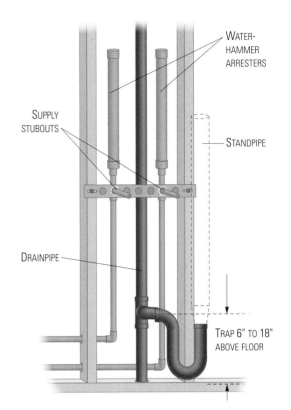

WATER-HAMMER ARRESTERS

SUPPLY STUBOUTS

STANDPIPE

DRAINPIPE

TRAP 6" TO 18" ABOVE FLOOR

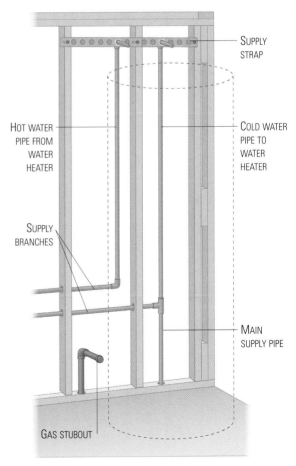

SUPPLY STRAP

HOT WATER PIPE FROM WATER HEATER

COLD WATER PIPE TO WATER HEATER

SUPPLY BRANCHES

MAIN SUPPLY PIPE

GAS STUBOUT

Test gauge

TESTING YOUR WORK

Once you've roughed-in your new pipes, you'll need to test your extensions for leaks using the methods described below. The building inspector will probably want to run these tests, too, but you can increase your odds for approval by first running them yourself.

After the building department has inspected and approved your work, patch the wall, ceiling, or floor coverings as outlined on the facing page.

SUPPLY TESTING: Simply cap off each pipe, turn on the water, and look closely for leaks. Usually this visual test is all you need.

If a potential leak might spray water where it could do damage during the test, you can install a test gauge on the supply line instead. The test gauge has a small, capped nipple; simply screw an air pump (even a bicycle pump) to this nipple and inflate the line with 50 pounds of air pressure. If the pressure drops, you have a leak. To trace it, apply soapy water to the connections (see page 85); bubbles mark the spot.

Did you find a leak? Try tightening the connections; disassemble and replace fittings, if necessary. If you need to cut and repair copper or plastic supply pipe, see page 185.

DWV TESTING: There are two methods for testing drain-waste and vent pipes, and both are a hassle to run. First, there's the water test: new drainpipes are capped off, water is poured in from a roof vent, then the pipes are inspected for leaks. A leak should be readily apparent, but that's the problem—all that water could do a lot of damage. Although this test is commonly used for new construction, it's rarely done when remodeling.

The pressure test, which the inspector may run—or have you run—is used most often for testing extensions of existing lines. First, the pipes are capped or sealed with test plugs, then either an inflatable ball (called a weenie) or a test cap (called a Jim cap) is inserted into a cleanout and pumped with 5 pounds of pressure. If the pressure drops within 15 minutes, you have a leak. To find the leak, run the soapy water test; again, bubbles mark the spot.

Pumps, weenies, and test gauges are available at many rental yards, or you can buy them yourself.

FINISHING UP

Once your pipes are roughed-in, some holes may need patching. If you've notched into walls or ceilings in the process of plumbing, now is also the time to make them look like new again. Here are some tips for putting everything back together.

REPAIRING PLASTER: Patching around trap outlets and supply stubouts is a simple matter. Use a wide-blade putty knife to apply commercial plaster compound. Try to match the texture of the surrounding wall.

For larger holes you'll have to nail on some backing (such as lath), clean and moisten the edges of the hole, and, in some cases, apply more than one coat of plaster compound.

REPAIRING GYPSUM WALLBOARD: For small repairs, simply use a wide-blade putty knife and some spackling compound.

To replace a large section, you'll need to cut a piece of new wallboard to fill the hole. If there are no studs or joists underneath on which to nail the replacement piece, add some wooden blocks for support.

Attach replacement wallboard with drywall screws or nails, dimpling the surface slightly at the fastener heads as shown at top right. Use a wide-blade putty knife to spread joint compound across the dimples. With joint tape and compound, cover the edge joints around the replacement as shown.

Apply a second coat of compound to the nail heads and tape, feathering the edges of the first coat to produce a relatively smooth surface. Let dry, then sand the nail dimples and joints.

For a smooth wall, you may have to apply a third coat to both the joints and the nail heads and sand again. To duplicate a skip-trowel texture, apply a large amount of joint compound with a broad palette knife and draw the blade over the surface in one direction. A plaster texture can be created with the same tool by applying the compound in a semicircular motion. Use a paintbrush to duplicate a stipple finish.

Let dry, then paint the surface.

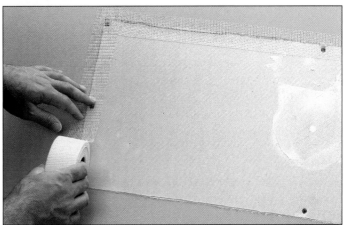

To repair wallboard, first screw a patch to wall studs or ceiling joists, driving fasteners slightly below the surface (top). Fill fastener holes with joint compound, then tape the joints (center). Finally, gently spread compound atop the tape (bottom).

FINISH WORK

At long last, it's time to hook up those fixtures and appliances that prompted your plumbing plans to begin with. In new construction, this so-called finish work is completed once walls, floors, and ceilings are in place. Be sure that new pipe runs and stubouts are anchored, capped, and tested; if not, see Chapter Five, "Rough Plumbing," beginning on page 60, for pointers. Of course, to simply replace an old faucet with an updated version, you can turn to the appropriate section in this chapter and go right to work.

Be sure to turn the water off before beginning—either at fixture shutoff valves or at the main house shutoff (see page 152). Also shut down power to any electrical appliance, such as a disposer, dishwasher, or water heater, that you're installing and test that it's off. When the job's done, turn utilities back on and check your work

THE KITCHEN SINK COMPLEX

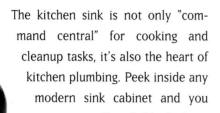

The kitchen sink is not only "command central" for cooking and cleanup tasks, it's also the heart of kitchen plumbing. Peek inside any modern sink cabinet and you will probably find not only a trap and supply tubes, but also fittings for a disposer, a dishwasher, an icemaker, and more. Here's how to install the sink and all those new appliances.

KITCHEN SINKS

Common sink materials include stainless steel, enameled cast iron or steel, composites, and solid-surface acrylics. Vitreous china is also making a comeback. For smaller auxiliary sinks or "bar" sinks, you'll find more decorative, higher-maintenance surfaces, such as copper or brass.

The traditional one-piece sink measures about 22 inches deep and 24 or 25 inches wide. Double- or one-and-a-half-bowl sinks average 33 inches wide; triple-bowl versions, or those with integral drain boards, may be as wide as 42 inches.

When you select your sink, be sure the holes in it will accommodate the type of faucet you plan to install (see pages 100–101), as well as any other sinktop accessories. A kitchen sink will normally have three holes for a simple faucet or four holes to accommodate a faucet and a spray hose, a hot water dispenser, or an air gap for a dishwasher. The distance between the holes is either 4, 6, or 8 inches.

The standard "deck-mounted" kitchen sink fits into a specially cut hole in the countertop. If you're replacing a sink, you may choose any model that's the same size as or larger than the present sink; if it's a larger sink or a new installation, you'll have to make the sink cutout first.

Three basic sink styles prevail: self-rimmed, frame-rimmed, and recessed (unrimmed). Most new sinks are self-rimmed; these have a molded overlap that's supported by the countertop. Heavy enameled models simply sit in sealant atop the opening, but most lightweight stainless-steel sinks also include mounting lugs to secure them from below.

A frame-rimmed sink has a surrounding channel that holds the sink to the countertop. The channel, which is fastened to the countertop, supports the sink.

Some recessed sinks perch on a lowered "shelf" in the countertop substrate; these are sometimes called flush-mounts. Others are under-mounted and held from below by metal clips. The flush-mount version, which is common with tile countertops, is detailed on the facing page. An under-mount sink is shown on page 108.

A fourth type, the integral sink, is part of the countertop and comes in both solid-surface and stainless-steel versions. Normally, you'll just set these atop the cabinet in a bead of adhesive (see page 110).

MAKING A SINK CUTOUT: For a new installation, you'll first need to cut a hole in the countertop. Trace either a template (included with the new sink) or the bottom edge of the frame onto the exact spot where the sink will

SELF-RIMMED SINK (CERAMIC)

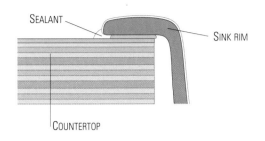

SEALANT
SINK RIM
COUNTERTOP

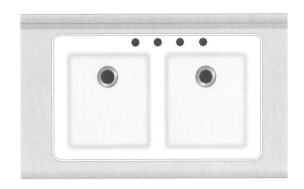

SELF-RIMMED SINK (STAINLESS STEEL)

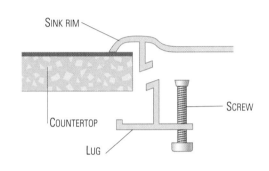

SINK RIM
SCREW
COUNTERTOP
LUG

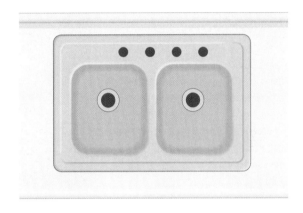

FRAME-RIMMED SINK

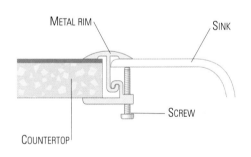

METAL RIM
SINK
SCREW
COUNTERTOP

RECESSED SINK

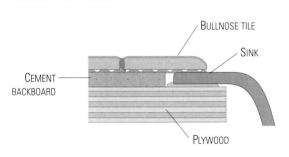

BULLNOSE TILE
SINK
CEMENT BACKBOARD
PLYWOOD

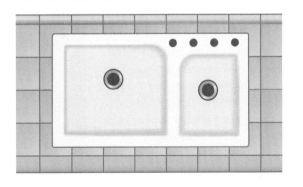

sit. For details, see below. Typically, the edge of the cutout is set back 1½ to 2 inches from the front edge of the countertop. Drill pilot holes in each corner of the outline, then insert a jigsaw into one of the holes to start the cutout.

INSTALLING THE NEW SINK: It's easiest to mount the faucet (pages 100–101) and hook up the strainer assembly (pages 102–103) before setting a new sink in the countertop.

To install a self-rimmed sink, apply a ½-inch-wide strip of plumber's putty or silicone sealant along the edge

INSTALLING A SELF-RIMMED SINK

1 Mark the opening

First trace a template or the outline of the sink onto the exact spot on the countertop where the sink will sit. If it's the outline you're tracing, you'll probably need to measure in from the lines an inch or so and draw a parallel set—otherwise, your sink could fall through the opening! To prevent splintering, you may wish to tape along the outline.

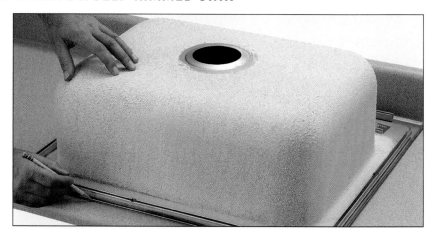

2 Cut the countertop

Drill pilot holes in the corners of the outline, then use a jigsaw to cut along the lines. If your top includes a backsplash, you may not have room in back for the saber saw; use a reciprocating saw or handsaw instead.

3 Mount the strainer and faucet

It's simplest to attach as much hardware as you can before installing the sink, saving awkward work later below the countertop. We're installing the sink faucet and supply tubes (pages 100–101) plus the sink strainer and tailpiece (see pages 102–103 for details).

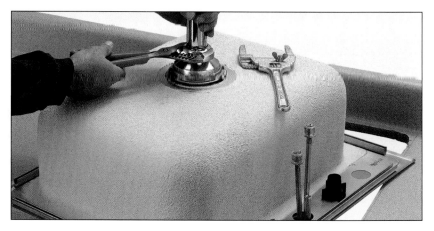

of the countertop opening. Set the sink into the cutout and press it down. Smooth excess putty. The installation sequence for a self-rimmed sink is shown below.

For a frame-rimmed sink, apply a ring of plumber's putty around the top edge of the sink. Fasten the frame to the sink, following the manufacturer's instructions; some frames attach with mounting screws, others with metal extension tabs that bend around the sink lip. Wipe off excess putty.

A recessed sink should also be embedded in a bead of putty or silicone sealant and anchored with any clamps or lugs provided.

Finally, hook up the supply tubes (page 101) and drain trap (page 103). Turn on the water and check for leaks.

4 Apply sealant

Run a bead of silicone sealant or plumber's putty around the edge of the opening, right where the sink's rimmed lip will sit. It's easiest to apply sealant with a caulking gun.

5 Position the sink

Gently lower the sink into the opening: you may need extra hands, especially if you're installing a heavy cast-iron model. Press the sink rim down onto the countertop, fine-tune alignment, then clean up excess sealant.

6 Add mounting lugs

If your sink model comes with mounting lugs or clamps, attach them from below, following the manufacturer's instructions. Most stainless-steel sinks include lugs; heavier enameled sinks simply sit in sealant atop the opening.

CENTER-SET FAUCET

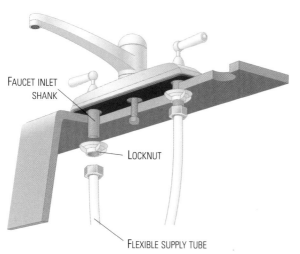

FAUCET INLET SHANK

LOCKNUT

FLEXIBLE SUPPLY TUBE

SINGLE-CONTROL FAUCET

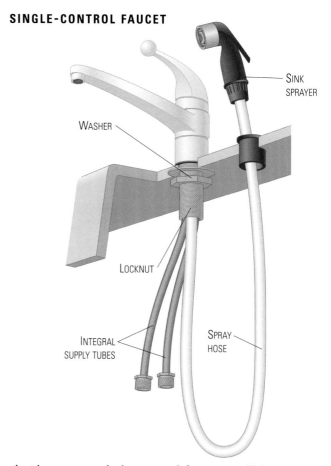

SINK SPRAYER

WASHER

LOCKNUT

INTEGRAL SUPPLY TUBES

SPRAY HOSE

KITCHEN FAUCETS

Kitchen sink faucets are available with single, center-set, or spread-fit controls. A single-control fitting has a combined faucet and lever or knob controlling water flow and temperature. A center-set control has separate hot and cold water controls and a faucet, all mounted on an "escutcheon," or base. A spread-fit control has separate hot and cold water controls and a faucet, independently mounted. Single-control and center-set models are shown above.

Faucets are either deck-mounted or wall-mounted. Most modern faucets are the deck-mounted type, seated on the rear of the sink and secured from below. When shopping, you may find the selection bewildering. You may choose from a varied lineup of single-control faucets—valve, disk, ball, and cartridge—as well as center-set or spread-fit faucets and styles ranging from antique reproductions to futuristic compression models. All are interchangeable as long as the new faucet's inlet shanks are spaced to fit the holes on the sink. Choose a new unit that comes with clear installation instructions, and a well-known brand that will have repair kits and replacement parts available for future use.

If you're replacing an old-fashioned wall-mounted faucet, you face a different decision: either to buy an updated style or to switch to a deck-mounted type. If you

decide to use a deck-mounted faucet, you'll be adding several steps to the installation process; at minimum, you'll need to reroute pipes from the wall into the kitchen cabinet and then patch the wall.

Clean the surface of the sink where the new faucet will sit. Some faucets come with a rubber gasket on the bottom; if yours doesn't, apply a bead of plumber's putty to the base, as shown on the facing page. Some plumbers pack the entire faucet base with putty for extra protection, even if it has a gasket.

Set the faucet in position, feeding the integral supply tubes, if attached, down through the appropriate sink hole. Press the faucet onto the sink's surface. Install any required washers and locknuts from below. Attach a spray hose according to the manufacturer's instructions.

Connect flexible supply tubes to the faucet's inlet shanks or integral tubes and to the hot and cold shutoff valves, gently bending the tubes as necessary to make the connections.

INSTALLING A KITCHEN FAUCET

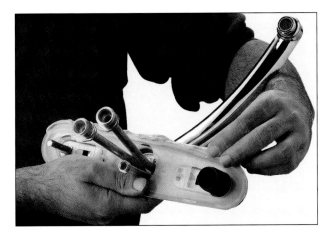

1 Apply plumber's putty

First, roll a string of plumber's putty between your hands. Then shape it around the outside of the faucet body where it will meet the sink or countertop.

2 Mount the faucet

Most faucets have one or more sets of locknuts that secure faucet to the sink or top from below. Simply hand-tighten plastic wingnuts; if possible, snug up metal locknuts with a wrench.

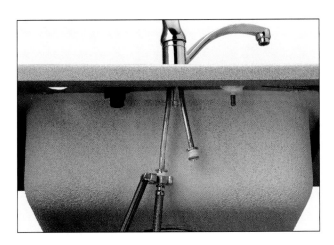

3 Connect supply tubes

Run flexible supply tubes from the fixture shutoff valves to the faucet inlet shanks or integral supply tubes. We're tightening the couplings with a basin wrench, a handy tool for such undersink adventures.

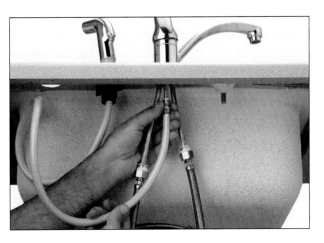

4 Attach a spray hose

If your faucet includes a sink sprayer, first thread its hose through a sink hole from above, then connect the hose to the faucet body below the sink. You may need to bend the supply tubes outward to gain access to the spray-hose threads.

What About Supply Tubes?

Flexible supply tubes make undersink faucet hookups much, much easier than they used to be. For a closer look at choosing and using these handy tubes, see "Adding Shutoff Valves" on page 109.

Center-outlet drain

End-outlet drain

TWO DRAINS IN ONE

A double-bowl sink requires one of two drain configurations, both shown above. If the drain is centered below both bowls, look for an assembly that includes a center outlet T-fitting and symmetrical waste arms. If the drain is offset, use a waste T and a long waste elbow. These setups are both available as kits, which include all the parts you'll need. 🔧

DRAIN HOOKUPS

The elements of a typical kitchen sink strainer and trap are shown below. Traps come in plastic (ABS or PVC), chrome-plated brass, and 17-gauge brass. You may purchase strainers, tailpieces, traps, and waste arms (sometimes called drain elbows) individually or buy multiple pieces in a kit. If you have a double sink, use one of the configurations shown at left. For details on drain setups with disposers and dishwashers, see pages 104–105.

INSTALLING A BASKET STRAINER: To install a strainer assembly, first apply a bead of plumber's putty to the underlip of the strainer body, then press it down into the sink opening. If the strainer body is held in place by a locknut, place the rubber gasket and metal washer over the strainer body from below, screw on the locknut, and tighten it by hand. Hold the strainer body from above while you snug up the locknut, preferably with a spud wrench. If the strainer body is held in place by a "quick-fit" retainer, fit the retainer over the strainer body and tighten all three screws.

DRAIN ASSEMBLY

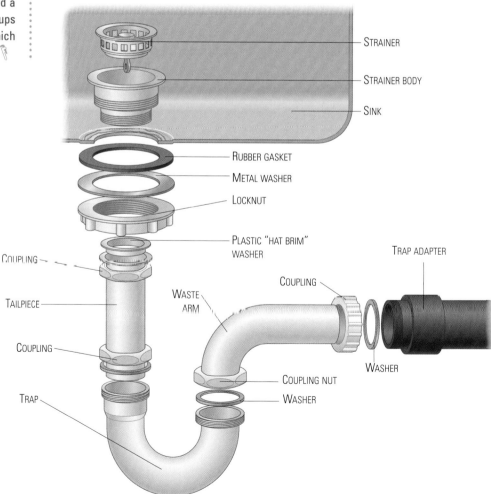

STRAINER

STRAINER BODY

SINK

RUBBER GASKET

METAL WASHER

LOCKNUT

PLASTIC "HAT BRIM" WASHER

COUPLING

TAILPIECE

COUPLING

TRAP

WASTE ARM

COUPLING

TRAP ADAPTER

COUPLING NUT

WASHER

WASHER

HOOKING UP THE TRAP AND WASTE ARM: First, attach the tailpiece to the strainer body with a coupling, as shown below right. Tailpieces come in different lengths; you may also cut one to fit, if necessary.

The next step, attaching the trap and waste arm, involves working the parts back and forth to get the right length and angle to align with both the tailpiece and the drain stubout. Measure and cut the waste arm as required to meet the drain stubout correctly.

The number one rule for traps is: Don't overtighten. Generally speaking, the couplings on plastic traps need hand-tightening only; metal couplings may need a half-turn or so past hand-tight, using a pair of adjustable pliers. If in doubt, err on the loose side: hand-tighten, turn on the water, and check for leaks. If you discover one, tighten the offending coupling slightly, then recheck.

HOOKING UP THE DRAIN

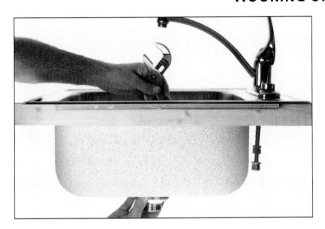

1 Secure the strainer

First run a fat bead of plumber's putty around the top of the sink opening, then press the strainer down into it. Add the gasket, washer, and locknut from below. If the strainer spins, wedge the twin handles of a wrench into the strainer (as shown) while you tighten.

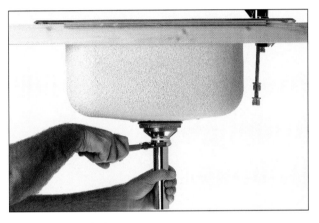

2 Add the tailpiece

Next add the tailpiece, securing it to the strainer's threaded body with a washer and coupling nut. Use slip-joint pliers to tighten the coupling. Tailpieces come in several lengths or can be cut to exact length; you can also buy extensions to make them longer.

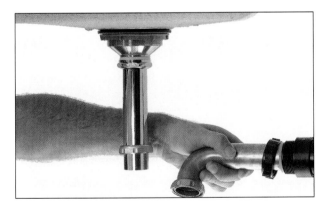

3 Position the drain elbow

If you haven't already, cement a threaded trap adapter onto the drain stubout coming from the wall. Slip the trap's coupling and the trap adapter's coupling onto the waste arm, then push the arm into the trap adapter. Like the tailpiece in Step #1, you can buy different lengths of waste arm, or you can cut one to exact length.

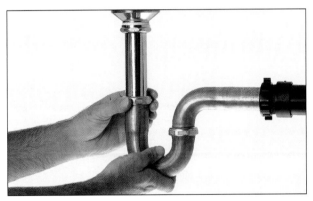

4 Add the trap

Hold the trap in place, fitting it to both tailpiece and waste arm. To help align things, slide the trap up onto the tailpiece, slide the waste arm in and out of the trap adapter, and adjust the trap from side to side. Once things are aligned, tighten the coupling nuts—first by hand, then with slip-joint pliers.

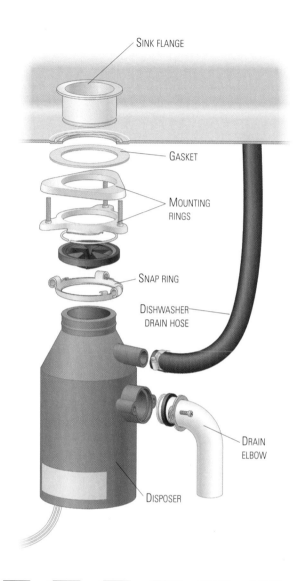

SINK FLANGE

GASKET

MOUNTING RINGS

SNAP RING

DISHWASHER DRAIN HOSE

DRAIN ELBOW

DISPOSER

WARNING When working with water-using electrical appliances, you should always be aware of the danger of possible electrical shock. Water and watts don't mix. Shut off the power before beginning any work. If you're replacing a disposer, turn off the electricity to that circuit and unplug the disposer or disconnect the wiring before removing the unit. If the disposer is wired in, don't touch bare wire ends with hands or tools, even if the power is off; handle them by the insulation only.

GARBAGE DISPOSERS

Installing a disposer takes a few hours, but the basic connection is not difficult. Most units fit the standard 3½- or 4-inch drain outlets of kitchen sinks and mount somewhat like a sink strainer (see pages 102–103). Plug-in disposers require a 120-volt receptacle under the sink and a separate wall switch adjacent to the sink. If your model has no plug, you or an electrician must hard-wire the unit directly from a nearby junction box.

MOUNTING THE DISPOSER: A disposer comes with its own sink flange and mounting assembly. Run a bead of plumber's putty around the sink opening and seat the flange in it. Then, working from below, slip the gasket, mounting rings, and snap ring up onto the neck of the sink flange. The snap ring should fit firmly into a groove on the sink flange to hold things in place temporarily.

Uniformly tighten the slotted screws in the mounting rings until the gasket fits snugly against the bottom of the flange. Remove any excess putty from around the flange.

Attach the drain elbow to the side of the disposer unit. Lift the disposer into place, aligning the holes in the unit's flange with the slotted screws in the mounting rings. Rotate the disposer so that the drain elbow lines up with the drain stubout. Tighten the nuts securely onto the slotted screws to ensure a good seal.

MAKING THE HOOKUPS: Fit a coupling and washer onto the drain elbow, then secure the trap to it. Add a waste arm on the other end of the trap to adapt to the drain stubout. For details, see pages 102–103. You may need to cut the waste arm to make the connection. Tighten all the connections, then run water down through the disposer to check for leaks. Tighten any loose connections.

At this point, either plug the disposer into a grounded receptacle or shut off the power and wire the unit directly, following the manufacturer's instructions. To be completely safe, it's important to test the unit to make sure it has been properly grounded.

Air gap

Waste T-fitting

Dual-outlet
shutoff valve

DISHWASHERS

Like a garbage disposer, a dishwasher connects to the sink drain—in fact, it often empties directly through the disposer. You'll also need to tap into the hot water supply pipe and provide a 120-volt circuit for power. Some dishwashers plug into a 20-amp, GFCI-protected receptacle inside the sink cabinet; others are hard-wired.

CONNECTING TO THE SUPPLY PIPE: Begin by shutting off the water supply, either at the shutoff valves under the sink or at the main house shutoff (see page 152). Drain the supply pipes by turning on the sink faucet or faucets. Cut into the hot water pipe and install a T-fitting or a special dual-outlet shutoff valve (shown at right) to isolate the water supply to the dishwasher. Run a flexible supply tube to the water inlet valve on the dishwasher.

MAKE THE DRAIN CONNECTION: Your dishwasher can drain either into the sink drain or into a garbage disposer. To route the waste water into a sink drain, you'll need to install a threaded waste T-fitting, as shown below right.

If you have a garbage disposer, you'll attach the dishwasher drain hose to the drain fitting on the disposer's side. First, turn off the electrical circuit that controls the disposer. Then, use a screwdriver to punch out the knockout plug inside the fitting. Use a hose clamp to secure the dishwasher drain hose to the fitting.

ADDING AN AIR GAP: Most codes also require you to connect an air gap (shown above right) to the dishwasher's drain hose to prevent contamination of the potable water supply system. To install an air gap, either use a vacant sink hole or bore a hole into the countertop. Insert the air gap through the hole from above and secure it by tightening the locknut with adjustable pliers or a spud wrench. Run one length of hose from the dishwasher to the air gap and another from the air gap to the waste T or disposer.

Plug in the new dishwasher, then slide it into place. Following manufacturer's instructions, complete the supply and drain hookups. Turn on the water supply to the dishwasher and check for leaks.

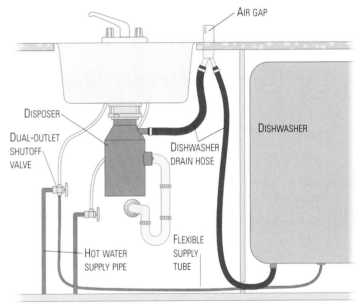

AIR GAP

DISPOSER

DUAL-OUTLET
SHUTOFF
VALVE

DISHWASHER

DISHWASHER
DRAIN HOSE

HOT WATER
SUPPLY PIPE

FLEXIBLE
SUPPLY
TUBE

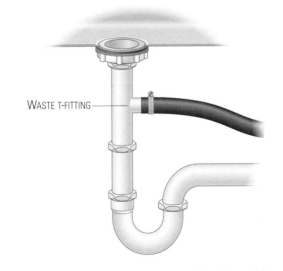

WASTE T-FITTING

HOT WATER DISPENSERS

Hot water dispensers are easy to install, incorporating just a stainless-steel faucet connected to an undercounter storage tank. The tank, which is fed by a nearby cold water pipe, has an electric heating coil that keeps water at about 200°F that's 50° hotter than water heated by the average water heater. Note: A hot water dispenser should not be installed where small children might reach it.

Most units plug into a 120-volt grounded receptacle installed under the sink. The faucet commonly fits in a hole on the sink rim or mounts directly on the countertop. With the latter type, you'll need to cut a 1¼-inch-diameter hole in the countertop near the sink.

To tap into the cold water pipe, shut off the water supply and drain the pipes by opening the faucet. Many dispensers come with a self-tapping supply valve that punctures the existing supply pipe, allowing you to tap into the supply line without cutting pipe and adding new fittings. If yours doesn't come with one, tap into the cold water pipe with a standard T-fitting and a shutoff valve with an outlet that matches your dispenser's water supply tube.

Install the water storage tank on a mounting bracket inside the sink cabinet.

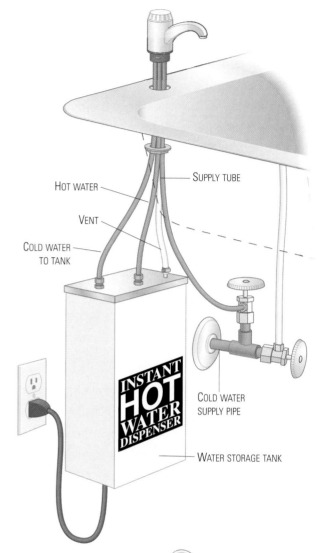

HOT WATER

SUPPLY TUBE

VENT

COLD WATER TO TANK

COLD WATER SUPPLY PIPE

WATER STORAGE TANK

SOME WATER FILTER FACTS

New, compact water purifiers look just like hot water or soap dispensers on the sink; the main unit fits below the sink like other water appliances.

Filtration systems vary widely. Reverse-osmosis filters are considered most effective, but their output is limited. Carbon filters are more compact and simpler to install but don't remove dissolved solids or bacteria. If you have questions about your water's composition, first have it tested, then choose the right system for the job.

An overview of a reverse-osmosis filter installation is shown at right. Connections are made with flexible tubing. Follow the manufacturer's instructions for installing the unit and for connecting it to the cold water supply pipe. One purifier can route clean water not only to the sink but also to a hot water dispenser and an icemaker. All you need to do is add a compression T to the tube that carries clean water from the filter and route flexible tubing to each additional appliance.

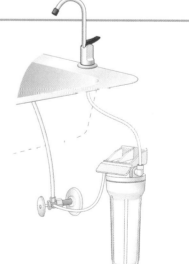

ICEMAKERS

A refrigerator's icemaker and/or chilled water dispenser is connected by $1/4$-inch flexible tubing to a cold water supply pipe. If the refrigerator can be easily reached from the sink complex, tap in there and route tubing behind or through the base cabinets. If the refrigerator is distant from the sink, look for another cold water supply pipe to tap into.

To make an undersink connection, use a saddle T or standard T-fitting and shutoff valve with a $1/4$-inch outlet. You may buy these pieces separately or in kit form. For remote locations, consider a recessed icemaker box, which includes a shutoff valve and a trim kit for mounting flush with the wall. Use $1/4$-inch copper, woven stainless, or woven vinyl tubing, and attach it to the refrigerator according to manufacturer's instructions.

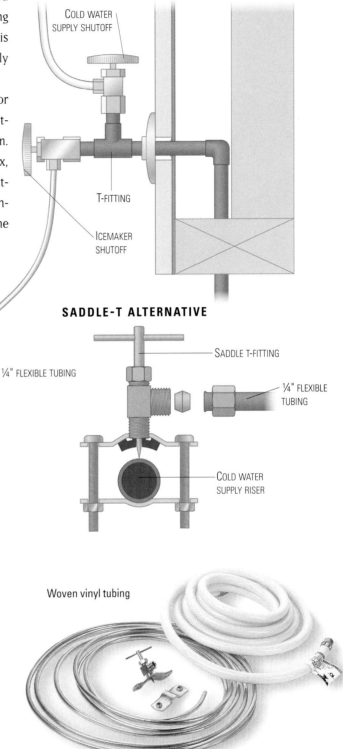

COLD WATER
SUPPLY SHUTOFF

T-FITTING

ICEMAKER
SHUTOFF

$1/4$" FLEXIBLE TUBING

SADDLE-T ALTERNATIVE

SADDLE T-FITTING

$1/4$" FLEXIBLE
TUBING

COLD WATER
SUPPLY RISER

REFRIGERATOR

ICEMAKER
INLET VALVE

Woven vinyl tubing

BATHROOM SINKS AND FAUCETS

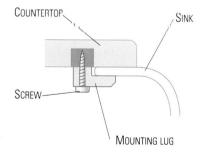

Bathroom sinks, faucets, and drain components have features that make installation somewhat different from hooking up kitchen sinks. Like kitchen sinks, many bathroom sinks are deck- (or vanity-) mounted, but in addition, you may choose from integral, pedestal, and wall-hung styles. Lavatory faucets are generally more petite than their kitchen counterparts, although styles are getting larger and more dramatic, and you may be working with smaller trap sizes ($1\frac{1}{4}$ inches instead of $1\frac{1}{2}$ inches). Many lavatory drains also include pop-up stoppers.

DECK-MOUNTED SINKS

When you're shopping for a deck-mounted sink, you'll have a choice of materials and styles: stainless or enameled steel, porcelain-coated cast iron, acrylic, and vitreous china, in different sizes and shapes. Most are available with holes for 4-, 6-, or 8-inch faucet assemblies.

A deck-mounted lavatory sink (shown above left) fits into a specially cut hole in a vanity top. Whether self-rimmed, frame-rimmed, or recessed (see below), a deck-mounted sink is sealed to the countertop with plumber's putty or silicone sealant, and sometimes with clips or lugs from below. If you're replacing an existing deck-mounted sink, measure the hole in the countertop and take the measurements with you when you shop.

For step-by-step installation pointers, see pages 98–99.

RECESSED SINK

  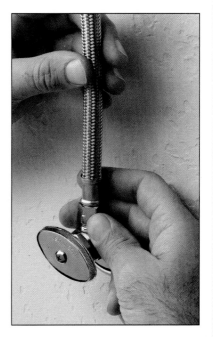

Installing a fixture shutoff valve is a three-step task. First, add a threaded nipple or supply adapter as required, then slip an escutcheon over the stubout (left). Next, secure the shutoff valve to the stubout, using either a threaded connector (center) or a compression ring and nut. Finally, run a flexible supply tube from each shutoff to the faucet (right), and tighten each coupling.

ADDING SHUTOFF VALVES

A shutoff valve simplifies turning off the water supply to a fixture for repairs or in case of an emergency. You just turn the valve handle clockwise until it's fully closed, open the faucet or faucets to drain the pipes, then go ahead with your job. Every sink, tub, shower, and washing machine should have shutoffs for both hot and cold water pipes. Toilets require only one shutoff valve because they use only cold water, and dishwashers need only one shutoff because they use only hot water. The shutoff valve for a dishwasher is usually located in the base cabinet below an adjoining sink. Other shutoffs are located right at the fixture or appliance.

When you shop for a shutoff valve, you'll need to choose either an angled valve or a straight one. Angled valves are used when the supply pipe, or stubout, comes out from the wall; straight valves are used for pipes that come up from the floor. The kind of stubout you have dictates the kind of valve and adapter fittings you need. A threaded pipe or pipe fitting naturally requires a threaded valve; an unthreaded copper stubout takes a compression valve.

Lengths of flexible supply tubing (shown below) save you the trouble of piecing pipe together to join valve to fixture. They come in woven stainless steel; woven vinyl; plain copper; and corrugated, chrome-plated copper; and are available in a variety of lengths with preinstalled fittings on each end. Err on the long side; a tube that's too long may simply be curved or even looped between shutoff and fixture.

Be sure the fittings at each end of your tubes match your fixture inlet shanks and your shutoff valve. Fittings are either threaded or compression, and are commonly available in ⅜-, ⁷⁄₁₆-, and ½-inch diameters.

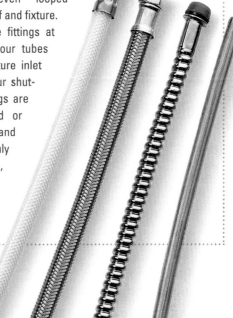

Flexible suppy tubes

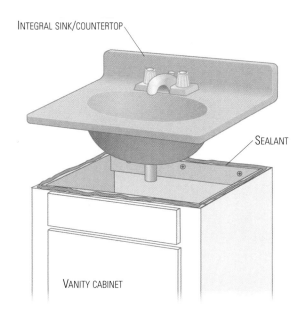

INTEGRAL SINK/COUNTERTOP

SEALANT

VANITY CABINET

INTEGRAL SINKS

One popular variation on the deck-mounted sink is the one-piece molded sink with integral countertop. This type is easy to install: you simply set it atop a cabinet and fasten it from below. Typical material options are solid-surface acrylic and cultured marble.

To install an integral sink, first cover the top edges of the vanity cabinet with a sealant or an adhesive recommended by the manufacturer. Place the countertop unit on the cabinet so that it's flush with the back edge. Make sure the overhang—if there is any—is equal on the left and right sides. Press along the countertop edges to complete the seal, then check around the perimeter and remove any excess sealant.

If your unit came with mounting brackets, use them to secure the countertop to the cabinet from below. Finally, seal the joint between the countertop and the wall with silicone sealant.

PEDESTAL SINKS

Pedestal sinks are making a big comeback in a wide range of traditional and modern styles. These elegant towers, typically of vitreous china, make great design accents and are usually easy to install.

Most pedestal sinks are made of two pieces—the sink and the pedestal, or base. First, position the pedestal with the sink on top in the desired location to determine its clearance from the wall; make sure the pedestal is centered in front of the drain stubout. Use the holes in the pedestal base to mark the locations of the hold-down bolts. Set the sink aside. Run a bead of plumber's putty or caulk around the bottom edge of the pedestal and bolt it in place.

It's a very good idea to preassemble as much of the sink hardware as you can before installing the sink—there's not much room to work behind a pedestal sink. Mount a faucet to the sink as shown on page 113. Attach supply tubes, drain body, pop-up stopper, and trap (see pages 114–115).

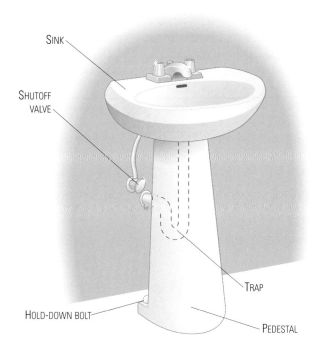

SINK

SHUTOFF VALVE

TRAP

HOLD-DOWN BOLT

PEDESTAL

Position the sink on the pedestal and, if required by the manufacturer, bolt the two together as directed.

Where a pedestal sink's trap, supply tubes, and shut-off valves will be visible, you may wish to buy decorative versions of these components to complement your other bathroom accents. These components are sometimes available in kits, or you may buy them separately.

WALL-HUNG SINKS

Wall-hung sinks are no longer as common as they used to be, but they're mounting a minor comeback and may still be found in many traditional designs.

For a first-time sink installation, you will need to mount a backing board. If the wall is uncovered, simply frame in a 2x6 or 2x8 between flanking studs, directly behind where the sink will be, as shown at right.

If remodeling, plan to remove a small section of the wall covering, then notch two studs to accommodate the backing board. Nail or screw the bracing board to the studs and patch the wall (see page 93).

Wall-hung sinks come with support hangers or angle brackets. Refer to the manufacturer's instructions to properly position the hanging device on the wall. Generally, the device will be centered, then leveled, over the drainpipe at the desired height (31 to 38 inches above the floor). Using woodscrews, fasten the hanging device through the wall's surface to the backing board.

Install the new sink flange and drain body (pages 114–115). Attach the faucet (pages 112–113), supply tubes, and pop-up assembly. Carefully lower the sink onto the hanger. Some hangers have projecting tabs that fit into slots under the sink's back edge. Angle brackets bolt up into the sink's base, but these can give way under heavy weights, so you may wish to install front supporting legs on the sink to give it extra stability. Fasten the legs, then screw the adjusting section of each leg downward until the sink is level at front and back. Caulk the sink-wall joint with a bead of silicone sealant. Connect the supply tubes to the shutoff valves (page 109), attach the trap, turn the water on, and tighten any leaky connections.

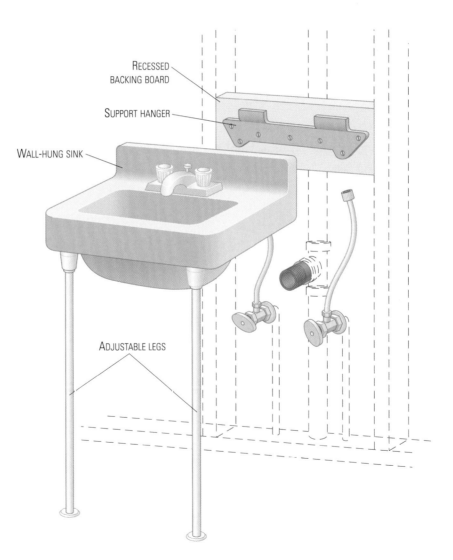

RECESSED BACKING BOARD

SUPPORT HANGER

WALL-HUNG SINK

ADJUSTABLE LEGS

INSTALLING BATHROOM SINK FAUCETS

Lavatory faucets are available with single, center-set, or spread-fit controls. A single-control fitting has a combined faucet and lever or knob controlling water flow and temperature. A center-set control has separate hot and cold water controls and a faucet, all mounted on an "escutcheon," or base. A spread-fit control has separate hot and cold water controls and an independently mounted faucet.

All models are interchangeable as long as the faucet's inlet shanks are spaced to fit the holes of the sink you'll be mounting the faucet on. Choose a new unit that comes with clear installation instructions, and a well-known brand that will have repair kits and replacement parts available for future use.

Clean the surface where the new faucet will sit. Most faucets have a rubber gasket on the bottom; if yours doesn't, apply plumber's putty before you set the faucet in position.

If your faucet comes with integral supply tubes (see drawing at right), carefully straighten the tubes before you mount the faucet; feed the tubes through the appro-

priate sink hole or holes. Press the faucet onto the sink and securely bolt it in place (see facing page). For a faucet like the one shown, screw the washers and locknuts onto the faucet inlet shanks by hand only.

Attach the flexible supply tubes to the faucet and to the shutoff valves with threaded nuts or compression fittings, gently bending the tubes to make the connections. Turn on the water and check for leaks.

SINGLE-CONTROL FAUCET

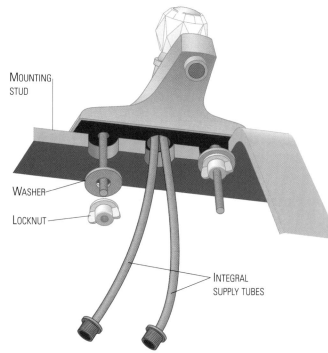

MOUNTING STUD

WASHER

LOCKNUT

INTEGRAL SUPPLY TUBES

SPREAD-FIT FAUCET

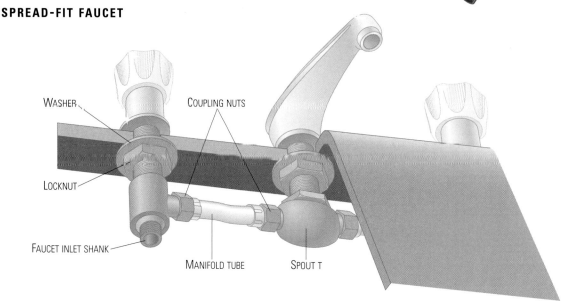

WASHER

COUPLING NUTS

LOCKNUT

FAUCET INLET SHANK

MANIFOLD TUBE

SPOUT T

INSTALLING A BATHROOM FAUCET

I Apply plumber's putty

Roll a chunk of plumber's putty between your hands, making a long, thin string; then apply the string to the outside of the faucet body where it will contact the sink or countertop.

2 Mount the faucet

Slip the faucet into the sink's mounting holes. Align the faucet front-to-back and side-to-side, then press it down onto the sink surface.

3 Secure the locknuts

Working from below, thread the locknuts onto the sink's inlet shanks or mounting bolts. Tighten plastic wingnuts by hand; use a wrench for metal nuts.

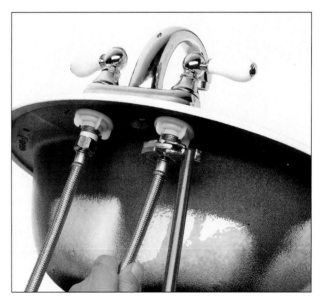

4 Attach supply tubes

Run flexible supply tubes from undersink shutoff valves to the faucet's inlet shanks (shown here) or integral supply tubes. Tighten the coupling nuts with a basin wrench or an adjustable wrench.

HOOKING UP DRAINS AND POP-UPS

Undersink drain connections include the sink flange and drain body, the trap and waste arm, and the pop-up stopper assembly.

INSTALLING THE SINK FLANGE AND DRAIN BODY: Drain bodies that include pop-up stoppers are made from either brass or plastic and are sold either as part of a new faucet or separately. The basic components are shown at left. Attach the drain's sink flange by running a bead of plumber's putty around the drain hole of the sink and pressing the flange into the puttied hole. Slip the locknut, metal washer, and flat rubber washer over the top of the drain body, in that order. Insert the threaded end of the drain body into the bottom of the sink and screw it onto the flange. Then, tighten the locknut with slip-joint pliers or a spud wrench until it is snug (but be careful not to over-tighten).

HOOKING UP THE TRAP AND WASTE ARM: Lavatory P-traps come in chromed brass, plastic ABS or PVC, and 17-gauge brass. To install one, first connect the trap to the drain body, then add the waste arm, working the parts back and forth to get the right length and angle to align with both the drain body and the drain stubout. Measure and cut the waste arm as required to meet the drain stubout correctly. If necessary, add a threaded trap adapter to the end of the drain stubout. Usually, the trap's slip fitting has enough play to line up with the drain body; if it doesn't, you can add a separate tailpiece to make up the difference.

The couplings on plastic traps need hand-tightening only; metal couplings may need a half turn or so past hand-tight, using a pair of adjustable pliers. If in doubt, err on the loose side: hand-tighten, turn on the water, and check for leaks. If you discover one, tighten the offending coupling slightly, then recheck.

ASSEMBLING THE POP-UP STOPPER: If you're installing a new pop-up, follow the manufacturer's instructions.

DRAIN AND POP-UP

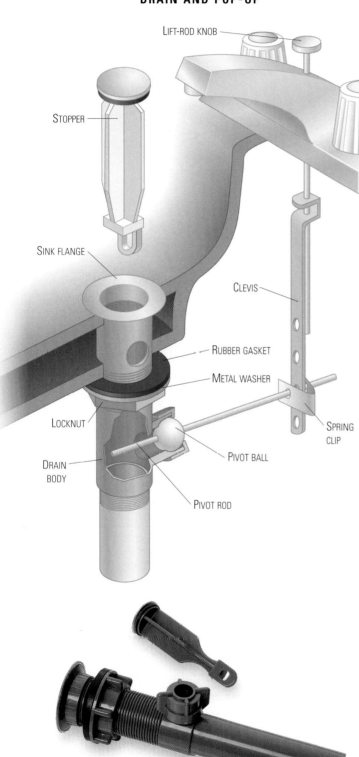

- LIFT-ROD KNOB
- STOPPER
- SINK FLANGE
- CLEVIS
- RUBBER GASKET
- METAL WASHER
- LOCKNUT
- SPRING CLIP
- PIVOT BALL
- DRAIN BODY
- PIVOT ROD

Generally, you first slip the stopper down through the sink flange and insert the pivot rod into it. Then, you secure the pivot rod with the fastenings supplied with the new drain assembly and connect the pivot rod to the clevis with a spring clip. Test the stopper: if it won't open or close properly, remove the spring clip and move the pivot rod to a higher or lower hole on the clevis. For a closer look, see below.

HOOKING UP A DRAIN AND POP-UP

I **Secure the flange and drain body**
Run plumber's putty around the sink opening, then slip the sink flange through the opening, pressing it down against the putty. Working from below, secure the drain body with rubber gasket, metal washer, and locknut. Tighten the locknut with slip-joint pliers.

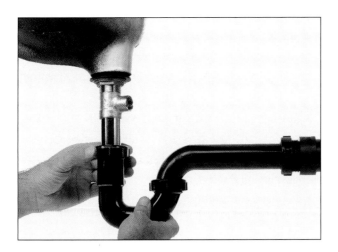

2 **Connect the trap**
Next, slip one end of a P-trap onto the tailpiece extending from the drain body, slip a waste arm into the drain stubout or trap adapter, and join the free end of the trap to the waste arm, as shown. Adjust heights and angles until things fit snugly, then tighten down all couplings.

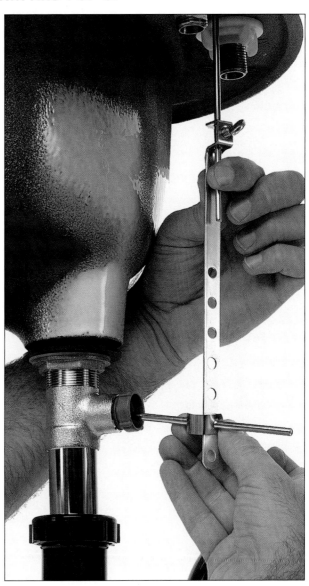

3 **Install the pop-up**
Slip the pop-up stopper down through the sink flange from above, and insert the pivot rod through the stopper end inside the drain body. Run the pivot rod through a hole in the long, flat clevis and secure it with a spring clip, as shown. Secure the clevis to the lift-rod that extends down through the faucet body.

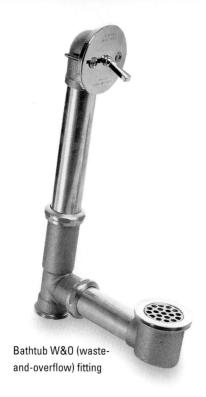

Bathtub W&O (waste-and-overflow) fitting

Tub-Moving Tips

A cast-iron tub is bulky and very heavy. If you decide to install one, plan to have at least four people to help lift it. If you're removing one, it can be broken into pieces with a sledgehammer and lifted out in sections.

One-piece tub-and-surround units, molded from plastic or fiberglass, are handy for new construction but are often too large to fit through existing windows and doorways. If you're remodeling, you may have to remove doors and even some trim to get any tub in or out.

TUBS AND SHOWERS

Whether you're replacing old fixtures or starting from scratch, tub and shower installations are complicated jobs. They take careful planning, precise carpentry, and a good bit of time. But the results are worth the trouble, especially if your installation will put an end to early-morning traffic jams in the bathroom. Home centers and plumbing supply stores carry tubs and showers in a wide variety of sizes, shapes, and materials.

BATHTUBS

If replacement is the issue, know the size of your existing fixtures before shopping. A standard tub is 60 inches long by 30 inches wide and about 14 inches deep. Larger sizes are available, at greater cost.

The familiar boxy tub is enameled steel, relatively inexpensive, and lightweight—and noisy, cold, and prone to chipping. Enameled cast-iron tubs are less noisy, warmer to the touch, and more durable, but they're more expensive and very heavy (they may require structural reinforcement).

Standard tubs come in two basic styles: recessed and corner. Recessed tubs fit between two side walls and against a back wall; they have a finished "apron," or front. Corner models have a finished front and a finished end; you can get a right- or left-handed version. Some more stylish tubs are finished on three sides, allowing placement along an open wall. Freestanding claw-foot tubs are also available.

In addition, new, lightweight acrylic (plastic) tubs are available in a wide range of shapes, sizes, and colors. These tubs are usually designed for platform or sunken installation. Acrylic tubs lack iron's structural integrity—be sure to provide solid support beneath one.

INSTALLING A NEW TUB: A bathtub filled with water is extremely heavy. Check local building codes for floor framing requirements and consider getting professional help for framing and support before you install a new tub.

Around its upper edge, your new tub will have a flange that fits against the wall studs. There will also be two precut holes: one for the drain, the other for the overflow. The faucet, spout, and shower head will mount on the wall above the tub. Piping for all these components must be in place and connected before you install the tub (see page 88).

BASIC BATHTUB COMPONENTS

MOLDED, THREE-PIECE TUB SURROUND

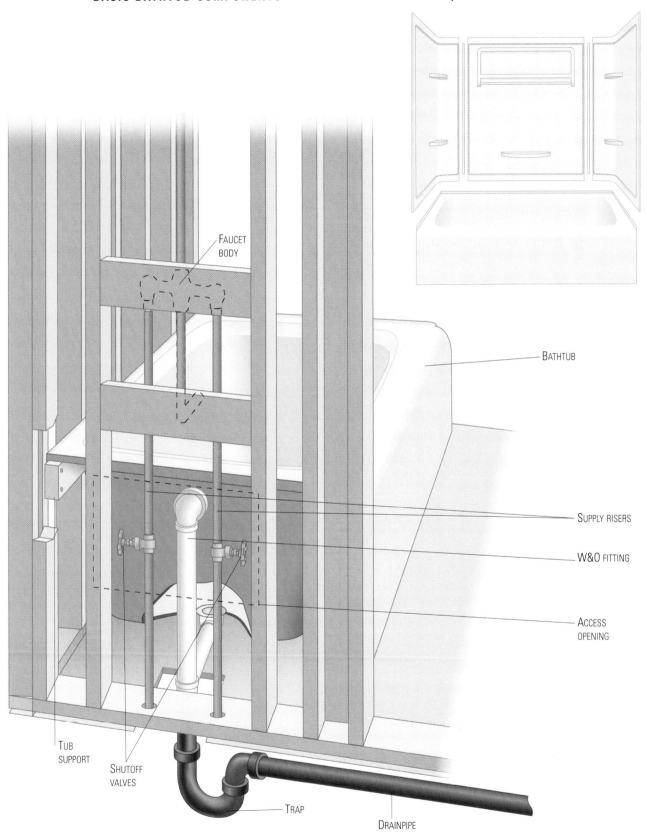

FAUCET BODY

BATHTUB

SUPPLY RISERS

W&O FITTING

ACCESS OPENING

TUB SUPPORT

SHUTOFF VALVES

TRAP

DRAINPIPE

For new installations, first mount horizontal 1x4s or 2x4s to the studs at the exact level where the tub flange can rest on them. Then wrestle the new tub into position. For a heavy cast-iron or steel tub, slide the tub along soaped wooden runners, and with the aid of several helpers, lift it so the flanges rest on the supports. Lightweight plastic tubs are much simpler to move.

Check the tub at both ends to see that it's level. If not, insert shims between the tub and wall supports or floor to level it. Plastic and steel tub flanges can be anchored to the studs with nails or screws; cast-iron tubs simply rest on the wood supports.

HOOKING IT UP: Next, connect the W&O (waste-and-overflow) fitting, the trap, and the drain assembly, working through an access door in an adjoining room or hallway, or through an opening under the floor. Be careful not to overtighten the nuts.

Before surfacing the tub wall, turn on the water and check the drain and supply pipes for leaks. Use moisture-resistant wallboard (such ceramic tile or fiberglass panels) as a base for the final waterproof wall covering; seal all joints between the tub and wall with silicone caulk to guard against water seepage. Complete the project by installing the spout, faucet handles, and, if you wish, a shower head (see pages 120–121).

(see pages 120–121)

W&O FITTINGS—TWO TYPES

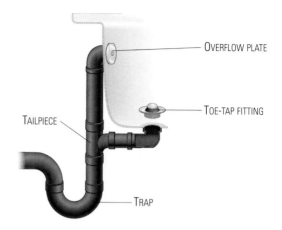

OVERFLOW PLATE

TOE-TAP FITTING

TAILPIECE

TRAP

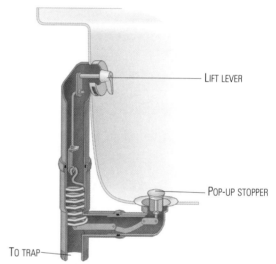

LIFT LEVER

POP-UP STOPPER

TO TRAP

WHIRLPOOL TUBS

Think of these hydromassage units simply as bathtubs with air jets. Unlike an outdoor spa, a whirlpool uses a standard hot water connection; once your soak is over, the water is drained. Most models resemble standard acrylic platform tubs; a pump and venturi jets are what create the whirlpool effect.

Although some professionals build custom whirlpool tubs from scratch and even retrofit old bathtubs, it's simplest to buy a complete whirlpool kit, which includes tub, jets, pump, and piping. Look for a unit that's UL-approved. Supply and drain connections are similar to those for standard tubs; in addition, you'll need to provide an electrical hookup—typically a dedicated 120-volt, 20-amp circuit with GFCI protection. Check local codes for installation specifics in your area.

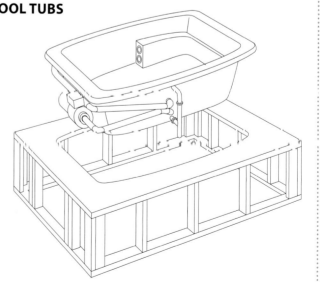

SHOWER STALLS

You may select a prefabricated shower stall, combine separate manufactured components, or build completely from scratch.

If your remodel calls for moving walls or doors, you may be able to fit a one-piece molded shower or tub-shower surround through the opening—although these units are really designed for new houses or additions. One-piece showers are available in fiberglass-reinforced plastic and synthetic marble. Some have ceilings. For comfort, choose a shower that's at least 36 inches square.

You may also mix and match base, surround, and doors. A shower base, or pan, may be purchased separately or in a kit that includes a two- or three-piece surround. Most bases are made of plastic, terrazzo, cast polymer, or solid-surface acrylic and come in standard square, rectangular, or corner configurations with a predrilled hole for the drain. Some include the drain flange. Of course, you could also have a tile professional float a traditional mortar base and line it with the tile of your choice.

A shower surround is essentially watertight wall paneling, often with amenities such as a soap tray and towel bar built in. The manufactured panels are sized for easy transport, then assembled and seamed on-site. They require solid framing for support.

Doors for showers and tub-shower enclosures come in a variety of styles: swinging, sliding, folding, and pivoting. If you're planning on a hinged door, be sure the shower stall or surround you choose has reinforced edging that's designed to support a door.

TWO SHOWER STYLES

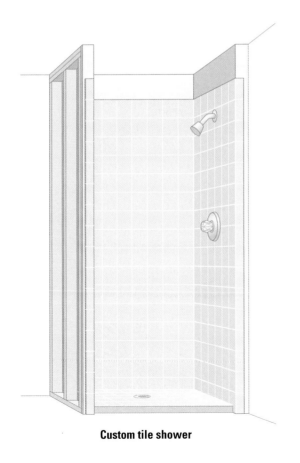

Custom tile shower

Molded one-piece shower stall

ADDING A SHOWER STALL: First, construct a frame to contain the shower unit. Be especially careful to make all measurements accurately and the framing square and plumb. Run supply pipes and drainpipes to the desired locations (see page 89) and install the shower riser and trap.

If necessary, drill holes through the surface of the stall or wall panel for the shower valve assembly and shower arm stubout. Refer to the manufacturer's installation instructions for exact locations and how-to information.

Slide a one-piece shower stall into place. Attach the stall as you would an acrylic tub, nailing the flange to the studs. It will probably take some maneuvering to line up the shower unit with the drain, shower head stubout, and faucet body. Many pros leave access behind and below the shower, then add these fittings after the shower is in place.

To install a molded shower base, it's best to first spread a layer of mortar over the area, then use the mortar to both support and help level the base. Position the base atop the drain outlet and connect base to drain by screwing in the shower drain flange. Cover the opening with rags. Once the base is secured, you're ready to cover the shower's side and back walls with tile or panels.

MAKING THE HOOKUPS: With the shower anchored in place, caulk around all openings; then attach the shower head, faucet handles, and escutcheon (base), as described below.

TUB FAUCETS AND SHOWER HEADS

Once the supply pipes, faucet body, and shower riser and arm are installed and the tub or shower is in place, it's a simple matter to add the faucet handles and tub spout and/or shower head. While assembly is straightforward, the specifics vary depending on make and model, so be sure to follow the manufacturer's instructions that come with your fittings. To avoid marring delicate faucet finishes

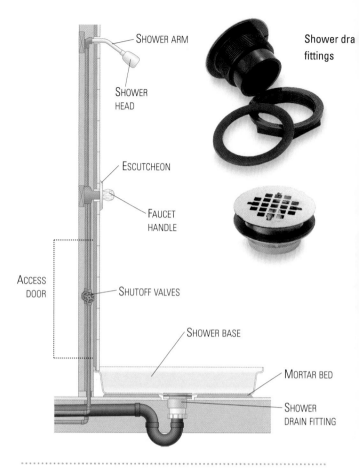

SHOWER ARM
SHOWER HEAD
ESCUTCHEON
FAUCET HANDLE
ACCESS DOOR
SHUTOFF VALVES
SHOWER BASE
MORTAR BED
SHOWER DRAIN FITTING
Shower drain fittings

Shower arm
Shower head
Tub spout

while tightening connections, it's a good idea to wrap your wrenches with masking or electrical tape first.

INSTALLING TUB FITTINGS: For tub-showers, you may opt for either single or separate controls. Tubs require a spout. Tub-showers need a spout, shower head, and diverter valve. Most fittings are wall-mounted, but you can find deck-mounted faucets and spouts, too.

Like sink faucets, tub-shower faucets are either compression-style or washerless; the two types are illustrated on page 163. With either kind, water is directed from the faucet to the tub or shower head by the diverter valve; some have a built-in diverter, while others have a knob on the tub spout.

A spout is easy to install: simply hand-screw it into place, then tighten with a tape-wrapped pipe wrench.

INSTALLING A SHOWER HEAD: Like a tub spout, a shower head simply hand-screws onto the shower arm stubout. Before installing a new shower head, clean the pipe threads and apply pipe-joint compound to prevent leaks.

Pressure-Balancing Valves

If you've ever experienced a pressure drop or an abrupt change in water temperature in the shower when someone flushes a toilet or starts the washer—or if you worry about small children being exposed to very hot water—you'll appreciate a new anti-scalding device on the market. The pressure-balancing (or temperature-limiting) mixing valve takes the place of a standard faucet body and shower control to prevent scalds via a built-in pressure-balancing diaphragm. These valves are already required for new construction by some codes and are a great safety feature for remodels.

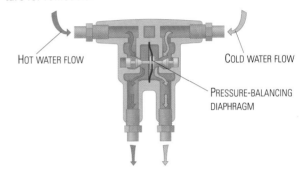

HOT WATER FLOW   COLD WATER FLOW

PRESSURE-BALANCING DIAPHRAGM

HOOKING UP A HAND-HELD SHOWER

A hand-held shower is an easy way to add or replace an over-the-tub shower, and it lets you direct the water as you please. One type of hand-held shower attaches directly to a shower arm; another is an integral part of a tub spout.

To install the shower head type, simply replace the existing shower head with a diverter valve, then fasten the hand-held shower hose to the outlet on the diverter. For a hand-held shower that hooks up to a tub spout, you'll need to replace the spout with one that has a diverter valve knob and built-in hose outlet (see at right).

Most hand-held shower kits come with some type of wall bracket for hanging the unit. Position the bracket at a convenient height. Mark and drill screw holes into the wall; if there's no wall stud to accept screws, use toggle bolts to fasten the bracket.

Note: To prevent water from siphoning back through a hand-held shower into the water supply, local codes may require the installation of a vacuum-breaker assembly. Manufacturers typically include instructions for installation of this device.

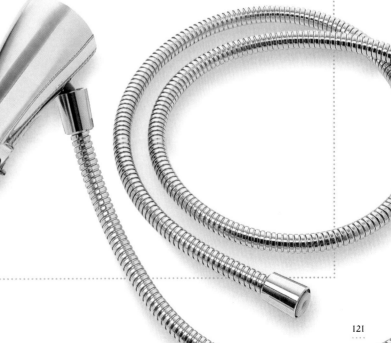

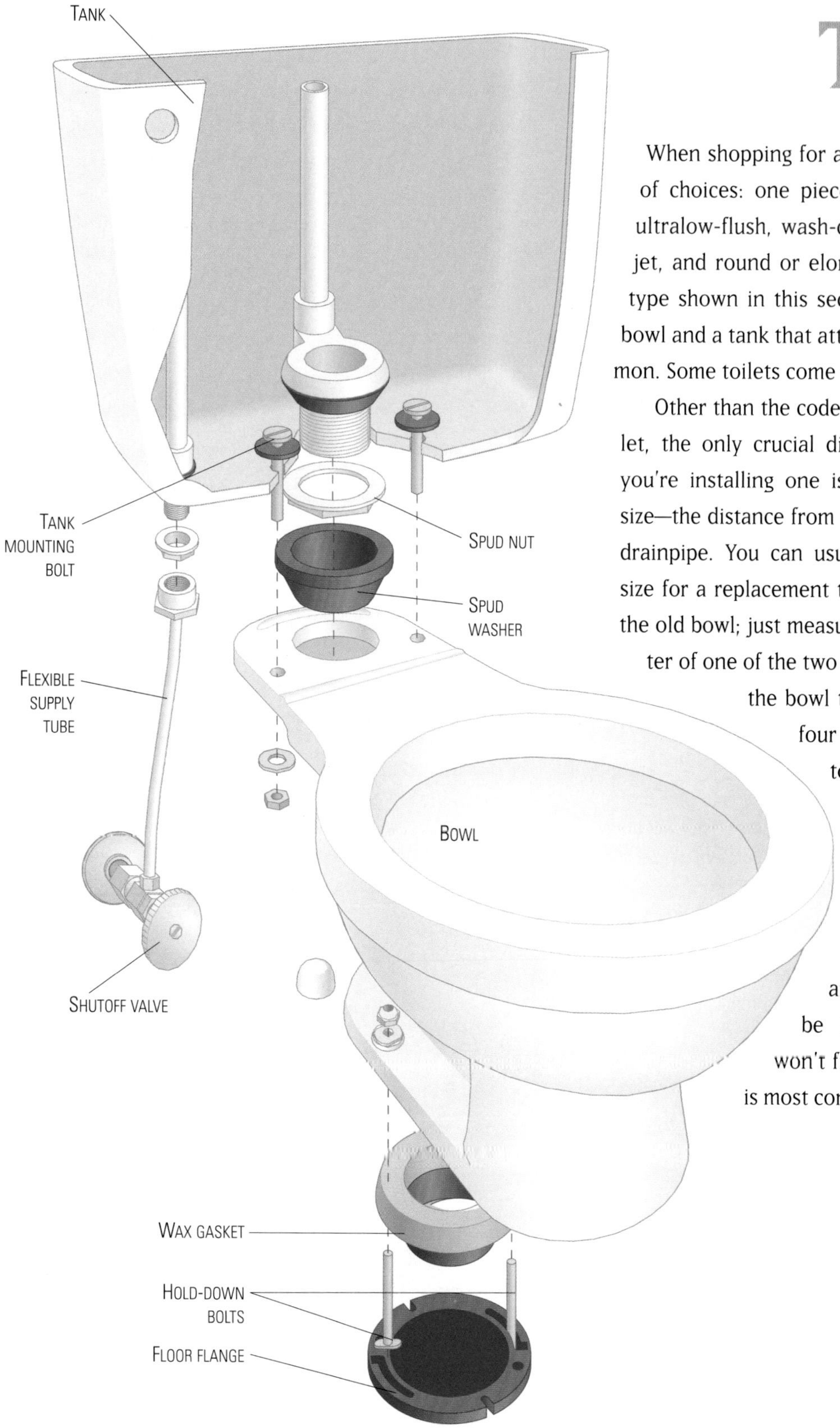

TOILETS

TANK

TANK
MOUNTING
BOLT

FLEXIBLE
SUPPLY
TUBE

SHUTOFF VALVE

SPUD NUT

SPUD
WASHER

BOWL

WAX GASKET

HOLD-DOWN
BOLTS

FLOOR FLANGE

When shopping for a toilet, you'll find a number of choices: one piece or two piece, wall hung, ultralow-flush, wash-down, reverse-trap, siphon-jet, and round or elongated bowl. The two-piece type shown in this section, with a floor-mounted bowl and a tank that attaches to it, is the most common. Some toilets come with seats; many don't.

Other than the code requirements for a new toilet, the only crucial dimension to consider when you're installing one is its offset, or roughing-in, size—the distance from the wall to the center of the drainpipe. You can usually determine roughing-in size for a replacement toilet without first removing the old bowl; just measure from the wall to the center of one of the two hold-down bolts that secure the bowl to the floor (if the bowl has four hold-down bolts, measure to the center of a rear bolt). The roughing-in distance for the new toilet can be shorter than that of the old fixture (there will just be a gap between the toilet and the wall), but it cannot be longer or the new toilet won't fit. A 12-inch roughing-in size is most common.

Pick out a model that's ready to install—one that has a flush mechanism already in the tank. Along with the toilet, you'll get the necessary gaskets, washers, and hardware for fitting the tank to the bowl, but you may need to buy hold-down bolts and a wax gasket. You'll need a new flexible supply tube, as well.

Toilet installation kits are available that have everything you'll need for the job, from wax gasket to supply tube. The contents of one kit are shown below.

You'll also need to buy a can of plumber's putty to secure the toilet base to the floor and the caps to the hold-down bolts.

Toilet Installation Kit

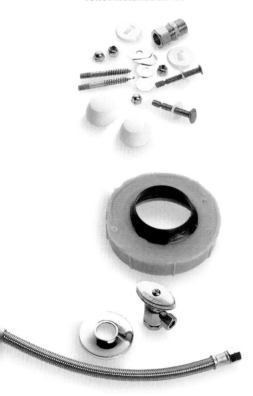

BIDET BASICS

Bidets are floor-mounted and plumbed with hot and cold water. They're best installed next to toilets. Styles and finishes are available that match new toilets, and units come with either a horizontal spray mount or a vertical spray in the center of the bowl. Some models have deck-mounted faucets; others use wall-mounted controls. Most bidets have a pop-up stopper that allows the unit to double as a footbath or a laundry basin.

Plumbing requirements for a bidet include hot and cold water supply pipes and a 1½-inch drain outlet. Some bidets drain through a floor outlet and floor trap, as shown below. Most new models, however, have built-in traps and exit through the wall. Designs vary, so be sure to consult the manufacturer's instructions for exact roughing-in dimensions and required hardware.

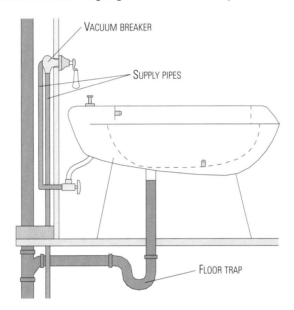

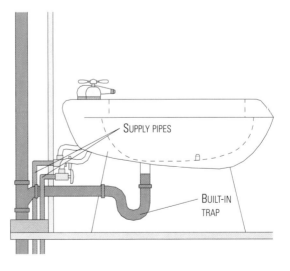

INSTALLING A TOILET

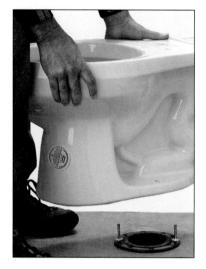

1 Position the wax gasket

First, place the new toilet bowl facedown on a cushioned surface, then slip a new wax gasket onto the toilet's outlet horn. Apply a bead of plumber's putty to the bowl's bottom edge.

2 Position the elbow

Pick the toilet up (easy on the back—it's heavy) and position it over the floor flange. Lower the toilet onto the flange, directing the hold-down bolts through the toilet's drilled openings on both sides.

3 Set the bowl atop the gasket

Press down firmly on the bowl, then rock the toilet side-to-side to seat the wax gasket against the floor flange. Check the bowl rim for level; if necessary, use metal shims to level the top.

4 Secure hold-down bolts

Slip washers and nuts onto the threads of the hold-down bolts sticking up above the toilet; tighten the nuts with an adjustable wrench. Place a dab of plumber's putty inside the hollow caps, then press them into place atop the bolts.

5 Attach the tank

Position any tank-mounting gaskets or hardware required, then thread the toilet tank's mounting bolts down through the drilled holes in the back of the bowl. Align the tank with the bowl and thread nuts onto the bolts—but don't overtighten.

6 Connect the supply tube

Finally, connect the fixture shutoff valve to the toilet's inlet shank with a flexible supply tube. Toilet tubes are shorter than those for faucets and often include a winged locknut at the top, which you simply hand-tighten.

INSTALLING THE NEW BOWL: First, set the new floor bolts in plumber's putty and insert them through the flange. Position the bolts so they line up with the center of the drainpipe.

Then, follow the installation sequence shown on the facing page. Turn the new bowl upside down on a cushioned surface. Place the new wax gasket over the toilet horn (outlet) on the bottom of the bowl. The tapered side of the wax gasket should face away from the bowl. If you use a wax gasket with a plastic collar, install the gasket with the collar away from the bowl. Make sure that the collar will fit into the toilet's floor flange. If it won't, substitute a wax gasket without a collar. Then, apply plumber's putty to the bottom edge of the bowl.

Remove the rag from the drainpipe. Gently lower the bowl into place atop the flange, using the bolts as guides. Press down firmly, while rocking and slightly twisting the bowl, to compress the wax.

Checking with a level, straighten the bowl; use thin pieces of metal to shim the bowl where necessary. Hand-tighten the washers and nuts onto the hold-down bolts.

ATTACHING THE TANK: Some new toilets come with tank components pre-installed, while others don't. If yours needs assembly, first fit the smaller rubber spud washer over the tank's threaded discharge tube and insert the tube through the flush-valve opening on the bottom of the tank. Thread the spud nut over the discharge tube and tighten it with a spud wrench. Then, slip the bigger spud washer over the end of the discharge tube. Place the rubber tank cushion, if there is one, on the rear of the bowl. Position the tank over the bowl and tighten the nuts and washers onto the mounting bolts.

Secure a wall-mounted tank to hanger brackets with bolts through the back of the tank. Assemble the large pipe that connects the bowl and tank and tighten the coupling nuts.

Use an adjustable wrench to snug up the hold-down nuts at the base of the bowl, but don't overtighten or you'll crack the base. Check that the bowl is still level. Fill the caps with plumber's putty and place them over the bolt ends. Smooth the puttied joint at the base of the toilet bowl.

HOOKING UP THE WATER SUPPLY: Now you're ready to connect the cold water supply stubout to the underside of the toilet tank. Install an angled shutoff valve on the wall stubout if there's not one there already, and attach a new flexible supply tube. Tighten the coupling nut on the other end of the supply tube to the threaded inlet shank on the tank. Most toilets use tubes with $7/16$-inch connectors. Finally, turn on the water, flush the toilet, and check for leaks.

PLUMBING UPHILL

If you're adding a toilet, shower, sink, or washing machine below the level of your main house drain, you have a puzzle to solve: how can you get waste water and/or sewage to flow into the drain? If you need only a few inches of extra height, you may be able to elevate the fixture on a platform. Otherwise, you'll need an electric pump, called a sewage ejector, to power waste up to a height where gravity can take over again.

A sewage ejector sits inside a well or sump, as shown below. Toilets typically require a 2-inch discharge pipe and a 2-inch vent, plus a check valve and a ball valve to prevent waste from flowing back downhill. A washing machine normally requires a 1-inch outlet, and a shower or sink a ¾-inch outlet. Check local codes. Sewage ejectors, sumps, and check valves are available at home centers and plumbing supply stores.

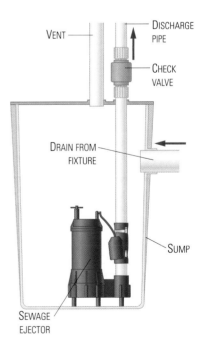

VENT — DISCHARGE PIPE
CHECK VALVE
DRAIN FROM FIXTURE
SUMP
SEWAGE EJECTOR

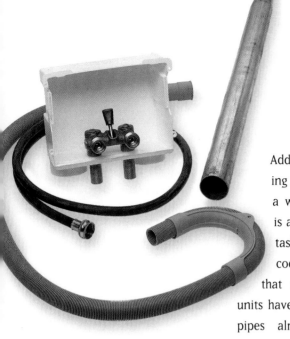

UTILITY ROOMS

Adding the plumbing connections for a washing machine is a straightforward task. Most building codes now require that new residential units have the connecting pipes already installed, but if you live in a home that's never had a washer, you can do the roughing-in yourself (see page 91).

You may need a new water heater if your old one begins to leak or show signs of rust and corrosion, or if you're building from scratch. For help hooking one up, turn to page 128.

WASHING MACHINES

If you're installing a washing machine in a new location, you'll need to run both hot and cold water supply pipes to the desired location, as detailed on page 91. In addition, each supply pipe needs a ¾-inch threaded connector and a shutoff valve (which may be one and the same). The simplest way to drain a washer is through a nearby sink or laundry tub; a washer's drain hose is designed to hook over the sink's edge. Otherwise, you'll need to drain the washing machine into a standpipe—a 2-inch-diameter pipe with a built-in trap that taps into the nearest drainpipe.

SUPPLY STRATEGIES: Hose bibb–style faucets are often used to serve a washing machine. Rather than using outdoor hose bibbs, it's best to look for "washing machine valves" (shown on the facing page), which include shutoff handles and threaded hose connectors and hang straight down. To install them, add threaded male adapters (copper to match copper pipes) or threaded nipples (plastic or galvanized to match those materials) at the end of the supply stubouts. Then, screw on valves to accept the machine hoses.

A single-lever shutoff valve turns off both hot and cold water simultaneously. This type of valve is sold

---

WATER SOFTENERS

All water softeners operate by substituting sodium (salt) for calcium, magnesium, or iron—any of which may cause hard water. A water softener not only eliminates soap scum but also prevents the buildup of harmful minerals in such water-using appliances as water heaters.

The softening unit may be attached to the main supply pipe in one of two places that are just past the point where the water enters

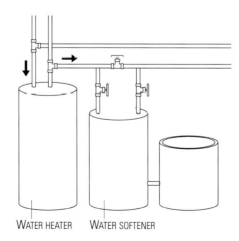

WATER HEATER   WATER SOFTENER

the house. It may be installed before the hot and cold water pipes branch off, so that all water is softened; or it may be installed only on the hot water branch, past the water heater. The latter strategy, shown at left, is a good choice for people who need to restrict their intake of salt. The softened water flows through hot pipes only—those used for bathing or washing, not for drinking or food preparation.

---

126   *Finish work*

WASHER HOOKUPS

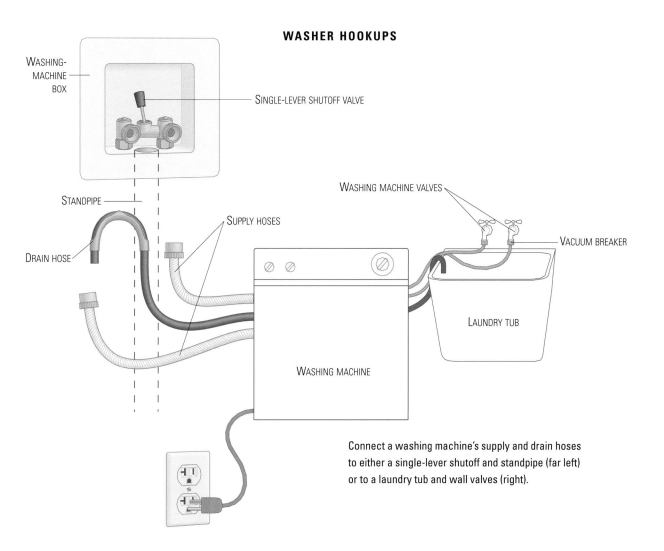

WASHING-MACHINE BOX

SINGLE-LEVER SHUTOFF VALVE

WASHING MACHINE VALVES

STANDPIPE

SUPPLY HOSES

VACUUM BREAKER

DRAIN HOSE

LAUNDRY TUB

WASHING MACHINE

Connect a washing machine's supply and drain hoses to either a single-lever shutoff and standpipe (far left) or to a laundry tub and wall valves (right).

separately or as part of a washing machine box, which is installed flush with the wall for a neat appearance. Some boxes include an outlet for the washer's drain hose. Attach threaded female adapters to each supply riser, then attach the valve. Screw on the washer hoses.

Many codes require that a vacuum breaker be connected to a washing machine's inlet valve; even if it isn't required in your area, it's a good idea to install one.

Note: It's prudent to close the shutoff valve or valves when the machine is not in use. This relieves the constant pressure on the supply hoses and the washer's inlet valve—and could prevent a flood.

DRAIN HOOKUP: If your washing machine isn't next to a sink or laundry tub it can drain into, you'll need to drain it through a 2-inch-diameter vertical standpipe that taps into a drainpipe. The standpipe should be taller than the highest level of water in the washer to prevent backup and siphoning of dirty water into the machine. They come in lengths from 34 inches to 72 inches; to determine the size standpipe you'll need, check the manufacturer's instructions. To install a standpipe, cut into a drainpipe and install a sanitary T-fitting and trap (see page 91 for details). Attach the standpipe to the trap (you may need a reducer fitting, as shown) and push the washing machine's drain hose about 6 inches down into the standpipe—make sure the hose won't be forced out of the pipe by the water pressure.

If you have a washing machine box with a built-in outlet for a drain hose, you'll need to secure the standpipe to the box before a finished wall covering is added.

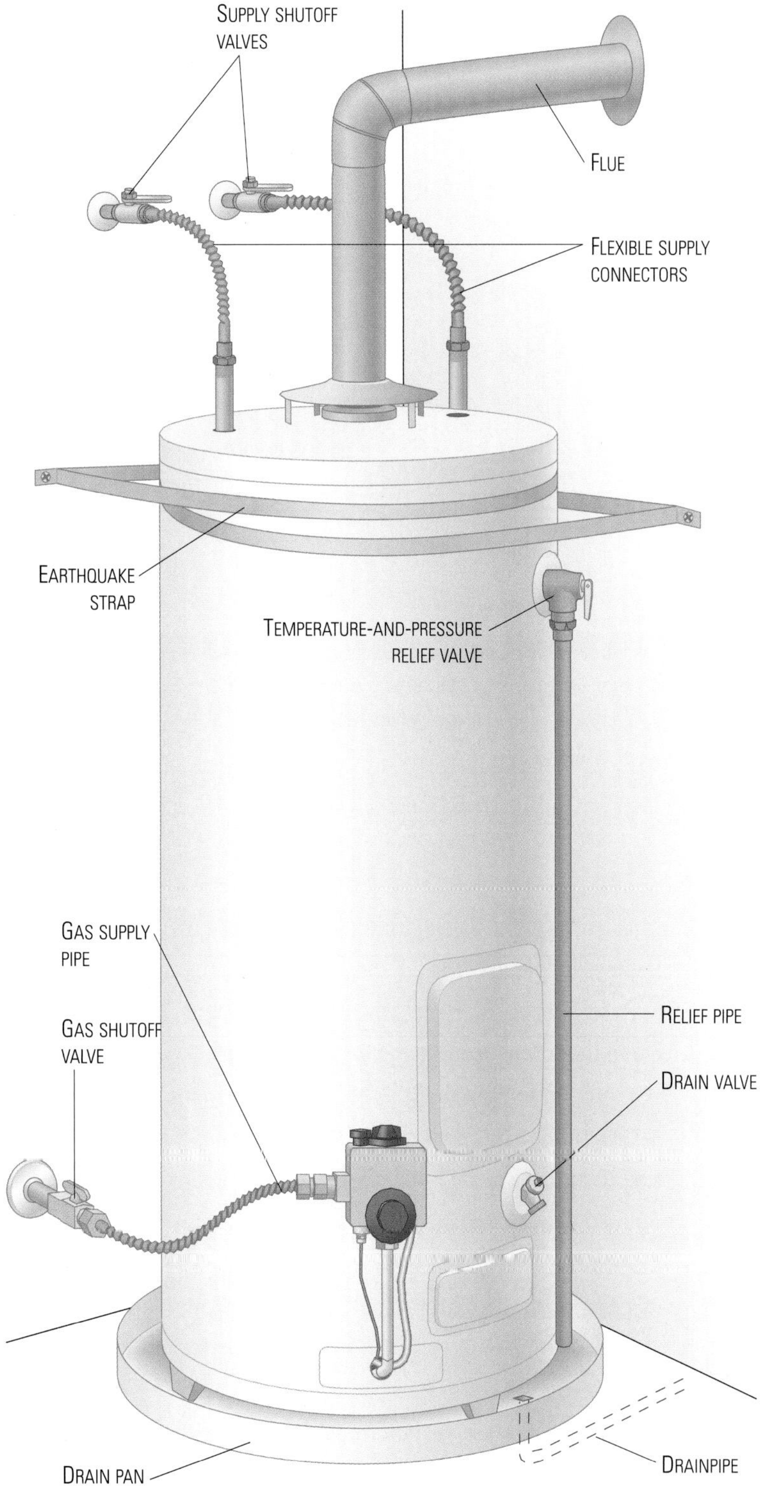

WATER HEATERS

If your plans call for replacing an aging water heater or adding a new one, choose a model that's fuel-efficient (new units list their yearly energy cost) and just large enough to meet your household's hot water needs. It's almost always preferable to select one that uses the same type of fuel as your old water heater. Although gas models are most efficient, the cost of running new gas supply lines may not justify switching from electric.

To add or relocate a heater, you'll need to rough-in a cold water supply pipe and a hot water outlet, then add either a gas line or an electrical power cable. If you're installing a gas heater, you'll also have to install a new flue. For help with the plumbing, see page 91. Electric water heaters use 240-volt electricity, so it's best to have an electrician handle the electrical work unless you're experienced.

SUPPLY SHUTOFF VALVES

FLUE

FLEXIBLE SUPPLY CONNECTORS

EARTHQUAKE STRAP

TEMPERATURE-AND-PRESSURE RELIEF VALVE

GAS SUPPLY PIPE

GAS SHUTOFF VALVE

RELIEF PIPE

DRAIN VALVE

DRAIN PAN

DRAINPIPE

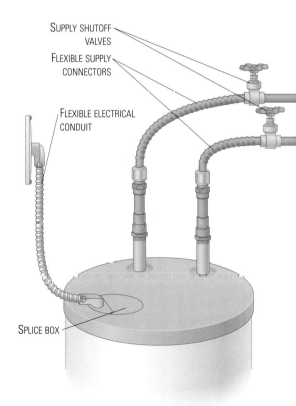

SUPPLY SHUTOFF VALVES

FLEXIBLE SUPPLY CONNECTORS

FLEXIBLE ELECTRICAL CONDUIT

SPLICE BOX

HOOKING UP A NEW HEATER: First, install shutoff valves (preferably full-flow ball valves) on both inlet and outlet pipes. Position the new heater and check that the unit is plumb and level; shim if necessary (old floor tiles work well). If your home is in an earthquake zone, you'll need to install secure straps around the water heater, screwing them to the framing to keep the water heater from tipping over. A metal drain pan will simplify future cleanups if the water heater overflows or leaks.

Use flexible connectors or unions to hook up the water and, for gas heaters, the gas line. (Flexible connectors are simplest to install but aren't allowed in some areas.) The connectors simply thread onto the 3/4-inch water pipes and bend as needed to make the hookup. If the supply pipes aren't threaded, add threaded male adapters and secure the connectors to them with an adjustable wrench.

Screw the temperature-and-pressure relief valve into its 3/4-inch side tapping and connect it to a properly plumbed relief pipe. To install a relief pipe, use rigid metal or plastic pipe that's the same size as the relief valve. This overflow pipe should extend—without bends, which could collect water and freeze—to within 6 inches of a floor drain or to a good drainage spot outdoors. Check with your local plumbing inspector.

For a gas heater, add the draft hood and flue, as shown on the facing page. Fasten the sections of a gas heater's vent pipe together with sheet metal screws driven through the overlaps at every joint.

ACTIVATING THE HEATER: With the connections made, open the water inlet valve to the heater. When the tank is filled with water, bleed the supply pipes by opening the hot water faucets to allow air to flow out of the pipes.

Test the temperature-and-pressure relief valve by squeezing its lever. Open the gas inlet valve or energize the electrical circuit to fuel the heater. For gas heaters, light the pilot according to instructions (they're usually printed on the control panel plate). Adjust the temperature setting as desired.

Finally, check all connections for leaks. If you're working on a gas heater, brush soapy water on the connections (see page 84)—bubbles indicate a gas leak.

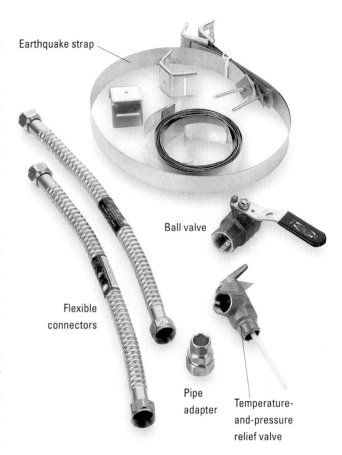

Earthquake strap

Ball valve

Flexible connectors

Pipe adapter

Temperature-and-pressure relief valve

Energy-Saving Tips

Lowering the temperature setting on your water heater to about 110° to 120° will help you save fuel without causing a noticeable difference in your laundry or bathing. Turn down the heater during the periods when your house will be empty or install an automatic timer that will adjust the thermostat during low- and peak-usage times.

Insulate the hot water supply pipes and wrap your new heater with a fiberglass blanket for maximum efficiency. For details, see page 183.

THE GREAT OUTDOORS

Ready for some fresh air? This chapter heads outside for such plumbing pursuits as hose bibbs, sprinkler and drip systems, garden pools, and fountains.

While outdoor installations use many of the same techniques as indoor jobs, there are some wrinkles—like those involving shovels—and you'll need to acquaint yourself with some new materials.

For each of these projects, you'll be tapping into the existing supply system, then running pipe to a new location. Whenever you extend a supply pipe outdoors, you'll need to add a backflow preventer (see page 133) that blocks outdoor waste water from heading back inside.

All that outdoor water needs to go somewhere, so we'll also be exploring your drainage options. Do not, in any case, tie into your existing DWV system—outdoor drainage must go elsewhere.

Schedule 40
PVC pipe

Schedule 80
PVC pipe

Flexible
PE pipe

Flexible
type L tubing

FIRST THINGS FIRST

Outdoor plumbing schemes, like indoor ones, revolve around two familiar concepts: supply and drainage. But when planning an outdoor project, you'll probably need to acquaint yourself with a few new materials. You'll also need to take a closer look at your landscape.

OUTDOOR MATERIALS

Compression fitting

Slip fitting   Threaded fitting

Plastic PVC pipe is the workhorse for outdoor extensions, sprinkler installations, and other irrigation projects. Schedule 40 PVC, the interior standby, is great for outdoor use, too—or you may substitute slightly thinner, slightly less expensive schedules. For aboveground use (where supply lines travel from house to ground or for vertical sprinkler risers), opt for threaded, charcoal-colored Schedule 80 pipe; these precut pieces are stronger and stand up to sunlight better than standard white PVC. Some plastic pipes are joined with standard slip fittings and solvent cement, while other connections call for threaded fittings, and still others for compression fittings. All three types of fittings are shown at left. You can also buy combination fittings—for example, a T-fitting with two slip outlets and one threaded outlet.

In some areas, flexible PE may be used for potable outdoor water systems; it's often used for drip irrigation as well. Join sections as necessary with barbed couplings, elbows, and Ts, as shown on page 24 (drip tubing is often joined with proprietary compression fittings).

Flexible copper tubing, type L, is the choice for main supply pipes running from the curb to the house and for extending the supply system from the house to an outbuilding, such as a detached garage or studio.

Outdoor drainage makes extensive use of plastic pipe and fittings, too. Many landscapers use PVC—usually either Schedule 40 in diameters up to 2 inches; or thinner, less expensive schedules in sizes up to 8 inches. Drainage needs are addressed on pages 148–149, where you'll find another player: flexible, corrugated drainpipe (both solid and perforated versions) in 10-, 50-, and 100-foot coils.

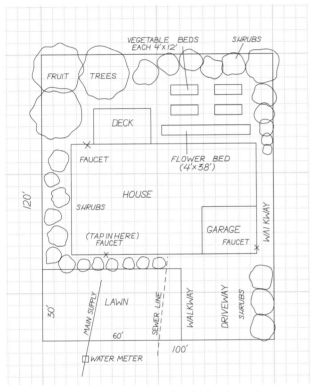

A base map of your property makes a handy planning tool.

WARNING Before you begin digging, be sure to ask your utility companies for the location of underground lines for gas, water, sewer, electricity, and other services so you can work around them. If your home isn't connected to a sewer, locate the septic tank and drainage field and avoid digging in those locations.

MAKING A MAP

If you're contemplating an outdoor project such as a sprinkler system and/or a drainage system, it's a good idea to make a scale drawing of your property like the one shown at left to serve as a base map.

Use graph paper to make a scale drawing of the areas to be watered or drained, marking locations and types of plants, any special water needs they have, and whether they're deep- or shallow-rooted. Pencil in water sources and structures and such obstacles as fences, walkways, and patios. Also note any slopes or other elevation changes, since they affect water distribution. The more detailed your map, the easier it will be to select the right components when you're ready to shop.

Now is the time to check with your building department for any necessary permits. Also investigate the various sprinklers, drip components, or drain fittings on the market; if you decide on a brand, pick up copies of the manufacturer's literature and/or any workbooks.

Backflow Preventers

Whenever you extend an indoor plumbing system outdoors, you need to install either a vacuum breaker or an antisiphon valve. Both are designed to prevent the backflow of "gray," or used, water into the house's water system, which could occur if pressure inside the interior system suddenly drops.

The vacuum breaker screws onto the end of an outdoor hose bibb; a garden hose screws onto the breaker. An antisiphon valve is required on sprinkler and drip systems or whenever an interior pipe system is extended to a location in the garden or to another building.

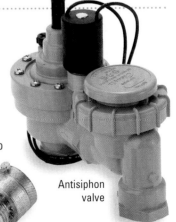

Vacuum breaker

Antisiphon valve

Decorative 90° hose bibb

"No-kink" hose bibb

Sillcock

Garden valve

INSTALLING OUTDOOR FAUCETS

Several models of outdoor faucets, known as hose bibbs, are available; most have threaded spouts for attaching hoses. Some have bodies with female threads and are screwed onto a pipe; others have male threads and are screwed into a threaded T-fitting or elbow. Most types fit onto horizontal pipes; garden valves fit vertical pipes. Some hose bibbs have an escutcheon, or notched flange, which allows the faucet to be mounted on an exterior wall (this type is often called a sillcock).

When installing a new faucet, first decide where you want it. The location should be convenient for outdoor watering and, if possible, high enough to clear a bucket. Also be sure to consider the location of the indoor cold water pipe you'll be tapping into (it's probably in your basement or crawl space). Plan carefully how you'll tap into the pipe, and organize all the pipe and fittings necessary before you begin. For pointers, see Chapter Four, "Pipefitting Know-how," beginning on page 44.

DRILLING THROUGH THE WALL: Before you start, check indoors to make sure you won't hit drainpipes, electrical lines, heating ductwork, studs, or floor joists. Avoid the foundation. If the water supply pipe is located below the foundation's top surface, plan to drill above the foundation and route the new pipes down to the water supply pipe. If possible, drill a small pilot hole from the inside out to mark the location. Select the right bit for the job: a spade bit for wood, a masonry bit for brick or stucco. Then, using an extension bit if necessary, drill through the wall from the outside, boring a hole large enough to fit the pipe that will be attached to the faucet.

CONNECTING THE FAUCET: Turn off the water at the main house shutoff (see page 152) and drain the pipes. Tap into the water supply pipe with a T-fitting and connect the new pipe and fittings. Unless you're using a freezeproof faucet (see the facing page), plan to add a stop-and-waste valve to the supply pipe that will feed the new hose bibb. A stop-and-waste valve is an indoor shutoff valve with a drain; it allows the outside water to be turned off inside a warm basement or crawl space and the water beyond to be drained so it won't freeze and cause the pipes to burst.

Run the new pipe through the wall (see below) and connect the faucet to it. Connecting pipes must be anchored to the house's framing near the wall, as well as all along the pipe run (see page 77). Fill any gaps around the pipe with silicone or foam sealant. When installing a flanged faucet, you can caulk the space around the pipe before screwing the flange in place.

Many codes require that you install a vacuum breaker or backflow preventer (page 133). This device, screwed on between the faucet spout and the hose itself, prevents the backflow of possibly polluted water into your supply system.

EXTENDING NEW PIPES OUTDOORS

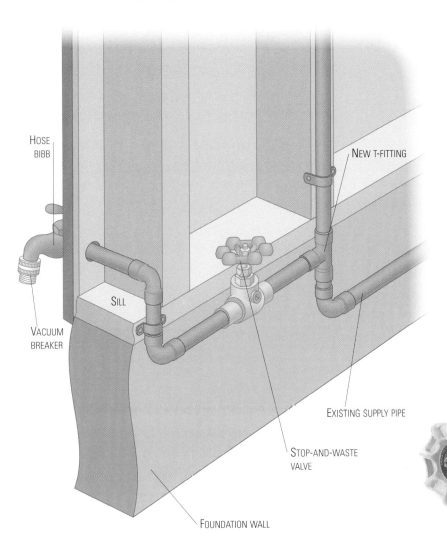

HOSE BIBB

NEW T-FITTING

SILL

VACUUM BREAKER

EXISTING SUPPLY PIPE

STOP-AND-WASTE VALVE

FOUNDATION WALL

Installing a Freezeproof Faucet

If you live in an area where winter temperatures often dip below freezing, it makes sense to install a freezeproof faucet. This type of faucet has an elongated body that extends well into a basement or crawl space and a valve seat located far back in the body. When you turn off the faucet, the water flow stops inside the house so it won't be exposed to the cold temperatures. Freezeproof faucets are self-draining. You install the unit at a slight tilt toward the ground outside, which allows any remaining water to run out after the faucet is turned off.

Freezeproof faucet

SPRINKLER SYSTEMS

Designing a successful sprinkler system requires some knowledge of hydraulics, soil types, plant growth needs, and irrigation equipment. But don't be discouraged—planning and installing sprinklers is well within the ability of most home plumbers.

Below are the basic components and techniques for installing a multicircuit sprinkler system. For details on drip irrigation, see pages 142–145. For help with particular problems or for expert advice, look in the yellow pages under "Irrigation Systems & Equipment," "Landscape Contractors," or "Sprinklers—Garden & Lawn."

GATHERING INFORMATION

To design an efficient watering system, you'll need to first prepare a fairly detailed base map of your property (see page 133), then determine the water-retaining characteristics of the soil and measure water pressure and water flow rate.

DETERMINING SOIL TYPE: Sprinkler systems work well in sandy soil and in loam. Clay soil holds so much moisture that excessive runoff and fungus growth occur when conventional sprinkler heads are used; if you have soil of this type, be sure to install low-flow heads instead.

....

Keeping It Simple

A permanent irrigation system may be overkill if you live in a rainy-summer climate, especially if you have just a few individual plantings to water during dry spells. Some homeowners go halfway: they simply automate their portable sprinklers and soaker hoses by connecting them to hose bibbs (pages 134–135) and the same kind of control valves and multiple-station timers used in underground sprinkler and drip systems.

If you're not sure of your soil type, wet some soil and squeeze it into a ball. If it crumbles, your soil is sandy. If some of the ball holds its shape, you have loam. If it sticks firmly together, it's clay.

CHECK WATER PRESSURE: Water pressure is measured in pounds per square inch (psi). Most sprinklers won't work efficiently if the psi is too low. To measure your home's water pressure, screw a water pressure gauge onto an outdoor faucet (see page 153) and, with all other water outlets turned off, turn the faucet on full. Record the psi at each outside faucet location, taking several readings throughout the day; use the lowest reading as a conservative basis when calculating sprinkler output.

CHECK WATER FLOW RATE: Flow rate, the amount of water that moves through pipes in a given period of time, is measured in gallons per hour (gph) or gallons per minute (gpm).

To determine flow rate, first fill a bucket with 1 gallon of water and mark this level on the bucket's inside wall. Empty the bucket, then place it under an outdoor faucet and count how many seconds it takes to fill to the line. Then, divide the total number of seconds into 60 to determine the gpm. Write this figure on your plan; you'll use it when plotting circuits.

Note that to use this method of measuring gpm, the outdoor faucet must be the same diameter as your supply pipe.

Generally, the total output of a circuit of sprinklers should not exceed 75 percent of the available water flow at the faucet; otherwise, the heads won't work properly and household water pressure may dip. If the sprinkler circuit requires a higher flow rate, the solution is to create several separate circuits, each directed by its own control valve.

A SPRINKLER SYSTEM OVERVIEW

Antisiphon control valve

Existing hose bibb

T-fitting

New supply pipe

Schedule 80 PVC risers

Flexible riser

Shutoff valve

Cutoff riser

Schedule 40 PVC pipe

Side-outlet elbow

Elbow fitting

T-fitting

Swing joint

SYSTEM COMPONENTS

The components you'll need to install a sprinkler system include antisiphon control valves, essential for preventing water from flowing back into your home's water supply; pipes and pipe fittings, usually made of PVC; risers; sprinkler heads; and a controller, or timer. Typical components are shown above.

The system begins at a cold water supply pipe, where you connect the new supply line with a T-fitting or compression T-fitting. Install a new shutoff valve on the new supply pipe (or at the end of the old pipe) so you can shut off the sprinkler system without turning off the water to your house.

The new supply pipe carries water to control valves with integral antisiphon devices. Each valve operates a circuit, or a separate set of sprinklers. Place the valves in a convenient, inconspicuous place, grouping them into what's called a manifold to avoid extra digging and make operation easier.

In an automated system, low-voltage wires run from the manifold to a controller, which may be anything from a simple mechanical timer to a complex digital system. The controller directs the watering cycle by automatically activating the control valves for the different circuits so they turn on for a preset time period. For details, see page 138.

PLOTTING YOUR SYSTEM

Planning your sprinklers on paper first will help you think the system through, guide you in ordering materials, and serve as a permanent record of where pipes are buried.

The two broad categories of sprinkler heads are spray and rotary. Spray heads operate at relatively low water pressure, from 15 to 30 psi; they're a good choice for precise, controlled watering of shrubs, irregular landscaping, and fairly small lawns. Rotary heads need more pressure to operate (from 30 to 70 psi) and throw water substantially farther—up to 90 feet; this makes them economical for very large lawns and landscaped areas.

Sprinkler heads also come in many different spray patterns, including full, half, and quarter circles, as well

Rotary head

Bubbler

Spray head

Pop-up head

as rectangular shapes. Some heads have adjustable patterns and throw distances. Low-flow nozzles reduce runoff, improve spray uniformity, and allow a larger area to be irrigated with a given amount of water.

For open lawn areas where foot traffic and mowing will occur, install pop-up heads that automatically rise

---

TIMER TIPS

The heart of an automated watering system—a controller, or timer—is a mechanical or electronic clock that automatically regulates the operation of each sprinkler circuit connected to it. For all but the smallest system, choose a multi-program controller that allows you to set watering frequency and duration.

Simple mechanical timers automate water shutoff, but because they have no power source or memory, you must set them every time you want to water. Electronic timers are far more accurate, and most have many useful features that mechanical timers don't offer. You'll probably need a multi-station model—one that has a circuit for each control valve. Dual- or multiple-program controllers let you water a lawn on a more frequent schedule than that needed for ground covers, trees, and shrubs. A rain- or moisture-sensing shut-off will override the programming if a certain amount of rain has fallen or if the soil is sufficiently moist. If your area is plagued by power outages, consider a timer with a battery

backup—otherwise, your timer settings will be wiped out every time the lights go out.

Low-voltage, insulated cable (typically AWG-14 or 18) that is approved for direct burial is used to connect the control valves to the timer. Color-coded multistrand wire makes it easy to remember what connects with what; a different color wire joins each valve to a station on the timer, and another color wire (the pros usually use white) links all the valves to the timer. Thus, if you have four valves, you'll need five-strand wire.

Connect the wire as shown below. Run the wire underground to the timer location. Leave plenty of slack as you lay the wire; the pros also loop the wire at each valve and at turns in the trench. When you get to the timer site, bring the wire aboveground and tack it along walls, joists, and other surfaces as needed.

Electronic timer, low-voltage cable

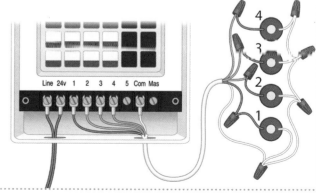

SOME SPRINKLER OUTPUT RATES

SPRAY HEADS (operating at 30 psi)

RADIUS OF THROW	8 FT.	10 FT.	12 FT.	15 FT.
ARC PATTERNS				
360° ●	1.00 gpm	1.60 gpm	2.40 gpm	3.60 gpm
270°	.75 gpm	1.20 gpm	1.80 gpm	2.70 gpm
240°	.70 gpm	1.00 gpm	1.60 gpm	2.40 gpm
180°	.50 gpm	.80 gpm	1.20 gpm	1.80 gpm
120°	.35 gpm	.50 gpm	.80 gpm	1.20 gpm
90°	.25 gpm	.40 gpm	.60 gpm	.90 gpm

ROTARY HEADS (operating at 40 to 50 psi)

RADIUS OF THROW	30 FT.	35 FT.	40 FT.	45 FT.
ARC PATTERN				
360° ●	1.00 gpm	1.80 gpm	2.70 gpm	5.20 gpm

when the water goes on and drop down when watering is finished.

Detail your proposed sprinkler system on a copy of the base map of your property (see page 133). Begin by noting where you need to locate sprinkler heads. To determine the spacing and the radius, or throw, for each head, check the manufacturer's workbook.

Next, break your system into separate circuits, or stations, keeping in mind the output rates shown above. Avoid placing rotary and spray sprinklers, shrub and lawn sprinklers, or low-flow and standard sprinklers on the same circuit.

Note that a T- or H-shaped circuit will deliver water more evenly to all heads than a straight-line circuit (the last head in a line typically receives less water pressure).

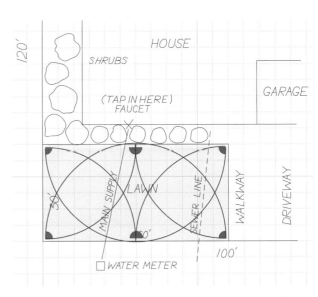

Use a compass to draw rounded spray coverage patterns, making sure they overlap sufficiently.

INSTALLING THE SYSTEM

Plumbing a sprinkler system with PVC pipe and fittings is not difficult; for help working with plastic pipe, see pages 46–47. Make sure that your base map shows the location of the control valves and all pipes and sprinkler heads.

DIG TRENCHES: The first task is to dig 8-inch-deep trenches for burying the pipe. To locate the trenches, run string between stakes or lay the pipes on the ground according to your plan and, using a shovel, mark their location on the ground. Dig the trenches with a flat spade or with a rented trenching machine. To salvage sod, gently work the spade beneath the sod layer and

peel the sod away before digging deeper. Keep the removed sod moist until you can put it back in place.

CONNECT TO THE SUPPLY PIPE: First, shut off the water at the main house shutoff (see page 152). Open a faucet at the low end of the system to drain the pipes. Then, use one of the three connection methods shown below.

ADD THE CONTROL VALVES: If the cold water supply pipe you'll be tying into is 1-inch in diameter or larger, you'll need to run 1-inch pipe to the control valves and circuits; if it's ³⁄₄-inch diameter, run ³⁄₄-inch pipe.

To install each control valve, you'll generally need two threaded Schedule 80 plastic risers; wrap the

---

TAPPING INTO THE SUPPLY SYSTEM

To supply a new sprinkler system, you'll have to tap into your existing cold water supply system at a faucet or along the main supply pipe, either outdoors or at a basement meter. Remember to shut off the main water supply first.

In mild climates, you may tap into an outdoor faucet (see below left). Simply remove the existing faucet, add a T-fitting, and attach a new faucet to the T. Install a shutoff valve as shown, then run new pipe to the sprinkler system.

You can also tap into the main supply pipe (see below center) before it enters the house; add a T-fitting and shutoff valve.

In cold-winter areas, you'll need to tap into the cold water supply pipe inside the house (see below right). Tie into the house side of the water meter with a T-fitting and install a shutoff valve beyond the T (choose a stop-and-waste valve so you can drain the system at this point; see page 135). To run the new line to the sprinkler system, drill a hole through the siding above the foundation.

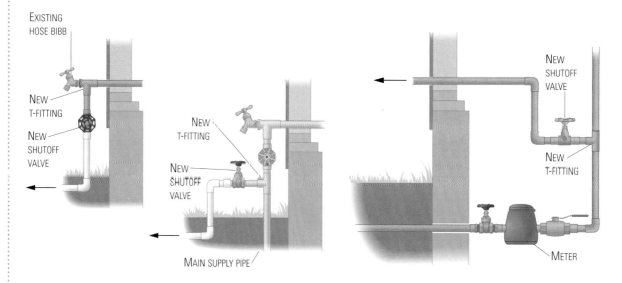

Connect to your cold water supply system either at an existing outdoor hose bibb (left); at the main supply pipe before it enters the house (center); or inside the basement or crawl space (right).

threads with pipe-thread tape and screw the risers into the valve; hand-tighten. Screw each riser into a slip-by-threaded T or elbow in the PVC sprinkler line. Most codes require that control valves be at least 6 inches above the ground and above the highest head in the circuit.

LAY THE PIPE: From the control valves, run the pipes for each circuit. Before cementing each slip-by-threaded riser T or elbow in place, screw in a riser so you can align the fitting properly with the surface of the ground. Don't add the sprinkler heads yet. When all piping is assembled, allow the solvent cement to cure for at least an hour.

ADD RISERS AND SPRINKLER HEADS: Open the shutoff valve that supplies the sprinklers. Next, briefly open the control valves to purge any dirt from the pipes. Wrap riser threads with pipe-thread tape, screw on the sprinkler heads, and adjust their positions. Turn the water on again to check for proper operation and any leaks.

If you're planning to install a mechanical or electronic controller (see page 138), now is the time to hook it up.

TEST THE SYSTEM: Before filling in the trenches, test the system—but first turn off any water running in the house so that you don't have a dishwasher or washing machine competing with your irrigation system. After you've switched on the water at the new shutoff valve, turn on each circuit manually. Check that each circuit works, and check that each spray head is spraying without obstruction. If necessary, check your timer's wiring connections or remove clogged sprinklers and check for dirt.

As you test the system, you may have to adjust a sprinkler's direction, throw, or spray pattern. Direction is often easily altered by turning the sprinkler body or tweaking the riser. Make sure that the spray patterns overlap. Follow the manufacturer's directions for adjusting a rotary sprinkler's arc.

BACKFILL THE TRENCHES: When the system is working properly, backfill the trenches. Fill each trench to just a little lower than the original soil or sod line, then flood it with water to settle the soil. Add more soil, mounding it slightly, then tamp with a hand tamper. In a lawn, replace any sod that you removed.

INSTALLING SPRINKLERS

1 Dig trenches
Remove sod and dig 8-inch-deep trenches for pipes. To keep trench lines straight, run string between two stakes.

2 Install control valves
Connect antisiphon control valves to the water supply, using Schedule 80 PVC risers; set each valve at least 6 inches aboveground.

3 Complete the circuits
Assemble the system from the control valve outward, fitting risers and heads to fittings as you go.

4 Test, then tamp
Flush out pipes with heads removed, then replace heads and test for leaks. When all is well, fill in trenches and tamp soil firmly.

½" fittings

Goof plugs

¼" fittings

Drip emitters

Flag emitters

DRIP SYSTEM DETAILS

Drip irrigation is the most practical, efficient way to water garden plants. In a typical system, water flows through lengths of flexible polyethylene tubing; emitters that you attach to the tubing deliver water just where you want it—near plant roots—in a gradual flow adjusted for each plant's water requirements. Drip systems eliminate water runoff and reduce water loss through evaporation and overspray by up to 70 percent. Used in conjunction with an automatic controller, or timer, such a system offers both flexibility and hassle-free control.

BASIC DRIP COMPONENTS

Following is a rundown of typical components and how they operate. You'll find installation basics on pages 144–145.

HEAD ASSEMBLY: The components that connect your water source to the drip system are known collectively as the head assembly. This includes a manual control valve or timer, a backflow preventer, a filter, and a pressure regulator.

A CONTROL VALVE turns the water to a drip circuit on and off. If you have a single drip line attached to an outdoor faucet (see below right), that faucet is your control valve. If your drip line is attached to a battery-operated timer at the hose bibb, your control valve is built into the timer. If the drip line

A DRIP SYSTEM OVERVIEW

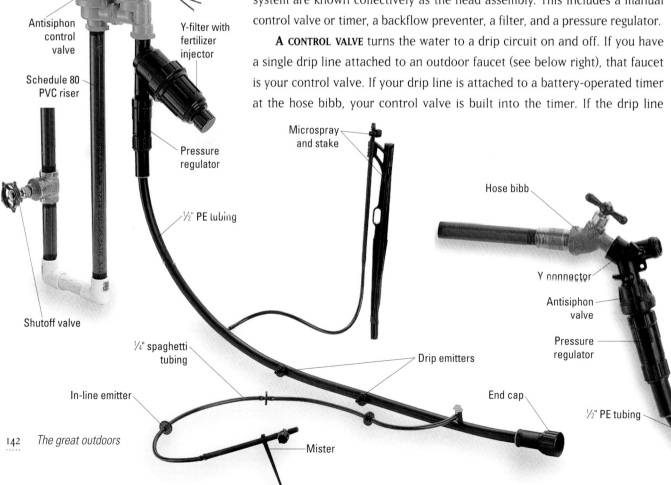

Antisiphon control valve

Y-filter with fertilizer injector

Schedule 80 PVC riser

Pressure regulator

½" PE tubing

Shutoff valve

Microspray and stake

Hose bibb

Y connector

Antisiphon valve

Pressure regulator

½" PE tubing

¼" spaghetti tubing

Drip emitters

End cap

In-line emitter

Mister

connects directly to your water line, a separate manual or remote-control valve is required for each circuit. Battery-operated and electronic timers connect to a remote-control valve via low-voltage cable, allowing you to schedule the water to turn on and off at appointed times. For timer details, see page 138.

A BACKFLOW PREVENTER keeps outside water from flowing back into the water supply. Most municipalities require that all irrigation systems include a backflow preventer. One common type is an antisiphon valve, which creates an air gap at a high point in the system.

A FILTER is necessary in all systems to prevent the small openings on the watering devices from becoming clogged. Small, in-line filters are the least expensive and are usually fine for small systems and clean water supplies, but you have to take apart the lines to wash the screens. Larger Y-filters allow for easy cleaning.

A PRESSURE REGULATOR adjusts household water pressure downward, allowing your drip system to run at its ideal 15 to 30 pounds per square inch (psi). A pressure regulator protects the fittings from blowing apart under excess force and allows the watering devices to work properly.

A FERTILIZER INJECTOR placed between control valve and pressure regulator puts fertilizer directly into the plants' water supply. Some filters have built-in injectors.

TUBING AND FITTINGS: These are the bones of your drip system. They carry the water from the head assembly to the different parts of the landscape.

DRIP TUBING, made of flexible black polyethylene (PE), is available in 1/2-inch (standard) and 3/8-inch diameters and is flexible enough to be snaked through plantings and looped around trees and shrubs. You may insert emitters directly into the tubing or install them in smaller tubing (microtubing) that branches off the main line. A special tool is used to punch through the wall of the tubing to install emitters.

MICROTUBING, sometimes called spaghetti tubing, is small-diameter (usually 1/4-inch) flexible polyethylene used to link individual sprayers or emitters to the larger drip tubing. Stakes are often used to hold it in place.

Ooze tubing

Laser tubing

FITTINGS are used to put together the system. Couplings allow you to join two sections of tubing; T-fittings let you branch off in different directions; and L-shaped fittings are useful for making sharp turns. End caps close off the ends of drip tubing, and goof plugs are indispensable for sealing holes you've punched in the wrong place.

WATERING DEVICES: Most let water drip or ooze onto the root zone; others spray water into the air like miniature sprinklers. Ooze tubing, laser tubing, and other porous tubing types double as pipes and emitters.

DRIP EMITTERS drip water directly onto the soil. Most have barbed ends that snap into the wall of the drip tubing or that push into the ends of microtubing. They typically dispense 1/2, 1, or 2 gallons per hour (gph), and manufacturers color-code them to make their output obvious. For help choosing the right emitters for your soil type and plants, see the chart on page 145.

OOZE TUBING, available in 1/2- and 1/4-inch diameters, leaks water from thousands of tiny pores.

LASER TUBING is 1/4 inch in diameter and features tiny emitter holes drilled by laser at regular intervals.

MICROSPRAYS are available in quarter-, half-, and full-circle patterns, as well as a bow-tie shape. These little heads are useful for covering tight or irregular spaces.

MINISPRINKLERS, also called spinners, cover larger areas than minisprays can, throwing water in circles measuring from 10 to 30 feet across.

MISTERS are used to raise the humidity or to water hanging plants or bonsai. Misters are often positioned above hanging plants so that the spray is directed downward. For in-ground plants, aim them upward.

INSTALLING YOUR DRIP SYSTEM

Hole Punch Pointers

When making holes in drip tubing for emitters and barbed fittings, use a punch designed for that purpose and make sure the tubing is lying straight—if it's twisted, the emitter could end up on top, causing water to run along the tubing instead of dripping down into the soil.

Position the hole so that the emitter will drip to the side or downward. Hold the punch at a right angle to the tubing to ensure a round hole that will seal tightly against the emitter's barb. You may find the piercing process to be easier if you slowly twist the punch as you push it into the tubing. On some punches, the tip may become clogged with extracted tubing; clear it out before punching again.

Because drip systems include lots of little parts, organizing them by size and type will make installation go more smoothly. Once you've sorted the parts, the most efficient way to connect them is to start with the head assembly and then position the water-distribution lines.

MAKING THE SUPPLY CONNECTION: There are two types of head assemblies: a hose-thread assembly and a pipe-thread assembly. Both are shown on page 142. A hose-thread assembly simply screws onto an outdoor faucet; you may want to install a Y-connector at the faucet and attach your system to one branch of it so the faucet may also be used for other purposes. A pipe-thread assembly is plumbed into a water supply line. For details, see page 140.

CONSTRUCTING THE HEAD ASSEMBLY: Hose-thread components naturally screw together in the proper direction, so there is no danger of assembling any part backward. The washers should seat properly when the parts are hand-tightened; don't use a wrench. For pipe-thread connections, look for directional arrows, and use pipe-thread tape for a tight fit.

LAYING THE LINES: Starting from the head assembly, lay the main tubing. Anchor it to the ground at intervals with plastic stakes sold with irrigation supplies. To avoid kinking the tubing, unroll it as you go rather than pulling it out of a coil lying on the ground, and leave a little slack for adjustments.

If you need to make a sharp turn, cut the tubing with pruning shears or a sharp utility knife and rejoin the ends with an elbow fitting. To branch the line, cut and rejoin the pieces in the arms of a T-fitting. Because ooze tubing and other soakers combine tubing with the watering devices, you may lay them now or wait until you install the emitters and microsprayers.

Try to keep dirt out of the tubing as you work. When all the lines are laid, turn on the water to flush them of dirt and debris. Once the water runs clear, you may turn off the water and close the main lines with end caps.

INSTALLING WATERING DEVICES: To install a drip emitter directly into 1/2- or 3/8-inch drip tubing, use your hole punch (see photo at left) to make a hole in the tubing and insert the barbed end of an emitter.

Another way to install an emitter is at the open end of microtubing run from the drip hose to the plant. To attach the microtubing to the drip line, insert a barbed connector in one end of the microtubing and push the connector into a hole you've punched in the drip hose. Then, insert the emitter into the other end of the microtubing and position it at the plant—you may want to use a special stake designed for this purpose.

To install a group of in-line emitters, simply string them together with microtubing, then secure the microtubing to drip tubing with a barbed insert. Then, use a goof plug or emitter to cap the microtubing's end.

Microsprays may be installed in various ways. A common method is to punch a hole in the drip tubing and insert a rigid microspray riser—you screw the head onto the riser top. Another option is to punch a hole and insert a barbed connector joining a short length of microtubing from the larger tubing to a stake. Some tubes are intended for support only; other types allow you to screw the spray head directly onto the stake.

Warm It Up

Polyethylene hose is much easier to unroll and install if you leave it in the hot sun for an hour to soften.

DRIP-EMITTER SELECTION GUIDE

	OUTPUT RATE	NUMBER OF EMITTERS	PLACEMENT
Vegetables, closely spaced	½–1 gph	1	every 12 inches
Vegetables, widely spaced	1–2 gph	1	at base of plant
Flower beds	1 gph	1	at base of plant
Ground covers	1 gph	1	at base of plant
Shrubs (2–3 ft.)	1 gph	1–2	at base of plant
Shrubs and trees (3–5 ft.)	1 gph	2	6–12 inches on either side
Shrubs and trees (5–10 ft.)	2 gph	2–3	2 feet from trunk
Shrubs and trees (10–20 ft.)	2 gph	3–4	3 feet apart, at drip line
Trees (over 20 ft.)	2 gph	6 or more	4 feet apart, at drip line

MICROSPRAY SELECTION GUIDE

FULL CIRCLE ●	HALF CIRCLE ◗	QUARTER CIRCLE ◢	BOW TIE ◆◀	OUTPUT RATE
8'	5'	5'	4'	6 gph
9'	6'	6'	5'	10 gph
11'	7'	7'	6'	17 gph
12'	8'	8'	7'	24 gph

GARDEN POOLS AND FOUNTAINS

Pumps and plumbing for garden pools have been improved to the point where even weekend plumbers can install them without much trouble. Following are guidelines for choosing a basic pump and using pipes, fittings, and accessories. For a look at two simple plumbing systems, see the facing page.

CHOOSING THE PUMP: The mechanical heart of a fountain or waterfall is merely a set of whirling blades that propel water through it.

Submersible pumps (like the one shown below) simplify plumbing to the extreme. They sit on the floor of a fountain or pool, often hidden only by the water itself, and operate silently—one advantage over other pumps. Flexible PE tubing or rigid PVC pipe carries water to the fountain spout or waterfall.

A larger, recirculating pump is frequently used when the pump must be operated continuously or when water has a long distance to go from pump to outlet—often the case with large waterfalls or streams.

All manufacturers give electrical specifications—amps, watts, and horsepower—for their products that indicate how much power they consume. But the practical measure of a pump's performance is its head, the volume of water it can pump vertically. Fountain spray jets are usually designed for a specific water pressure, but pump requirements for waterfalls and streams vary depending on the desired effect.

PIPEFITTING FOR POOLS: Whenever possible, opt for plastic pipe and fittings for both water supply and drain lines; plastic is easy to cut, is straightforward to assemble, and won't corrode like copper or galvanized steel. Small water features that are powered by submersible pumps may require only flexible PE tubing. But for larger pools, rigid Schedule 40 PVC pipe and fittings are the standby. ABS plastic may be used for larger drain lines.

Valves allow you to control the flow to a fountain or waterfall, divert water to a nearby drain, or shut down the entire system for repairs or maintenance. A gate valve is adequate for simple on/off use and for isolating a pump, filter, or drain line. Need to keep water flowing in one direction or maintain a pump's prime? Install a check valve. To control flow, opt for a ball valve. A three-way valve allows you to shut off the flow, send a controlled flow to a fountain head, or open up a line for draining the pool.

A small pool or fountain may not need a drain, especially if it has a submersible pump that can double as a sump pump. Larger pools, however, should have a main drain so the pool can be emptied for maintenance or emergency repairs. Drains come in a variety of shapes and sizes; swimming pool and

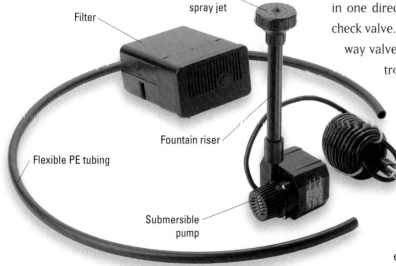

Filter

Fountain spray jet

Fountain riser

Flexible PE tubing

Submersible pump

GARDEN POOL COMPONENTS

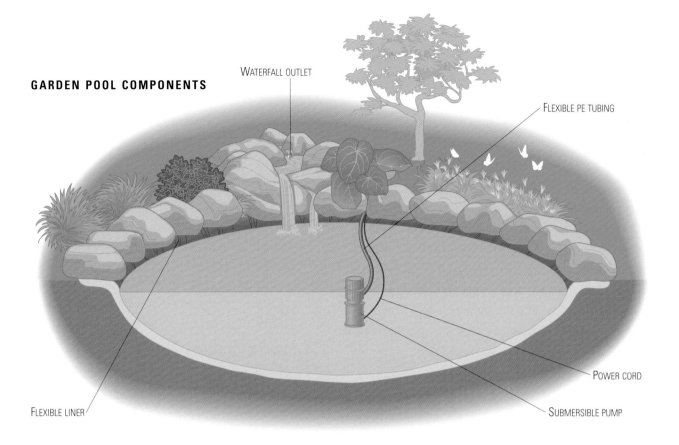

WATERFALL OUTLET

FLEXIBLE PE TUBING

POWER CORD

SUBMERSIBLE PUMP

FLEXIBLE LINER

spa suppliers are good places to find them. Make sure the pool floor slopes slightly toward the drain.

FOUNTAINS: Some spray fountains come as complete units, but others include the spray jet only, requiring a riser pipe—or a series of nipples and adapters—to achieve the proper height. To install a spray jet, fasten the riser tightly to a stake or support block, then screw the jet onto the riser's threads.

Typically, a wall fountain has no jet, but simply one or more pipe ends flush with the back wall. An example is shown at right. Cover the pipe end with a decorative noz-zle or figurine, or hide it between masonry units such as bricks or stones, leaving a narrow slot in mortar or grout.

A ball valve or three-way valve will maintain the flow to any fountain.

FILTERS: Whether they're cartridge, pressurized-sand, or biological, all filters require intake and outlet plumbing. Always position the filter on the outlet side of the pump unless you're using a separate pump and plumbing route just for the filter, which is a good idea for large pools. A separate ball valve on this line is handy.

WALL FOUNTAIN DETAILS

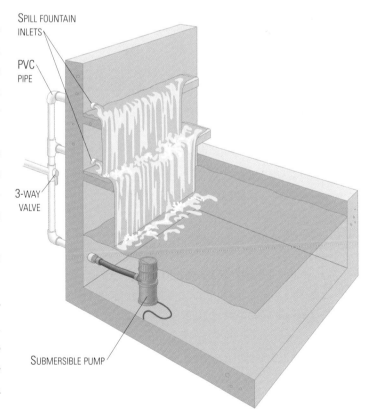

SPILL FOUNTAIN INLETS

PVC PIPE

3-WAY VALVE

SUBMERSIBLE PUMP

DRAINAGE DETAILS

When you add hose bibbs, sprinklers, or a drip system that delivers water to your landscape, you also need to plan for adequate outdoor drainage—to channel that water away from building foundations, patios, driveways, and low-lying garden areas. Complex grading and drainage schemes are jobs for a professional, but with a shovel and some basic plumbing skills, a homeowner can easily handle some smaller tasks. Here's how.

CHOOSING YOUR MATERIALS

Solid drainpipes direct water toward a dry well, storm drain, street, or other low spot where it can be safely discharged. These pipes may be either rigid plastic (typically PVC) or ribbed, flexible plastic (shown on the facing page). Perforated drainpipe, available in both rigid and flexible forms, absorbs rising runoff from the areas around it; and, depending on whether there's drainage gravel or an impermeable layer below, either channels water to a central point or gradually releases the excess as it travels through the pipe.

You'll find couplings, elbows, Ys, and Ts to match each pipe type. You'll also find a wide selection of both plastic and concrete drains, catch basins, matching grates, drainage channels, and downspout fittings.

What size pipe do you need? Strictly speaking, the minimum sizes for both vertical pipes (like those for draining a roof) and horizontal pipes (those serving a lawn or patio) depend on three main factors: the square footage of the area to be drained, the pitch of the drainage pipe (nominally 1/4 inch per foot), and the amount of rainfall expected (couched in terms of the worst "1-hour storm in a 100-year period"). Plumbing codes may include charts specifying these values. Sound confusing? It's a good idea to consult a local building inspector.

CHANNELING TECHNIQUES

Often, you can improve the drainage in one area by simply channeling excess water to another place for disposal. To channel water below the surface, use trenches containing gravel and/or drainpipes. Drain grates, catch basins, and dry wells serve as collection points.

LAYING PIPE: Rigid and flexible drainpipes direct water away from structures, downspouts, and low spots, and channel water to storm drains or dry wells (see below).

Place the pipe in a trench dug 12 inches deep (deeper in frost areas); slant it at least 1 inch for every 8 feet of trench. Put coarse gravel or small stones about 2 inches deep in the trench and lay the pipe on top. If you use perforated pipe, lay it with the holes downward so soil won't seep in and clog the pipe. Fill the trench with gravel. If you like, cover the gravel with soil or river rocks.

INSTALLING A CATCH BASIN: To drain water from a low-lying area, install a catch basin. Dig a hole at the lowest point and set a ready-made plastic or concrete box into it (many sizes are available). Set a matching grate on top and dig a sloping trench for a drainpipe to direct water from the basin toward a storm drain (if permitted) or dry well.

DIGGING A DRY WELL: A dry well provides a final destination for runoff in a low area where there's no other drainage alternative. Water that accumulates in the well gradually seeps into the ground below. To build a dry well, dig a 2- to 4-foot-wide hole at least 3 feet deep, keep the bottom above the water table. Cover the sides of the hole with geotextile fabric. Next, dig trenches for the drainpipes that will carry the water into the dry well. Fill the well with coarse gravel or small rocks, then cover it with impervious material, such as heavy roofing felt, and conceal it with a thin layer of topsoil.

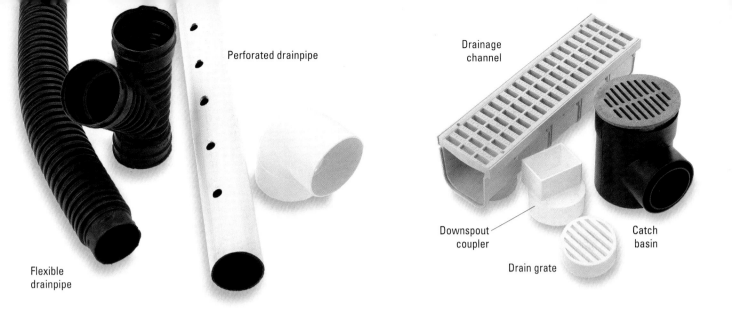

Flexible drainpipe

Perforated drainpipe

Drainage channel

Downspout coupler

Drain grate

Catch basin

A SAMPLE DRAINAGE SCHEME

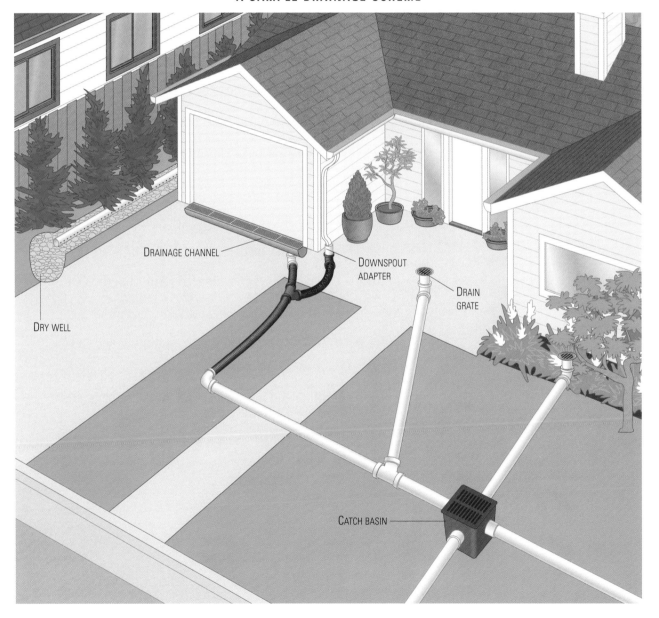

DRAINAGE CHANNEL

DOWNSPOUT ADAPTER

DRAIN GRATE

DRY WELL

CATCH BASIN

TROUBLESHOOTING AND REPAIRS

That constant drip, drip, drip from a faucet is not only annoying, but means wasted water—and it will surely just get worse. Why not fix it today? That's where this chapter comes in: it's all about solving those "classic" plumbing puzzles like clogged drains, frozen pipes, and running toilets. We even head outdoors for some sprinkler repairs.

Understanding the supply and DWV systems in your home will help you diagnose many of the problems you may encounter. So before you turn to the repair instructions on the following pages, it's a good idea to read Chapter One, "An Introduction to the Basics," beginning on page 6.

Note: When working on your supply system, you'll need to turn off the water at the fixture shutoff valves or at the main house shutoff. Need details? Simply turn the page and learn how.

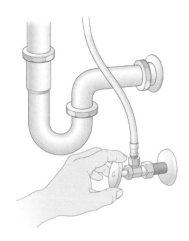

Fixture shutoff valve
Look for this valve directly under the fixture or appliance at the point where the water supply connects to it. Turn the handle clockwise to stop the flow. If there's no fixture shutoff, use the main house shutoff (see below).

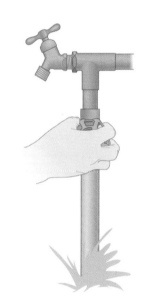

Main house shutoff
This valve, typically a gate or ball type, is close to where the water supply enters the house, either inside or outside. Know where this valve is and label it before any trouble arises.

Curbside utility shutoff
There's also a valve that allows the utility company to shut off the water meter for servicing; use it if there's an emergency on the house side of the meter. In cold climates you may need to dig down to a long, cylindrical buffalo box. In either case, you might need a meter key to turn the valve handle.

SHUTTING OFF THE WATER

The water supply may be turned off at a fixture shutoff valve or at the main house shutoff. A fixture shutoff valve turns off water just to that fixture. You'll usually find one directly below the fixture or appliance at the point where it connects to the water supply pipe (shown at left). A shutoff for a tub or shower may be reached via an access door in an adjacent wall or closet or, occasionally, in the ceiling or floor below the fixture. If the fixture does not have a shutoff valve, you'll need to turn off the water at the main house shutoff (shown center left).

The main house shutoff turns off the water supply to the entire house. Know where this valve is and label and test it before any trouble arises. The house shutoff is usually a gate-type valve (or, in newer houses, a ball-type valve) and is close to the point where the water supply enters the house, either inside or outside.

If there's a problem in the supply pipe between the street and main shutoff, you or your utility company may have to access a curbside box (shown below left), sometimes called a buffalo box. You'll need a long-handled meter key (see page 40) to close the recessed valve inside this box.

ADDING A SHUTOFF VALVE

If your house is not outfitted with fixture shutoff valves, installing a new one is not too difficult, and it will make any future repairs to that fixture much easier.

Essentially, you'll need to cut through the existing supply pipe, remove the cut pipe between fixture and stubout, then secure a new shutoff valve to the stubout. For basic pipefitting techniques, see Chapter Four, "Pipe-fitting Know-how," beginning on page 44. You'll find help with choosing and installing shutoffs on page 109. Lengths of flexible supply tubing save you the trouble of piecing new pipe together to join valve to fixture.

Before doing any work, turn off the water at the main house shutoff. Open a faucet downstream from where you're working to relieve the pressure, and put a bucket under the pipes you're removing.

THE HIGHS AND LOWS
OF WATER PRESSURE

Most appliances, valves, and fixtures that use water are engineered to take 50 to 60 pounds of pressure per square inch (psi). Mains deliver water at pressures as high as 150 psi and as low as 10 psi. You can determine your water pressure by attaching a water-pressure gauge (below) to an outside hose bibb.

Water-pressure gauge

LOW PRESSURE: The telltale sign of low pressure is a very thin trickle of water from faucets throughout the house. Chronic low pressure is typically found in homes on hills near reservoir level. Periodic low pressure may also occur during peak service hours regardless of the home's location.

The only way of increasing water pressure to a home is to install a booster system. However, flushing rusted pipes (explained below) or putting in larger sections of pipe will at least give you a greater volume of water. If your pipes are too small (see pages 164–165), consider replacing the section of pipe that leads from the outdoor utility shutoff valve to the main house shutoff; for example, if it's a ¾-inch pipe, replace it with a 1-inch pipe. If you have a water meter, you can also ask your utility company to install a larger meter.

Flushing the pipes will help you regain lost volume if the water flow in your house has become sluggish. To do this, follow these steps: Remove and clean aerators on faucets (page 162). Close the valve that controls the pipes you intend to clean; it may be the main house shutoff or a shutoff valve on the water heater. Fully open the faucet at the point farthest from the valve and open a second

faucet nearer the valve. Then, plug the faucet near the valve with a rag (but don't shut off the faucet). Reopen the valve and let water run full force through the farther faucet for as long as sediment continues to appear—probably only a few minutes. Finally, close the faucets, remove the rag, and replace the aerators.

HIGH PRESSURE: The symptoms of high pressure are loud clangs when the dishwasher shuts off or wild sprays when faucets are first turned on. High pressure usually occurs in houses on low-lying slopes of steep hills or in subdivisions where high pressure is maintained for fire protection.

Above-normal pressure can be corrected easily and inexpensively with the installation of a pressure-reducing valve, shown at right. This valve can reduce pipe pressure from 80 psi or more down to a manageable 50 to 60 psi. If you'd like to retain the high water pressure for outdoor hose bibbs and sprinklers, install the pressure-reducing valve downstream from them.

Pressure-reducing valve

To add a pressure-reducing valve, first shut off the water supply. Assemble the valve with the fittings necessary to connect the threads of the valve to the existing pipe. Then, remove a length of pipe on the house side of the main house shutoff that's long enough to accommodate the valve and the assembled fittings.

Install the pressure-reducing valve, following the instructions for pipefitting beginning on page 44. When the work is completed, you may turn the water back on. Be sure to check for any leaks in the new connections.

To reduce the water pressure, turn the adjusting screw at the top of the valve clockwise until the pressure is low enough to end bothersome pipe noises. Make sure the valve still supplies adequate water flow to the upper floors or to faraway fixtures in the house.

LEAKING COMPRESSION FAUCETS

If your faucet has separate hot and cold water handles that come to a spongy stop, it's a compression faucet. This type of faucet has a rubber seat washer secured to the base of a coarse-threaded stem. When you turn the handle to shut off the faucet, the stem screws down, compressing the washer against the valve seat in the faucet body. At the same time, a packing nut compresses the packing (either twine, a washer, or an O-ring) against the stem and prevents water from leaking around it.

Leaks in compression faucets may occur around one of the handles or the spout. Before beginning any repair work, turn off the water at the fixture shutoff valves or the main house shutoff (see page 152) and open the faucet to drain the pipes.

To fix a leak around a handle, remove the handle and tighten the packing nut. If that fails to stop the leak, replace the packing (see the facing page).

If the faucet leaks from the spout, either a washer is defective or a valve seat is badly worn or corroded. First, find out whether the hot or cold side needs work by turning off the shutoff valves one at a time; if the spout still leaks when you turn off a valve, that's the defective side. Take off the corresponding handle and remove the stem. Check the washer first. If it's worn, replace it. If the washer looks fine, a damaged valve seat could be causing the leak by preventing the seat washer from fitting properly. On most compression faucets, the valve seat is replaceable. If the seat is built into the faucet, it can be smoothed with a valve-seat dresser (see page 41).

Before you reassemble the faucet, lubricate the stem threads with silicone grease. If the threads are worn or stripped, consider replacing the stem.

COMPRESSION FAUCET

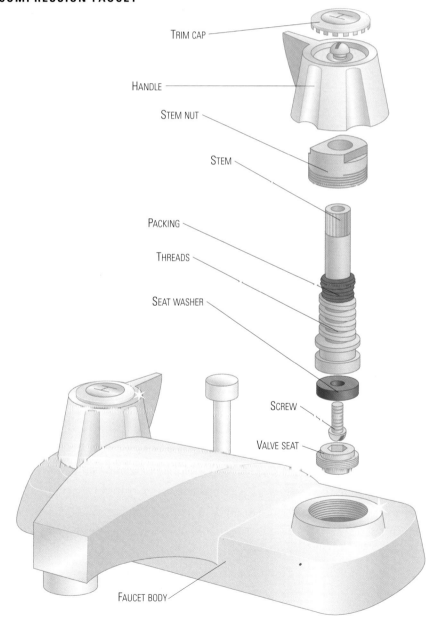

TRIM CAP
HANDLE
STEM NUT
STEM
PACKING
THREADS
SEAT WASHER
SCREW
VALVE SEAT
FAUCET BODY

DISASSEMBLING THE FAUCET

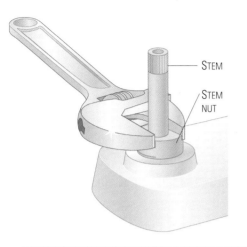

1 Remove the handle

With the handle removed, loosen the stem nut and stem by turning the nut counterclockwise with a wrench.

STEM
STEM NUT

STEM
PACKING
THREADS
SEAT WASHER

2 Inspect the stem

Unscrew the stem and lift it straight out of the faucet body. If the threads are damaged or worn, replace the stem; if not, check the packing for wear (see below left).

THREE PACKING DETAILS

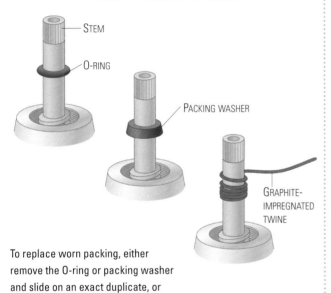

STEM
O-RING
PACKING WASHER
GRAPHITE-IMPREGNATED TWINE

To replace worn packing, either remove the O-ring or packing washer and slide on an exact duplicate, or scrape off the twine and wrap new packing clockwise around the stem.

REPLACING A SEAT WASHER

SCREW
SEAT WASHER

Swivel-head washer

Beveled washer

Flat washer

To remedy a cracked or worn seat washer, remove the screw and washer; install a duplicate washer. If the threads are too worn to hold a screw, snap in a swivel-head washer.

WORKING ON A VALVE SEAT

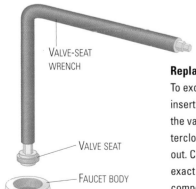

VALVE-SEAT WRENCH
VALVE SEAT
FAUCET BODY

Replace an old seat

To exchange a removable seat, insert a valve-seat wrench into the valve seat and turn it counterclockwise until the seat lifts out. Coat the threads of an exact duplicate with pipe joint compound and install.

Dress a nonremovable seat

To recondition a valve seat, grind down its burrs with a seat dresser. Insert the tool and turn it clockwise once or twice until the seat is smooth; remove metal filings with a damp cloth.

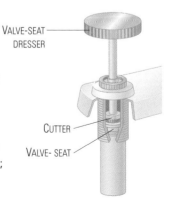

VALVE-SEAT DRESSER
CUTTER
VALVE- SEAT

SINGLE-HANDLE DISC FAUCET

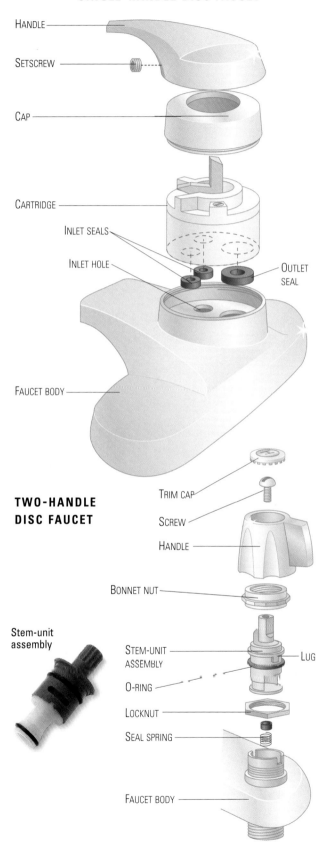

HANDLE

SETSCREW

CAP

CARTRIDGE

INLET SEALS

INLET HOLE

OUTLET SEAL

FAUCET BODY

TWO-HANDLE DISC FAUCET

TRIM CAP

SCREW

HANDLE

BONNET NUT

Stem-unit assembly

STEM-UNIT ASSEMBLY

LUG

O-RING

LOCKNUT

SEAL SPRING

FAUCET BODY

LEAKING DISC FAUCETS

The core of a washerless disc faucet is a ceramic disc assembly, sometimes called a cylinder. Openings in the disc line up with inlet holes to allow the flow of water. Disc faucets come in two versions: single-handle and two-handle. Before doing any work on either type, turn off the water at the fixture shutoff valves or the main house shutoff (see page 152).

SINGLE-HANDLE MODELS: With these faucets, the mix and flow of hot and cold water are controlled by two discs inside a sealed cartridge. Raising the faucet handle lifts the upper disc, controlling the flow; rotating the handle turns the lower disc, controlling the mix. The disc assembly seldom wears out, but if it does, you'll need to replace the entire cartridge. Most often, a worn inlet or outlet seal is the problem.

If you have a leak at the base of the faucet, one of the seals may be worn. Take the faucet apart as shown on the facing page; you'll find the set of seals under the cartridge. Replace them both with exact duplicates.

If the water flow is sluggish, first check the faucet aerator for clogged holes (see page 162). If that's not the problem, the faucet inlet and outlet holes may be obstructed by sediment buildup; in this case, scrape away any deposits.

When reassembling a dismantled faucet, be sure to realign the lugs in the disc assembly with slots in the base of the faucet.

TWO-HANDLE MODELS: These operate the same way as single-handle disc faucets except that they have a pair of cartridges, or stem-unit assemblies, plus a single rubber or plastic seal and a small spring on each side. Although cartridges in single-handle models rarely wear out, in two-handle models they may need to be replaced from time to time. More often, though, an inlet seal is the culprit.

If the faucet drips from the spout, the inlet seal and spring probably need replacing (see the facing page). If the faucet leaks from the handle, the O-ring or stem-unit assembly needs replacing (see the facing page).

WORKING ON A SINGLE-HANDLE MODEL

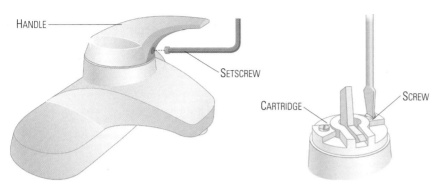

HANDLE

SETSCREW

CARTRIDGE

SCREW

CARTRIDGE

INLET SEAL

INLET HOLE

OUTLET SEAL

OUTLET HOLE

1 Remove the handle

First, lift the handle as high as it can go and loosen—but don't remove—the setscrew with a hex-head wrench. Take off the handle and cap.

2 Remove the cartridge

Loosen the two screws that fasten the cartridge to the faucet body. Then lift the entire cartridge unit straight up and off the body.

3 Replace the seals

Check the rubber inlet and outlet seals in the bottom of the cartridge for signs of wear; replace any worn ones with exact duplicates. Aligning the seals on the cartridge with the holes, replace the cartridge, then the cap and handle.

WORKING ON A TWO-HANDLE MODEL

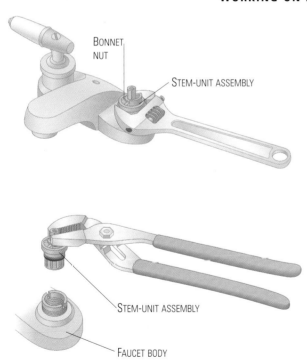

BONNET NUT

STEM-UNIT ASSEMBLY

STEM-UNIT ASSEMBLY

FAUCET BODY

1 Disassemble the faucet

Pop off the trim cap, if any, using a blunt knife or screwdriver. Undo the handle screw and pull off the handle. Use a wrench to remove the bonnet nut.

2 Examine the stem-unit assembly

Pull out the stem-unit assembly with pliers. If the O-ring is worn, replace it with an exact duplicate; lubricate the new ring with silicone grease before rolling it on. If the O-rings are sound, replace the stem-unit assembly.

3 Replace the seal and spring

Remove the seal and spring with a pair of long-nose pliers and replace them with parts designed for the same model of faucet. To reassemble the faucet, put the stem-unit assembly back, making sure to line up the lugs in the assembly with the slots in the base of the faucet.

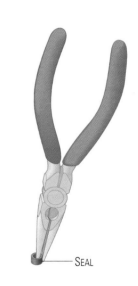

SEAL

FAUCET BODY

BALL FAUCET

LEAKING BALL FAUCETS

Inside every ball faucet is a slotted metal ball atop two spring-loaded rubber seals. Water flows when openings in the rotating ball align with hot and cold water inlets in the faucet body.

If the handle of a ball faucet leaks, first tighten the adjusting ring; if the leak persists, replace the cam above the ball. If the spout drips, the inlet seals or springs may be worn and need replacing. If the leak is under the spout, you must replace the O-rings or the ball itself.

Remember to turn off the water at the fixture shutoff valves or the main house shutoff (see page 152) before doing any work.

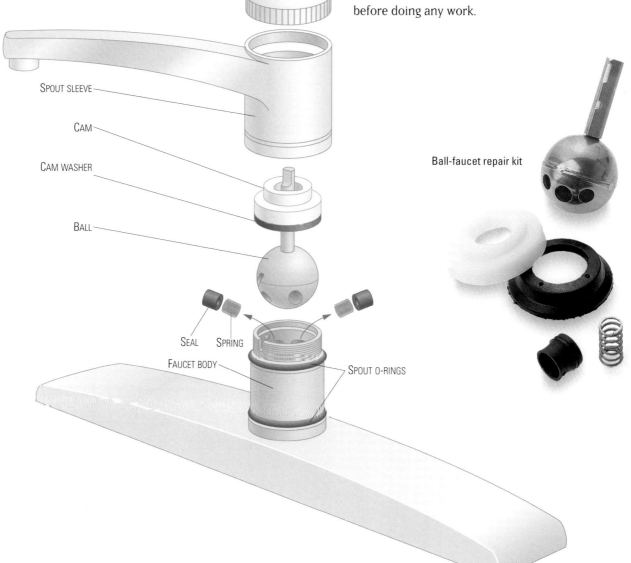

HANDLE

SETSCREW

ADJUSTING RING

CAP

SPOUT SLEEVE

CAM

CAM WASHER

BALL

SEAL   SPRING

FAUCET BODY

SPOUT O-RINGS

Ball-faucet repair kit

TIGHTENING THE ADJUSTING RING

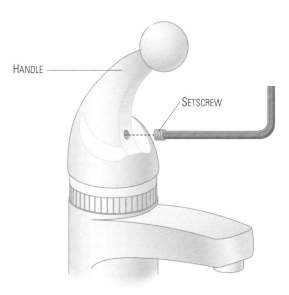

Remove the handle

I Loosen the setscrew under the faucet handle with a hex-head wrench and lift the handle off.

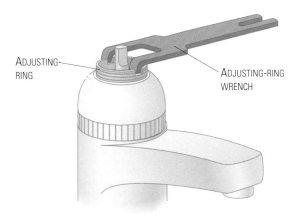

Tighten the ring

2 Tighten the adjusting ring in the cap by turning it clockwise with an adjusting-ring wrench as shown or a kitchen knife inserted in the notch.

REPLACING FAUCET PARTS

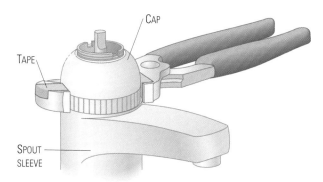

Disassemble the faucet

I Unscrew the cap using tape-wrapped slip-joint pliers. Lift out the ball and cam; underneath are the inlet seals and springs. Remove the spout sleeve to expose the faucet body.

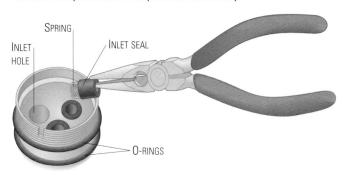

Inspect seals and rings

2 Lift out the inlet seals and springs, using long-nose pliers. With a pocketknife, remove any sediment in the holes; replace the inlet seals. Examine the O-rings and replace them if they're worn.

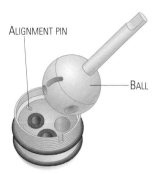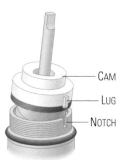

Inspect the ball

3 If the old ball is corroded, replace it. When you install the new ball, carefully line up the slot in the ball with the alignment pin in the faucet body.

Replace the cam

4 Fit the lug on a new cam into the notch on the faucet body. Replace the spout sleeve and cap, tighten the adjusting ring, and replace the handle.

CARTRIDGE FAUCET

LEAKING CARTRIDGE FAUCETS

These washerless faucets have a series of holes in the stem-and-cartridge assembly that align to control the mix and flow of water. Usually, leaks occur because of worn O-rings or a faulty cartridge.

First, look at the O-rings on the faucet body. If they're worn, replace them. If they're in good shape, remove the cartridge (see the facing page). If the cartridge is worn, replace it with an identical one.

Cartridges vary, so read the manufacturer's instructions before installing a new one. The most common type has a flat side on the stem that must face the front—otherwise, the hot and cold water supply will be reversed. Be sure to fit the retainer clip snugly into its slot.

If a faucet is hard to turn, lubricating the cartridge O-rings should fix the problem.

Before doing any work, remember to shut off the water supply (see page 152).

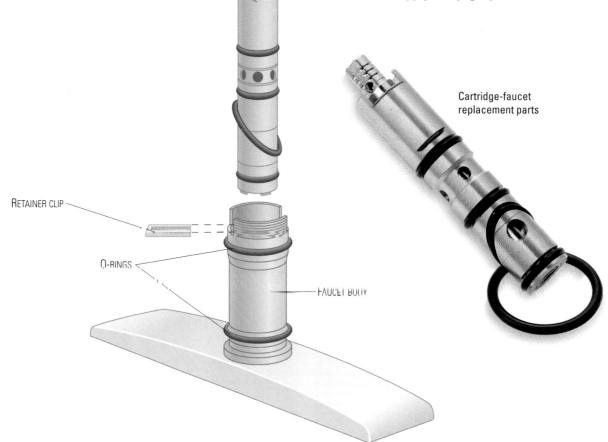

TRIM CAP

SCREW

CAP

HANDLE

SPOUT SLEEVE

RETAINER NUT

CARTRIDGE

RETAINER CLIP

O-RINGS

FAUCET BODY

Cartridge-faucet
replacement parts

TAKING THE FAUCET APART

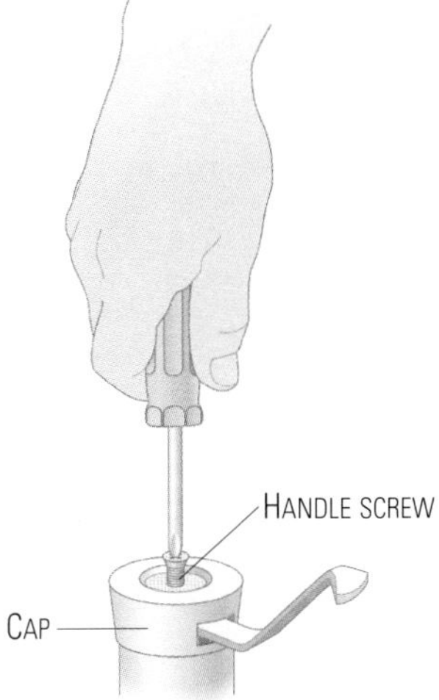

1 Remove the handle

Loosen the handle screw with a screwdriver; lift off the cap and handle. Then remove the retainer nut.

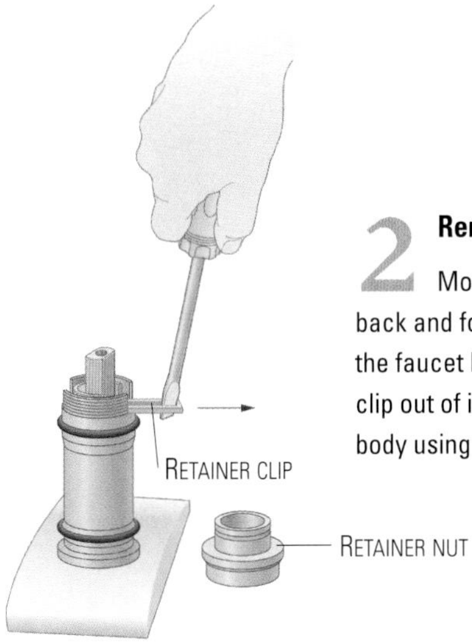

HANDLE SCREW

CAP

2 Remove the retainer clip

Move the spout sleeve back and forth, and gently pull it off the faucet body. Pull the retainer clip out of its slot in the faucet body using a screwdriver or pliers.

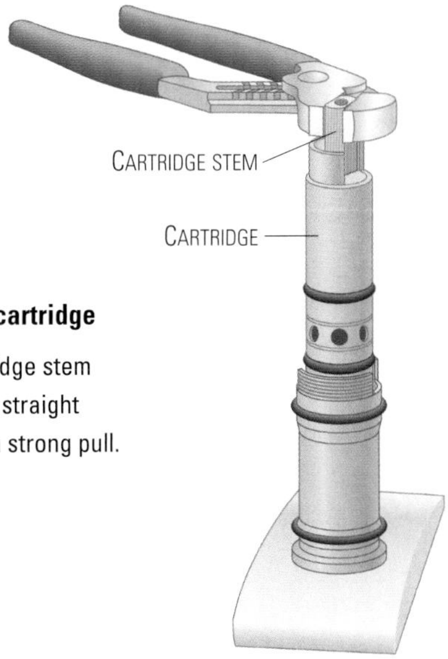

RETAINER CLIP

RETAINER NUT

CARTRIDGE STEM

CARTRIDGE

3 Remove the cartridge

Grip the cartridge stem with pliers and pull it straight out—it may require a strong pull.

MAKING REPAIRS

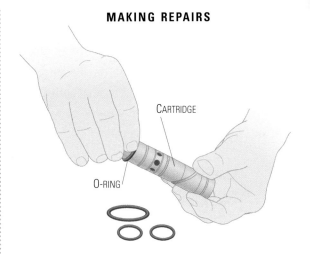

CARTRIDGE

O-RING

Changing an O-ring

Examine the O-rings on the cartridge and replace them if they show signs of wear. Apply silicone grease to the new O-rings before installing them.

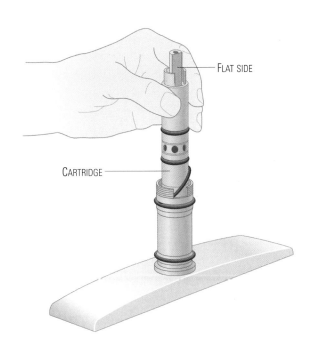

FLAT SIDE

CARTRIDGE

Replacing the cartridge

If the O-rings are in good shape, it's the cartridge that's seen its day. Buy an exact duplicate and push it down into the faucet body. If there's a flat side, be sure it faces forward. Reassemble the faucet, making sure to fit the retainer clip snugly into its slot in the body of the faucet.

CLEANING A FAUCET AERATOR

If the flow from your faucet is sluggish, the trouble may be the faucet aerator. This device, at the tip of most faucet spouts, mixes air and water for a smooth flow. But minerals or dirt particles in the water sometimes build up on the screen and disc, blocking the flow.

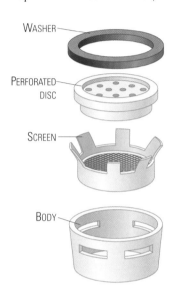

If mineral deposits are present or if aerator parts are damaged, it's best to replace the aerator. But if dirt is the problem, you can simply clean the parts. Unscrew the aerator from the end of the spout (to loosen stubborn connections, douse them with penetrating oil) and disassemble. Clean the screen with a brush and soapy water; use a pin or toothpick to open any clogged holes in the disc. Flush all parts with water before reassembling.

SINK SPRAYERS

Sink sprayers are attached to the faucet by a coupling nut under the sink. Sprayers have nozzle aerators that may clog, causing the diverter valve to malfunction. You can clean the aerator in the same way you would a faucet aerator—by disassembling it, cleaning the screen with a brush and soapy water, and using a pin or toothpick to clean out holes in the disc.

Leaks may occur at three different places: the spray head, hose, or diverter valve inside the base of the faucet that reroutes water from the spout to the sprayer. Before doing any work, remember to shut off the water supply (see page 152).

FIXING A SPRAY HEAD LEAK: If the hose leaks at the spray head, try tightening the fitting at the base of the

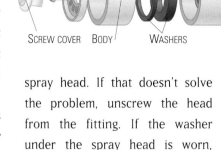

spray head. If that doesn't solve the problem, unscrew the head from the fitting. If the washer under the spray head is worn, replace it, then flush out the hose.

REPLACING A LEAKY HOSE: If the hose leaks where it attaches under the sink, undo the fitting from the tip of the hose by first removing the retainer clip (see drawing at right). Then, undo the coupling nut under the sink using rib-joint pliers or a basin wrench (or unthread the hose if it connects directly into the base of the faucet without a coupling nut). Getting at the coupling nut can be awkward; you'll need to lie on your back under the sink. Once the coupling nut is detached, inspect the entire length of the hose for kinks or cracks. If you find defects, replace the hose with a new one of the same diameter. Nylon-reinforced vinyl is the most durable.

CLEANING A DIVERTER VALVE: If the sink sprayer won't work or has reduced flow, the diverter valve may be clogged with deposits or scale. To check, you'll need to take off the faucet spout to get at the diverter. Some spouts simply unscrew; for others, you may need to take apart the handle. Once you have access to the inside of the faucet body, loosen the screw atop the diverter valve just enough to lift the valve from the seat. Take the valve apart and clean its outlets and surfaces with an old toothbrush and water. Soaking the part in vinegar or commercial lime-dissolver will help get rid of scale.

TUB AND SHOWER FAUCETS

Like sink faucets, tub and shower faucets can be either compression- or cartridge-style (washerless). Either way, water is directed from the faucet to the tub or shower head by a diverter valve; some, as shown at right, have built-in diverter valves, while others have a knob on the tub spout. This latter type is easy to replace—just grip the old spout with a tape-wrapped wrench and turn it counterclockwise to remove it, then hand-tighten the new spout into place.

Before taking a tub faucet apart, turn off the water at the main house shutoff (see page 152) and open a faucet that is lower than the level of the tub faucet to drain the pipes. Also review the instructions on sink faucets, which are similar to tub faucets.

To work on a recessed tub faucet, first unscrew the handle and remove the escutcheon. To access the stem nut in a compression faucet, you may need to chip away the wall's surface and then grip the nut with a deep shower socket (see page 41).

SHOWER HEADS

A shower head simply screws off the shower arm stubout, so accessing or replacing the internal parts is easy. If a shower head is leaking or spraying wildly, unscrew it and tighten all connections with slip-joint pliers (wrap the jaws with tape to avoid damaging the finish). If that doesn't solve the problem, replace the washer between the shower head and the swivel ball.

If water flow is sluggish, there's likely a clog in the screen or faceplace. Remove the center screw and clean the faceplate and screen with a toothbrush and vinegar.

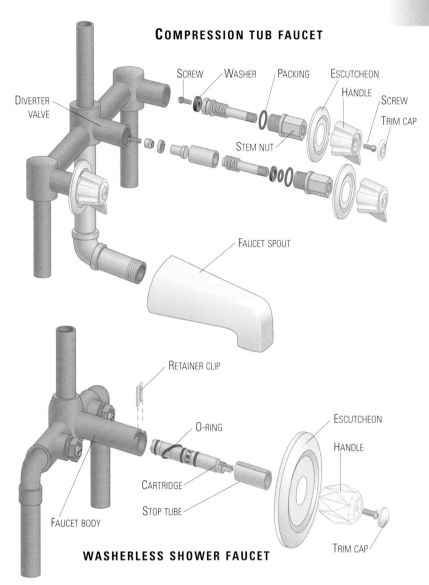

COMPRESSION TUB FAUCET

DIVERTER VALVE · SCREW · WASHER · PACKING · ESCUTCHEON · HANDLE · SCREW · TRIM CAP · STEM NUT · FAUCET SPOUT

WASHERLESS SHOWER FAUCET

RETAINER CLIP · O-RING · ESCUTCHEON · HANDLE · CARTRIDGE · STOP TUBE · FAUCET BODY · TRIM CAP

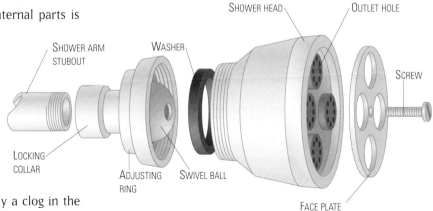

SHOWER HEAD · OUTLET HOLE · SHOWER ARM STUBOUT · WASHER · SCREW · LOCKING COLLAR · ADJUSTING RING · SWIVEL BALL · FACE PLATE

Flexible plastic trap

Flexible rubber trap

Tailpiece extensions

90° trap elbow

45° trap elbow

TACKLING TRAP PROBLEMS

Traps are the workhorses of the DWV system. They remain filled with just enough water to keep sewage gases from coming up your drainpipes and into the house. Unfortunately, because of their shape and function, traps are often the first plumbing parts to cause leaks or clogs.

If the trap of a sink, tub, or shower leaks, the cause could be corrosion or stripped fittings. If a clog remains after you have attempted to clean it out (pages 168–171), you can suspect a mineral buildup inside the trap. For any of these problems, the solution is to install a new trap and possibly a new fixture tailpiece.

Traps come in assorted sizes and shapes. Ordinarily, home plumbing systems use P-traps, either the swivel type shown here (consisting of a J-bend pipe and a waste arm or elbow) or, in some homes, a fixed type that includes both trap and waste arm in one piece. If you discover an old-style S-trap, which exits the floor rather than the wall, you're not required to replace it with a P-trap unless you are remodeling or altering part of your plumbing system. You will find replacement S-traps at many plumbing supply houses and home centers.

Trap materials vary, as do sizes and shapes. Replacement traps may be brass, chrome, or plastic, but brass and plastic ones last longest. New traps are sold as complete units, including washers and threaded couplings. You can also buy these fittings separately. If possible, buy a new trap that's the same size as the old one.

If the existing trap is attached to the tailpiece with a short extension and unthreaded slip couplings, you'll need to buy a new extension along with your new trap. A trap adapter is necessary to secure a waste arm to an unthreaded drain stubout.

A tailpiece that is cracked or corroded must be replaced. Fortunately, replacements are available separately, not just as part of a trap assembly.

Before doing any work, turn off the water at the fixture shutoff valves or the main house shutoff (page 152) and open a faucet at the low end of the system to drain the pipes.

FUDGING A TRAP CONNECTION

Despite your best efforts, you may be unable to find a standard replacement trap that readily lines up with your existing tailpiece, drain elbow, and wall stubout. Don't force unruly trap parts together, screw them tight, and hope for the best—they'll probably leak.

Fortunately, there are other options, as shown above. A flexible trap, made from ribbed plastic or rubber, can help bridge a mild misalignment between an existing tailpiece and a drain elbow. Tailpiece extensions, available in several lengths and in both threaded and unthreaded versions, are designed to fill vertical gaps between tailpiece and trap height. You can also buy 45° and 90° elbows made from the same materials as traps and drain elbows; use these to fine-tune a tricky angle between the trap and an off-center drain stubout.

REPLACING A TRAP

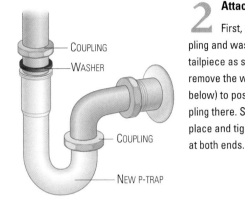

1 Remove the old trap

To replace a swivel P trap, first position a pail to catch water. Loosen the couplings at the tailpiece and waste arm with a tape-wrapped wrench. Pull off the old trap.

2 Attach a replacement

First, slide the new coupling and washer on over the tailpiece as shown. If required, remove the waste arm (see below) to position a new coupling there. Set the trap in place and tighten the couplings at both ends.

REPLACING A TRAP: The first step in removing the old trap is to remove the cleanout plug, if there is one, using an adjustable wrench (place a pail under the trap). Use a spud wrench or taped slip-joint pliers to loosen the couplings that attach a swivel P-trap to the tailpiece and waste arm. Carefully pull off the trap.

Slide a new coupling and washer on over the tailpiece. If the waste arm has a raised shoulder, you may need to briefly remove the arm in order to slip on a coupling there. Set the new trap in place and tighten the couplings at both ends by hand. That should do it for plastic couplings; finish tightening metal couplings with a spud wrench or slip-joint pliers. Be careful not to strip or overtighten the couplings. Turn the water back on and check all connections for leaks while the fixture drains.

REPLACING A TAILPIECE: To remove the tailpiece, unscrew the couplings that fasten it to the trap and the sink drain, and push the tailpiece down into the trap. Loosen the couplings at the drainpipe or waste arm and turn the entire trap at the drainpipe a quarter turn (see below right), just far enough to allow room to remove the tailpiece. You can now pull the old tailpiece out of the trap and replace it with a new one of the same length.

Coat all threads with pipe-joint compound to ensure a watertight seal, then tighten the couplings. Restore water pressure, run some water, drain, and look for leaks.

ADDING A NEW WASTE ARM

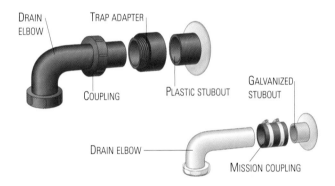

If the waste arm needs replacing along with the trap, loosen the coupling holding it to the drain stubout. Secure the elbow to a plastic stubout with a threaded adapter and coupling (top left). If the stubout is unthreaded galvanized pipe, you can use a Mission coupling (top right) to bridge the gap.

REPLACING A TAILPIECE

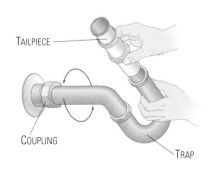

To remove the old tailpiece, unscrew the sink drain and trap couplings; push the tailpiece into the trap. Loosen the drainpipe coupling; swivel the unit and remove the tailpiece. Attach a new one.

SINK STRAINERS

There are two types of sink strainers, as shown below. One is held in place by a locknut, the other by a retainer and three thumbscrews. Leaks may be caused by an improper seal between the strainer body and the sink. Check whether the strainer body is loose; if it isn't, you'll likely need to replace the metal or fiber washer or the rubber gasket between the locknut or retainer and the sink bottom. This will require disassembling the strainer from under the sink.

DISASSEMBLING A STRAINER: Unscrew the coupling with a spud wrench or slip-joint pliers to free the tailpiece. To loosen the lugs on a locknut strainer, use a hammer to tap an old screwdriver against the lugs, or use a spud wrench. Be careful not to damage the sink. Remove the locknut, the washer, and the rubber gasket from the bottom of the strainer body. Lift the strainer from the sink. To remove a retainer-type strainer, simply undo the

three thumbscrews on the retainer and disassemble in the same way as for a locknut type.

SEALING THE DRAIN OPENING: Thoroughly clean the area around the drain opening. Check the rubber gasket and the metal or fiber washer for wear; get exact replacements if needed. Apply a ⅛-inch-thick bead of plumber's putty around the underlip of the strainer body and insert it into the sink opening. Press down firmly for a tight seal between the sink and strainer.

REASSEMBLING THE STRAINER: If the strainer is held in place by a locknut, work from beneath the sink to place the rubber gasket and metal washer onto the strainer body, and hand-tighten. Have a helper hold the strainer from above to prevent it from turning while you snug up the locknut with a spud wrench. If you're working alone, place the handles of a pair of pliers in the strainer (see page 103) for counterforce while you tighten the nut. Replace the coupling and connect it to the tailpiece. Wipe any excess putty from the sink's surface.

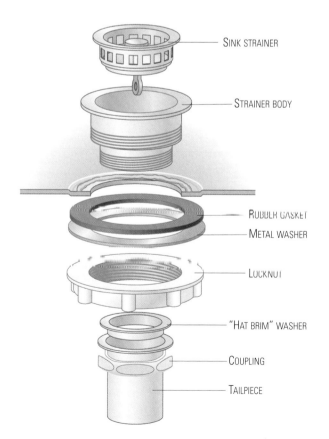

SINK STRAINER
STRAINER BODY
RUBBER GASKET
METAL WASHER
LOCKNUT
"HAT BRIM" WASHER
COUPLING
TAILPIECE

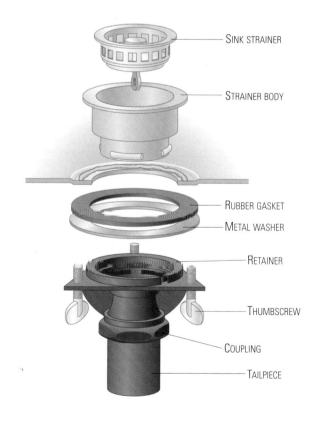

SINK STRAINER
STRAINER BODY
RUBBER GASKET
METAL WASHER
RETAINER
THUMBSCREW
COUPLING
TAILPIECE

SINK AND TUB POP-UPS

As its name implies, a bathroom pop-up pops up or down to open or close the drain depending on the position of the lift rod. The lift rod connects to the pivot rod to raise and lower the stopper. Although the mechanism is simple, its several moving parts need adjusting every so often. The lift rod and clevis can be adjusted to fix a pop-up that doesn't close properly or open fully. The spring clip that holds the pivot ball in place may need adjustment to prevent leaks.

Sink Stoppers

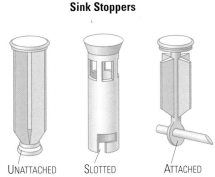

UNATTACHED SLOTTED ATTACHED

REPAIRING A SINK POP-UP: If the stopper doesn't open far enough for proper drainage, loosen the thumbscrew and retighten it lower on the lift rod; if there's not enough room left on the rod, you'll need to move the spring clip and pivot rod to a lower hole.

If the pop-up stopper isn't seating snugly, pull it out. The unattached type shown above must be pulled out; the slotted type must be twisted to free it; for the attached type, you'll need to undo the spring clip and pull out the pivot rod to remove the stopper. Clean the stopper of any hair or debris. Check its rubber seal; if it's damaged, pry it off and slip on a new one. If the pop-up still doesn't seat correctly, loosen the thumbscrew, push

the stopper down, and retighten the screw higher up. When the drain is closed, the pivot rod should slope downhill from clevis to drain body.

If the pop-up is seating properly but water is still leaking out of the basin, try tightening the retaining nut that holds the ball in place. Still leaking? Replace the washer behind the ball, then adjust the pivot rod so the pop-up seats properly.

SERVICING A TUB POP-UP: If the stopper of a lift-lever unit doesn't seat properly or if water drains slowly, remove the pop-up stopper and rocker arm, shown below, by pulling the stopper straight up. Then, unscrew and remove the tub's overflow plate and pull the entire assembly out through the overflow. For a stopper that isn't seating well, loosen the adjusting nuts and slide the middle link up to shorten the striker rod. The striker spring rests unattached on top of the rocker arm. For a sluggish drain, lower the middle link to lengthen the assembly. Before reassembling, clean the pop-up stopper.

Note: Instead of a pop-up assembly, some tubs have a strainer and an internal plunger that blocks the back of the drain to stop the flow of water. The adjustments to the lift mechanism are identical to those for a pop-up assembly.

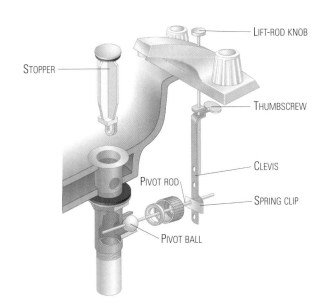

STOPPER
LIFT-ROD KNOB
THUMBSCREW
CLEVIS
PIVOT ROD
SPRING CLIP
PIVOT BALL

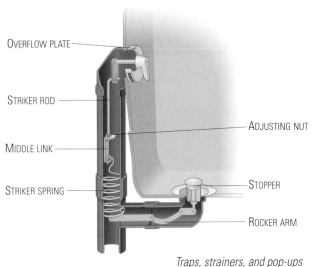

OVERFLOW PLATE
STRIKER ROD
MIDDLE LINK
STRIKER SPRING
ADJUSTING NUT
STOPPER
ROCKER ARM

CLEARING SINK CLOGS

If a sink is blocked and no other drains in your home are affected, you're probably dealing with a clog in the trap or the drainpipe leading from the fixture. If more than one drain won't clear, something might be stuck in the main drain (see pages 172–173).

A kitchen sink usually clogs because of a buildup of grease and food particles that get caught in it. A dose of scalding water is often effective against grease buildups. If the water doesn't help, it could be that some small object—a coin or small utensil—is caught in the drain. To check, remove (and thoroughly clean) the sink's pop-up stopper or the strainer (pages 166–167).

If these simple measures fail, try using a sink plunger to clear the pipe, as detailed at right. If the plunger also fails, you'll need to use a drain-and-trap auger, also called a snake, which is a flexible metal coil that you feed through the pipes until it reaches the clog; the end of the coil snags the clog and dislodges it or pulls it right out.

USING A SINK PLUNGER

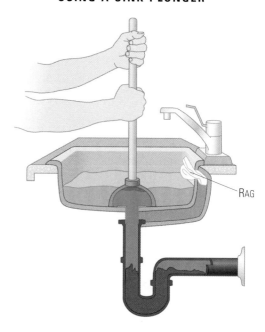

First fill the clogged sink with enough water to cover several inches of the plunger cup. Use a wet rag to block off all other outlets. To dislodge the clog, pump the plunger vigorously up and down.

Drain-and-trap auger

Sink plunger

EFFICIENT PLUNGING: When using a sink plunger to clear a drain, don't make the typical mistake of pumping up and down only two or three times, expecting the water to whoosh down the drain. Choose a plunger with a suction cup large enough to cover the drain opening completely. Fill the clogged fixture with enough water to cover several inches of the plunger cup. Then, use a wet rag to block off all other nearby outlets (the overflow vent, the second drain in a double sink, or adjacent fixtures). Coat the rim of the plunger cup with petroleum jelly to ensure a tight seal, and insert the plunger into the water at an angle so that little air gets trapped under it. Then, holding the plunger upright (see above), apply 15 to 20 forceful downstrokes; the last motion should be a vigorous upstroke, snapping the plunger off the drain and, ideally, drawing the clog with it. Repeat the process two or three times before giving up and trying the auger.

USING AN AUGER: To use an auger, first insert it down through the sink drain. If that doesn't clear the clog, put the auger in through the trap cleanout, if there is one. If that doesn't work, remove the trap entirely (see page 165). You may find that you're able to solve the problem simply by cleaning out the trap with a flexible brush, such as a bottle brush, and soapy water. If that fails, the clog is farther down the line, and you'll need to insert the auger directly into the drainpipe.

If your sink has a garbage disposer and the disposer drainpipe clogs, disassemble the trap and thread an auger into the drainpipe. If both basins of a double sink with a garbage disposer clog, snake the auger down through the one without a disposer.

If running an auger through the sink drainpipe doesn't work, the clog is probably too deep in the pipes to reach through the drainpipe. This means you're dealing with a main drain clog (see directions on pages 172–173).

Feed the drain-and-trap auger, or snake, into the drain, trap, or pipe until it stops. If the auger has a handgrip (as shown at right), position it about 6 inches above the drain or pipe opening and tighten the thumbscrew. Rotate the handle clockwise to break the blockage. (Never rotate counterclockwise, as that may damage the cable.) As the cable works its way into the pipe, loosen the thumbscrew, slide the handgrip back, push more cable into the pipe, tighten again, and repeat. If the auger has no handgrip, push and twist the cable until it hits the clog. The first time the auger stops, it probably has hit a turn in the drainpipe rather than the clog. Guiding the auger past a sharp turn takes patience and effort; keep pushing it forward, turning it clockwise as you do. Once the head of the auger hooks the blockage, pull the auger back a short distance to free some material from the clog, then push the rest on through.

After breaking up the clog, pull the auger out slowly and have a pail ready to catch any gunk that is brought out. Flush the drain with hot water. Dry the auger and coat it with a lubricant before putting it away.

USING AN AUGER

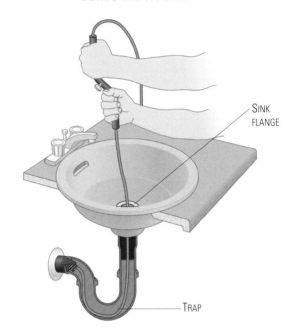

To snake through the sink, first remove the pop-up stopper (page 167) or the sink strainer. Insert the auger in the drain opening and twist it down through the trap until you reach the clog.

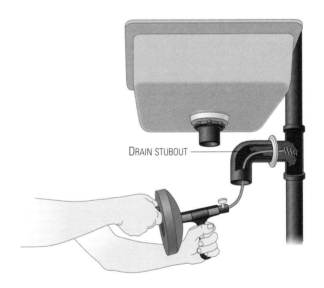

To snake through the drainpipe, first remove the trap (page 165), spilling the contents into a pail. Feed the auger as far as possible behind the wall until it hits the clog.

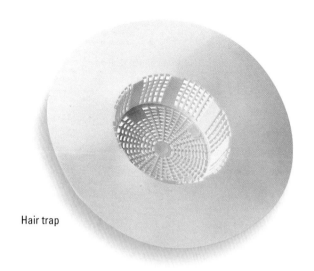

Hair trap

CLEARING OUT CLOGGED TUBS AND SHOWERS

Hair and soap scum are the usual causes of problems in bathroom drains. To help prevent clogs in tubs and showers, you can install a hair trap. One type of hair trap (shown at left) simply sits in the drain; another requires replacing the pop-up.

When a tub or shower drain does clog up, check whether other fixtures are affected. If they are, work on the main drain (pages 172–173). If only the tub or shower is clogged, work on it. First, try plunging (page 168), then remove the strainer or pop-up and clean it (page 167). If the drain still won't empty, use an auger or a balloon bag (page 172), inserting the bag past any openings in the drainpipe where other pipes enter.

PREVENTING DRAIN CLOGS

The best way to deal with clogs is to prevent them. Be alert to warning signs, such sluggish drains. It's easier to clear a drain that's slowing down than one that's stopped completely.

SOME MAINTENANCE TIPS: A kitchen sink usually clogs because of a buildup of grease and food particles that get caught in it. To keep the problem to a minimum, don't pour grease down the drain. Another villain is coffee grounds—throw them out; don't wash them down.

Clean out sink strainers and pop-ups regularly. Some strainers are held in place by screws. Instructions for servicing a pop-up are on page 167.

Every few months, remove the overflow plate on a tub and pull up the pop-up assembly to reach the spring or rocker arm. Remove accumulated hair and soap scum and rinse the assembly thoroughly with warm water. Some tubs and showers have strainers that are screwed into the drain opening. Remove these strainers with a screwdriver and reach down into the drain with a bent wire to clear out accumulated debris. Scrub the strainer before putting it back in place.

If invasive tree roots are a problem in your yard, you may need to call in professionals [a plumber or professional drain-cleaning firm] once a year or so to clear the pipes. They'll use an electric auger to cut out the roots.

USING CHEMICAL CLEANERS: Chemical cleaners are most successful when used occasionally for clog prevention. They may also help clear a partial block—where water is still draining somewhat—but they should never be used on fixtures or drains that are stopped completely. They are hazardous and may cause injury to eyes and skin; frequent use may also eventually damage your pipes.

Many chemical drain cleaners are on the market: choose an alkali (usually containing lye) to cut grease, an acid to dissolve soap and hair. Read and follow the instructions on the label. Work in a well-ventilated room and wear rubber gloves and goggles. Don't mix chemicals; mixing an acid and an alkali cleaner is potentially dangerous. Don't look down the drain after pouring in a chemical; the solution frequently boils up and gives off toxic fumes. And don't plunge if you've recently used a chemical.

Consider using equal parts baking soda and vinegar instead of a commercial cleaner to prevent buildup of soap and hair. Dump the baking soda down the drain first, followed by the vinegar. Let the mixture fizz, then flush the drain with boiling water.

TIPS FOR CLEARING TUBS AND SHOWERS

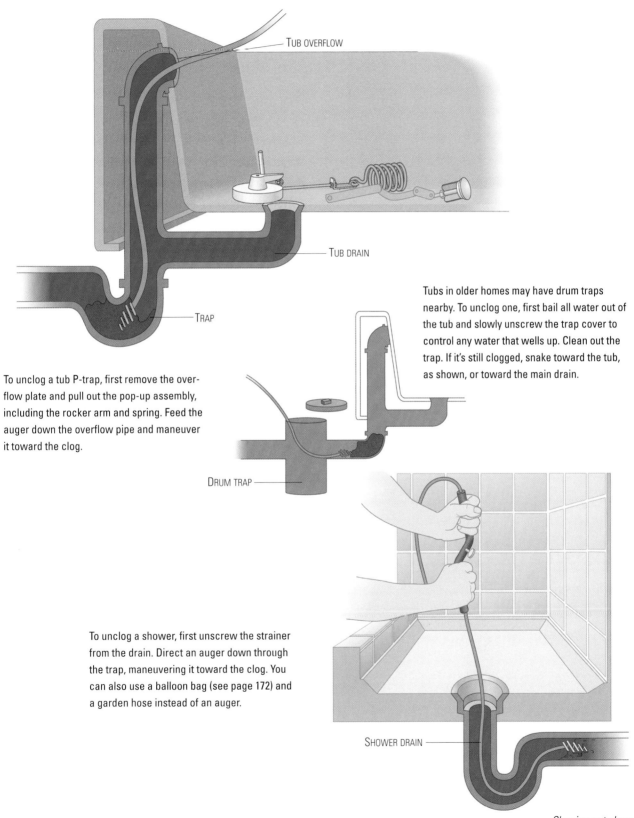

TUB OVERFLOW

TUB DRAIN

TRAP

DRUM TRAP

SHOWER DRAIN

Tubs in older homes may have drum traps nearby. To unclog one, first bail all water out of the tub and slowly unscrew the trap cover to control any water that wells up. Clean out the trap. If it's still clogged, snake toward the tub, as shown, or toward the main drain.

To unclog a tub P-trap, first remove the overflow plate and pull out the pop-up assembly, including the rocker arm and spring. Feed the auger down the overflow pipe and maneuver it toward the clog.

To unclog a shower, first unscrew the strainer from the drain. Direct an auger down through the trap, maneuvering it toward the clog. You can also use a balloon bag (see page 172) and a garden hose instead of an auger.

Balloon bag

UNCLOGGING A DRAIN FROM THE ROOF

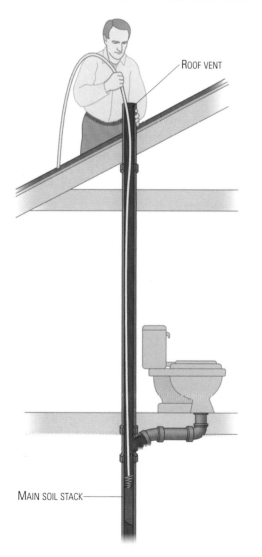

ROOF VENT

MAIN SOIL STACK

Thread an auger through the vent stack to the soil stack, working it from side to side. Exercise caution on the roof.

MAIN DRAIN CLOGS

If more than one drain won't clear, something is stuck farther along in a branch drain, the soil stack, or the main drain leading to the sewer or septic tank, causing all the fixtures upstream of the clog to stop up.

To troubleshoot a clog, first try using a drain-and-trap auger to reach the clog from one of the branch cleanouts; in most new buildings, branch cleanouts are usually installed wherever a branch of the drainage system makes a sharp turn. If that doesn't work, trace the pipes from the plugged fixtures to the main soil stack—the vertical pipe to which all the branches connect—and clear the soil stack from above, through the roof vent, or from below, through the main cleanout. A clog in the main drain may also be cleared through the main cleanout or the house trap.

If none of these methods does the job, you may choose to rent a power auger, which is longer and more powerful. Know your drain's diameter when you go to rent an auger and be sure to ask for explicit safety instructions. Always plug the auger into a GFCI-protected outlet, enlist a friend to help you run the auger, and use caution.

If you don't want to use a power auger, it's time to call a plumber or professional drain-cleaning firm, which may decide to try cleaning the soil stack through the vent stack from the roof; because of the danger involved in working on a slick roof with an unwieldy power tool, this job should not be attempted by amateurs.

OPENING THE MAIN CLEANOUT: The main cleanout, usually a Y- or T-shaped fitting, is near the bottom of the soil stack where it meets the main drain. Look for it in the basement or crawl space, or on an outside wall near a toilet. Put on rubber gloves and have pails, mops, and rags handy. Then, slowly, remove the plug with a pipe wrench (see facing page) to release the water a little at a time and prevent flooding.

Try to clear the clog first by using a hand-operated drain-and-trap auger (see page 169 for instructions). If that doesn't work, try a balloon bag and garden hose

WORKING FROM A MAIN CLEANOUT

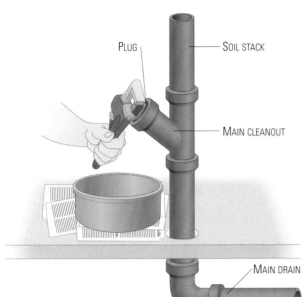

PLUG

SOIL STACK

MAIN CLEANOUT

MAIN DRAIN

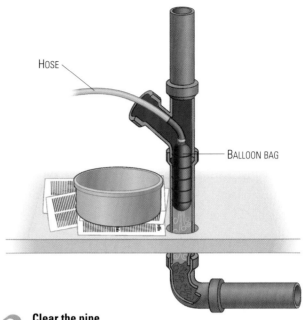

HOSE

BALLOON BAG

1 **Remove the cleanout plug**

Put on rubber gloves and set up a pail or newspaper to catch waste water. Slowly remove the cleanout plug with a pipe wrench, releasing any water a little bit at a time.

2 **Clear the pipe**

Try using an auger (page 169). If this doesn't work, try a balloon bag and hose, as shown; buy a bag that matches the diameter of your drain. Once the drain is clear, flush it with water .

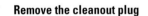

instead. Don't leave the hose in the drain any longer than necessary—a sudden drop in pressure could back-siphon sewage through the hose into the water supply. Once the drain is clear, flush it with water. Coat the plug with pipe-joint compound and recap the cleanout. Clean and disinfect all tools and materials.

PROBING THE TRAP: The house trap, if there is one, is located in the basement, crawl space, or yard near where the main drain leaves the house. Two adjacent cleanout plugs extend up to the floor or ground level.

Before opening the house trap, put on rubber gloves and spread newspapers or rags around the cleanout. With a pipe wrench, slowly loosen the plug nearest the outside sewer line. Probe the trap and its connecting pipes with an auger (right). Be prepared to withdraw the auger and cap the trap quickly when water starts to flow. When the flow subsides, open both ends of the trap and clean it out with an old wire brush. Recap and flush the pipes with water from an upstream cleanout.

WORKING FROM A HOUSE TRAP

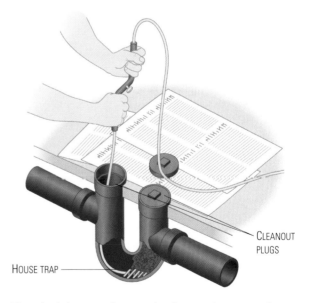

CLEANOUT PLUGS

HOUSE TRAP

First, slowly loosen and remove the cleanout plug nearest the outside sewer line. Probe the trap and its connecting pipes with an auger. Work slowly, and be prepared to cap the trap quickly when water flows.

TROUBLESHOOTING A TOILET

The workings of a flush toilet remain a mystery to most people until something goes awry. Knowing how a toilet operates is essential to troubleshooting problems.

Basically, two assemblies are concealed under the lid: a flush-valve assembly, which controls the flow of water from the tank to the bowl, and an inlet-valve assembly, which regulates the filling of the tank. The toilet bowl includes a built-in trap. When someone presses the flush handle, a trip lever in the flush-valve assembly raises the lift-rod wires or chain connected to the tank stopper. As the stopper goes up, water rushes through the valve seat into the bowl via the flush passages under the rim of the toilet bowl. The water in the bowl yields to gravity and is siphoned out of the built-in toilet trap into the drainpipe.

As the tank empties, the float ball descends and the stopper drops into the flush-valve seat. The float ball trips the inlet valve open, letting a new supply of water into the tank through the tank-fill tube. As the water level in the tank rises, the float ball also rises until it gets high enough to shut off the flow of water. If the water fails to shut off, the overflow tube carries excess water into the bowl to prevent flooding.

On the following pages are instructions for making toilet repairs. Before beginning any toilet repair—unless you're simply adjusting the float arm—you'll need to shut off the water at the fixture shutoff valve, flush the toilet to empty the tank, and sponge out any remaining water.

ANATOMY OF A TOILET

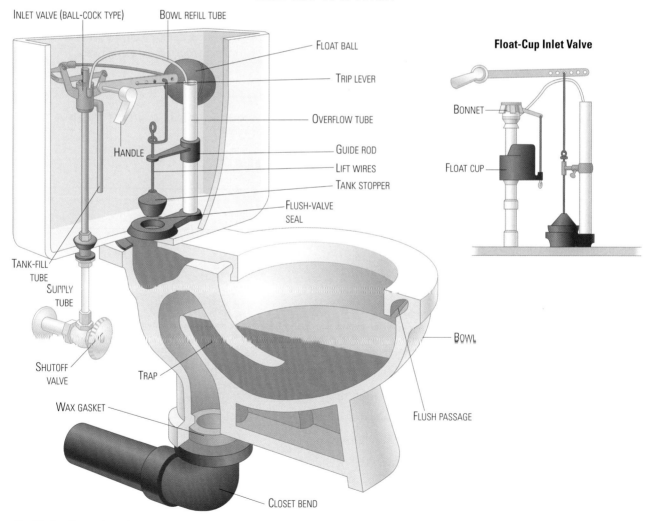

INLET VALVE (BALL-COCK TYPE)
BOWL REFILL TUBE
FLOAT BALL
TRIP LEVER
OVERFLOW TUBE
HANDLE
GUIDE ROD
LIFT WIRES
TANK STOPPER
FLUSH-VALVE SEAL
TANK-FILL TUBE
SUPPLY TUBE
SHUTOFF VALVE
TRAP
WAX GASKET
CLOSET BEND
BOWL
FLUSH PASSAGE

Float-Cup Inlet Valve

BONNET
FLOAT CUP

NOISY TOILETS

If your toilet whines or whistles as the tank fills with water after a flush, the problem may be restricted water flow or a defective inlet-valve assembly.

First, check to make sure the fixture shutoff valve is fully open. Still noisy? You may need to oil the trip lever or replace part or all of the inlet-valve assembly.

The inlet valve in your toilet tank may be one of several types. Two common varieties—ball cock and float cup—are shown on the facing page. If the inlet valve is faulty, you may be able to replace just the washers or

seal, or you may need to replace the whole assembly, which isn't difficult to do. You can replace a ball-cock style with a similar model, but you may be happier with a new float-cup assembly; this type is inexpensive, easy to install and adjust, and nearly trouble-free. Be sure any replacement assembly is designed to prevent back-flow from the tank into the water supply—look for one marked "antisiphon" or "meets plumbing codes."

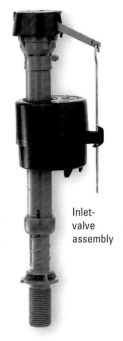

Inlet-valve assembly

REPAIRING AN INLET VALVE

To stop ball cock leaks, remove the retaining pins in the ball-cock lever and lift out the float arm. Remove the plunger from the ball cock and replace defective washers.

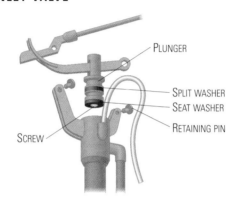

PLUNGER
SPLIT WASHER
SEAT WASHER
RETAINING PIN
SCREW

REPLACING AN INLET-VALVE ASSEMBLY

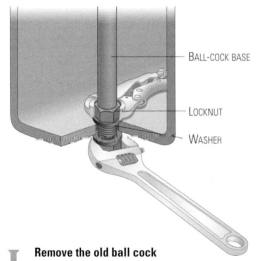

BALL-COCK BASE
LOCKNUT
WASHER

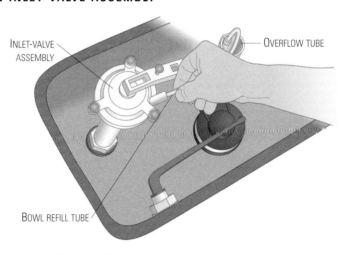

INLET-VALVE ASSEMBLY
OVERFLOW TUBE
BOWL REFILL TUBE

1 Remove the old ball cock

Using pliers and a wrench, loosen the locknut holding the inlet-valve assembly to the tank. Unclip the bowl refill tube; holding onto the base, remove the inlet-valve assembly.

2 Install a new unit

Install the new antisiphon inlet-valve assembly according to the manufacturer's instructions. Position the bowl refill tube in the overflow pipe.

ADJUSTING TOILET TANK WATER LEVEL

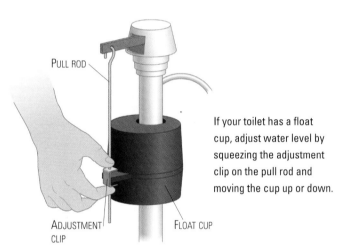

Bending a float arm downward lowers the water level in the tank so the toilet doesn't continue to run. The float ball sometimes develops cracks or fills with water. If this happens, unscrew the ball and replace it.

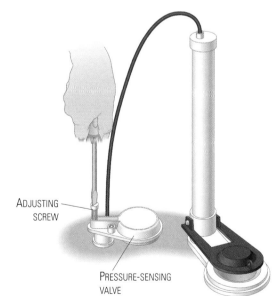

If your toilet has a float cup, adjust water level by squeezing the adjustment clip on the pull rod and moving the cup up or down.

If you have a pressure-sensing valve, turn the adjusting screw clockwise to raise the water level, counterclockwise to lower it. One turn should change the level by about 1 inch.

RUNNING TOILETS

If water in your toilet tank trickles incessantly and the problem isn't in the inlet-valve assembly (see page 175), you may need to adjust or replace the float mechanism or one or more parts of the flush-valve assembly: the overflow tube, valve seat, tank stopper, guide rod, or lift wires. Or you may need to replace the entire assembly.

FLOAT MECHANISM: If your toilet has a ball-cock inlet-valve assembly, bending the float arm downward or away from the back of the toilet tank may stop the water from running. If the float ball is filled with water, it should be replaced.

If you have a float-cup assembly, see the drawing at left for adjustment details. Some new toilets have a pressure-sensing device instead; for help with this device, see the drawing at bottom left.

FLUSH-VALVE ASSEMBLY: A defective or badly fitting valve seat or stopper may cause a running toilet. If the valve seat is rough and pitted, scour it smooth. If the tank stopper isn't seating properly, try adjusting the guide rod and lift wires or chain. You may need to replace the stopper (see the facing page).

If a metal overflow tube is cracked, replace it.

If the toilet is still running, replace the entire flush-valve assembly as shown on the facing page. First, remove the bolts, then the gaskets, to separate the tank from the bowl. Insert the discharge tube of the new valve assembly through the tank bottom, position the overflow tube, and tighten the locknut to hold it in place. Reattach any guide rod, lift wires, and other hardware that your assembly requires. Finally, install the stopper, aligning it with the center of the seat.

REPLACING A TANK STOPPER

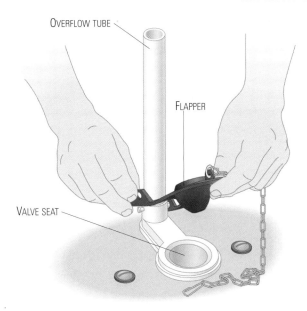

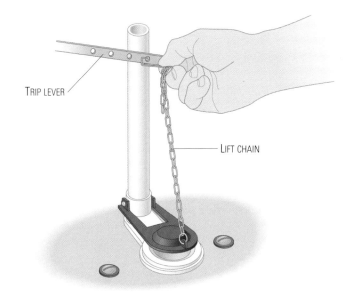

1 Remove old stopper, add new flapper

First remove the old stopper and guide rod, then install a new flapper, sliding its collar to the base of the overflow tube. Position the flapper over the valve seat.

2 Make adjustments

Adjust the length of the new flapper's lift chain and hook it on the tip of the trip lever, leaving about ½ inch of slack when the flapper is in place on the flush valve.

Detecting a Running Toilet

A toilet that runs constantly can waste more than a thousand gallons of water a day. Of course, you can hear a toilet that runs this heavily. A toilet that leaks slowly is harder to detect. Even an imperceptible toilet leak may waste as much as 40 gallons each day.

To check your toilet for a leak, remove the tank lid and add about 12 drops of colored dye to the water inside. (Blue food coloring will work, or ask your water company for dye tablets.) Then, wait 5 minutes to see if the dye flows into the bowl. If it does, water is escaping either through the top of the overflow tube or past the tank stopper and valve seat.

REPLACING A FLUSH-VALVE ASSEMBLY

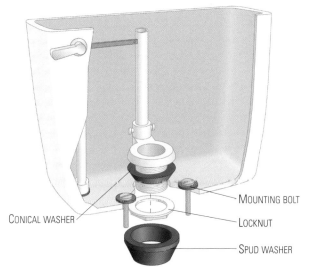

For a bowl-mounted tank, first remove the tank mounting bolts and gaskets; lift off the tank. Unscrew the locknut under the tank after removing the spud washer. Then remove the conical gasket and flush valve assembly. To install the replacement, assemble the conical gasket and locknut; position the overflow tube; then tighten.

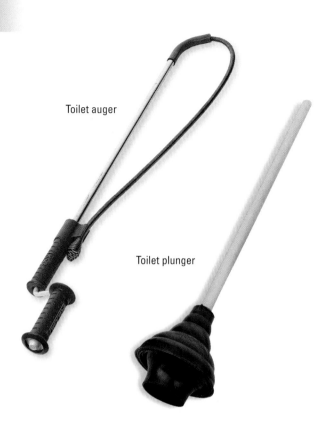

Toilet auger

Toilet plunger

CLOGGED TOILETS

The usual cause of a clogged toilet is an obstruction in the trap. To remove it, first bail out or add water so that the bowl is half-full. Then, use a funnel-cup toilet plunger specifically designed to fit the bowl's trap. If that doesn't work, use a toilet auger. If these tools don't clear the clog, you might try using a drain-and-trap auger (snake) or a balloon bag in the nearest cleanout (see page 173).

Preventing an Overflow

If the toilet bowl is filled to the brim, do not flush the toilet again. If a toilet is about to overflow, quickly reach into the tank and push the stopper or flapper down into the valve seat, which will prevent any more water from filling the bowl. Hold the stopper down while you turn off the water at the fixture shutoff valve.

UNCLOGGING A TOILET

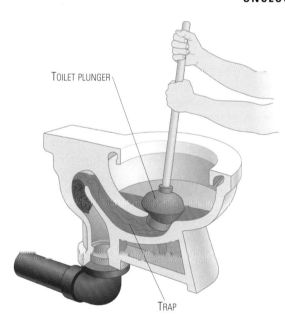

TOILET PLUNGER

TRAP

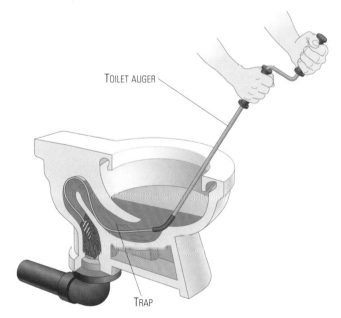

TOILET AUGER

TRAP

Using a toilet plunger
A toilet plunger has a special funnel-cup tip to fit the bowl. To loosen a clog, pump the plunger up and down a dozen times and then pull off sharply on the last stroke; the alternate pressure and suction should loosen the obstruction.

Using a toilet auger
If the plunger doesn't work, use a toilet auger. It has a curved tip that starts the auger with a minimum of mess and a protective housing to prevent scratching the bowl. To maneuver the auger, simultaneously push it and turn the handle.

LEAKS, TANK SWEATING, AND FLUSH PROBLEMS

Other toilet problems you may need to repair include leaks, tank sweating, and certain flush problems.

Some repairs require an empty tank. When this is the case, turn off the water at the fixture shutoff valve, flush the toilet, and sponge the tank dry before making the repair.

LEAKS: Toilet leaks are a common problem but may be confused with tank sweating (see far right). For a tip on how to detect leaks, see the box at right.

To stop a leak between the tank and bowl of a bowl-mounted toilet tank, tighten the mounting bolts in the tank or replace the bolts' gaskets (shown below).

If there's still a leak when the toilet is flushed, remove the tank, reversing the steps shown on page 177, and replace the spud washer on the bottom of the flush valve.

When a bowl leaks around its base, first try tightening the hold-down bolts that anchor it to the floor. If that doesn't stop the leak, you'll have to remove the bowl and replace the wax gasket that seals the bowl to the floor (shown below center).

TANK SWEATING: This problem occurs most often in the summer when cold water from the tank cools the porcelain, and warm, moist air condenses on the outside. Tank sweating encourages mildew, loosens floor tiles, and rots subflooring.

An easy solution is to insulate the inside of the tank by first draining and drying it, then gluing to the inside walls a special liner sold at plumbing stores or one made of foam rubber or polystyrene pads. A more costly remedy, and one that will add to your energy costs, is to install a tempering valve that mixes hot water with the cold water entering the tank.

FLUSH PROBLEMS: A loose handle or trip lever may cause an inadequate or erratic flush cycle. Adjusting the setscrew (see below right) on the handle or replacing the handle often solves the problem. Clogged flush passages under the bowl's rim may also be restricting water flow. Clean obstructed passages with a piece of wire.

Leak or No Leak?

If you can't tell whether your toilet is leaking around the tank bolts or just sweating, add food coloring to the tank water. Wait an hour, then touch the bolt tips and nuts under the tank with white tissue. If the tissue shows coloring, you have a leak; if it doesn't, the moisture is just condensation.

THREE REMEDIES FOR TOILETS

Leaky tank
Tighten the bolts between the tank and bowl of a bowl-mounted tank or replace their gaskets if damaged.

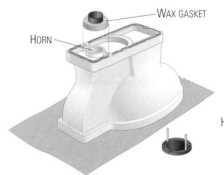

Leaking wax gasket
If the toilet leaks at its base, install a new wax gasket on the toilet horn to make a watertight seal with the floor flange.

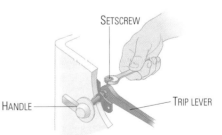

Tightening the handle
Tighten the setscrew on the handle or trip lever if a loose handle is causing an inadequate flush.

GARBAGE DISPOSER BREAKDOWNS

The two types of garbage disposers are batch-feed (activated by turning a stopper) and continuous-feed (controlled by a wall switch). Problems with either type usually involve jams or clogs, and occasionally leaks.

If your disposer makes a loud whirring noise or stops, it has jammed. Turn it off and wait 5 minutes, then firmly press the reset button on the bottom of the motor housing. (Machines without buttons are designed to reset automatically.)

If the disposer still doesn't work, see if it's designed to be unjammed from below—check the housing for a small crank (or a socket for a hex-head wrench) to turn the flywheel. Or it may have a reversing switch. If neither of these features is present, make sure the disposer is turned off, then angle a broom handle against an impeller blade and work the blade back and forth until you dislodge the jam. Then, press the reset button.

To clear a clog in a single-bowl sink with a disposer, disassemble the trap (see page 165) and thread a drain-and-trap auger (snake) into the drainpipe. If both basins of a double sink are clogged, snake down from the one without a disposer.

CAUTION If you're dismantling a disposer, unplug the unit or shut off power at the service entrance panel. Never put your hand in the disposer—use pliers or kitchen tongs to remove an object. And never pour a chemical drain cleaner into a disposer or you may damage the unit.

Before making dishwasher repairs, shut off power to it at the service entrance panel. Turn off the dishwasher's water supply under the sink before working on the inlet valve or disconnecting the water hose.

Water dripping from a disposer usually indicates one or more gaskets are worn and need to be replaced.

Many professionals service disposers in the home. If you need to bring a unit to the shop for work, first disconnect it from the power source, then separate the disposer from the drain elbow and loosen the mounting screws to release it from the support flange.

DISPOSER DETAILS

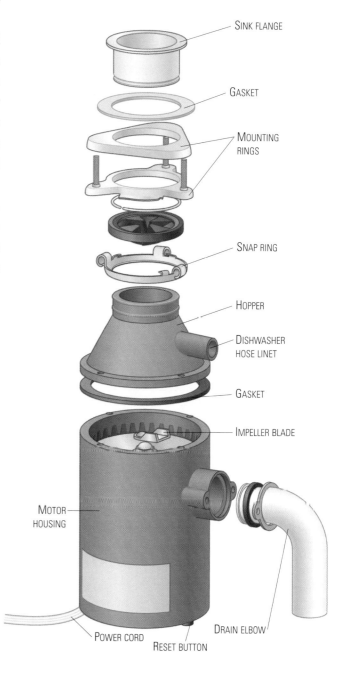

DISHWASHER DILEMMAS

If a dishwasher isn't cleaning, the cause is likely the result of water temperature that is too low (140°F is ideal), hard water (less than 15 grains of hardness is optimal), or an insufficient amount of detergent (the recommended amount is 1 teaspoon per each grain of water hardness).

Most plumbing-related dishwasher problems involve leaks or clogged water-inlet valves or drains. If the dishwasher won't drain, the cause is probably a plugged strainer basket, a clogged drain, or a dirty air gap (see below). Dishwasher leaks can usually be traced to either a faulty hose connection or a door gasket that isn't sealing. If your dishwasher won't fill, check to see whether the water-inlet valve is closed or whether the inlet-valve screen is simply clogged.

Troubleshooting other dishwasher problems is tricky because of the difficulty in determining which component might be the culprit. For starters, use the illustrations below to orient yourself to the various parts and their locations. With the exception of mechanical defects, such as faulty timers or switches, which are best left to technicians to repair, many dishwasher problems are easy enough to tackle on your own. Most parts are expensive, but they carry manufacturer's warranties that may extend up to 10 years.

If your dishwasher has an air gap, you may need to clean it occasionally to dislodge bones, seeds, or bits of food that may be blocking it. Dishwasher water discharges through a drain hose connected to one side of the air gap; another drain hose runs from the air gap to the sink trap or disposer. To clean the air gap, lift off the cap, unscrew its cover, and insert a long piece of wire, pushing it straight down. This may also help if the dishwasher is slow to drain or if suds ooze from the cap.

DISHWASHER COMPONENTS

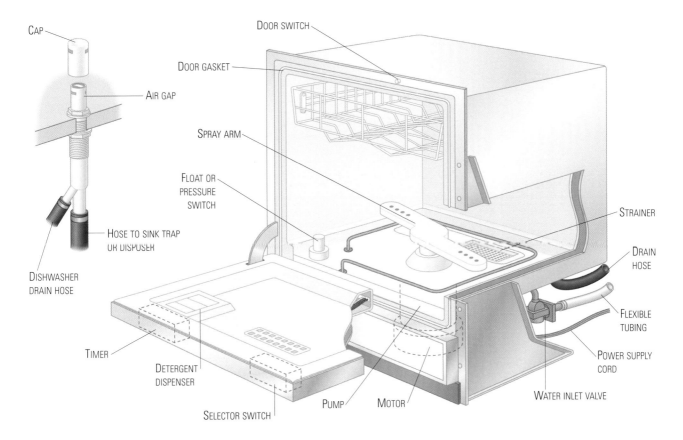

CAP
DOOR SWITCH
DOOR GASKET
AIR GAP
SPRAY ARM
FLOAT OR PRESSURE SWITCH
HOSE TO SINK TRAP OR DISPOSER
DISHWASHER DRAIN HOSE
STRAINER
DRAIN HOSE
FLEXIBLE TUBING
POWER SUPPLY CORD
WATER INLET VALVE
TIMER
DETERGENT DISPENSER
SELECTOR SWITCH
PUMP
MOTOR

TROUBLESHOOTING A WATER HEATER

When a hot water faucet is turned on, heated water is drawn from the top of the tank and is replaced by cold water that is delivered to the bottom via the dip tube. As the water temperature drops, a thermostat activates the heat source—a burner in a gas heater, heating elements in an electric unit.

A gas heater has a flue running up the center and out the top to vent gases. An electric heater needs no venting. In both types of heaters, a special anode attracts corrosion that might attack the tank's walls.

Problems with traditional, storage-type water heaters are usually announced by noises, leaks, or water that's too hot or not hot enough. Often you can correct the problem yourself. For guidelines, see below. Problems with on-demand heaters require professional repair.

With a gas heater, knowing how to relight the pilot is very important in case it goes out. Directions vary, so follow the instructions on the tank. A gas heater has a thermocouple, a thermoelectric device that senses whether the pilot is on and shuts off the gas if the pilot light goes out.

GAS WATER HEATER   **ELECTRIC WATER HEATER**

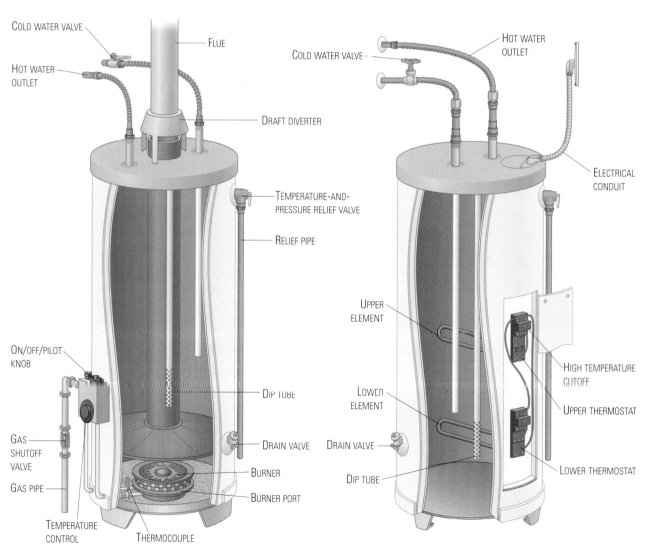

Twice a year, inspect the flue assembly to make sure it is properly aligned and its joints are sealed. Then, check for obstructions in the flue itself: with the burner on, place your hand near the draft diverter; air flowing out indicates an obstruction that should be removed.

When an electric heater has problems, suspect the high-temperature cutoff, the heating elements (upper and lower), or the thermostats that control them. The high-temperature cutoff and the thermostats are concealed behind an access panel on the side of the water heater.

If the high-temperature cutoff has tripped due to water that's too hot, the solution may be as easy as pushing the reset button in the access panel; however, because of the potential danger in working with high-voltage power, other repairs warrant a service call.

ROUTINE MAINTENANCE: To prevent sediment accumulation, every 6 months open the drain valve at the bottom, letting the water run into a bucket until it looks clear (you'll drain about 5 gallons); see the following instructions for draining a tank. Annually test the temperature-relief valve, which guards against hazardous pressure buildup, by lifting or depressing its handle; water should drain from the overflow pipe. If it doesn't, shut off water to the heater, open a hot water faucet somewhere in the house, and replace the valve.

CAUTION: If steam or boiling water comes out of the valve or the hot water faucets, shut the heater off at

WARNING   If you smell a slight odor of gas near a gas water heater, turn off the gas inlet valve and ventilate the area. If the odor is strong or if it persists, leave the house immediately and call the gas company.

once. And if you ever hear a rumbling sound, assume the heater is overheating and turn it off.

WATER TEMPERATURE: Water heaters are often set to heat water to 150° or 160°F. By lowering the setting to about 120°F, you can increase safety and save substantially on your fuel bills without affecting laundry or bathing. Dishwashers require higher temperatures to clean properly, but many models today are equipped with their own water-heating devices.

DRAINING AND FLUSHING A TANK: Turn off the gas or power, close the cold water valve, and attach a hose to the drain valve to route water into a drain or outdoors. Open the drain valve and open one hot water faucet to let in air. When all the water has drained, turn the cold water valve on and off until the water from the drain looks clear. Then, close the drain valve and the hot water faucet, open the cold water valve, and turn the power back on.

KEEPING THE HEAT IN

If you have an old water heater and wish to save energy, consider installing an insulating-foam or fiberglass heating jacket; kits are available.

To minimize heat loss from your hot water system, insulate hot water pipes—especially those that pass through unheated or drafty areas. Several types of pipe insulation are available; two of the most common are shown at right. Polyethylene foam jackets fit around most standard pipes and are fastened with tape. Another type of insulation is foil-backed, self-adhesive foam tape, which you spiral-wrap around the pipe.

To install polyethylene foam jackets, simply fit the jackets around the pipes (the jackets are pre-slit); cut to fit at T-junctions and elbows. Use duct tape to seal the joints.

Before you apply insulation tape, clean the pipe with a mild detergent solution. Wrap the tape snugly around the pipe at a 45° angle, overlapping as you go.

FIXING LEAKING PIPES

A higher-than-normal water bill might be the first indication that you have a leaking pipe. Or you might hear the sound of running water even when all the fixtures in your home are turned off.

If you suspect a leak, first check all the fixtures to make certain the faucets are tightly closed. Then, go to the water meter, if you have one. If the lowest-quantity dial on the meter is moving, it means you're losing water somewhere in the system. If you don't have a water meter, you can buy or borrow a mechanic's stethoscope, which will amplify any sound of running water when it's held up to a pipe.

LOCATING THE LEAK: If you hear water running, follow it to its source. If you don't hear it, look for stains. If water has stained the ceiling or is dripping down, the leak will probably be directly above. Occasionally, though, water may travel along a joist and then stain or drip at a point some distance from the actual leak. If

water stains a wall, it means that there's a leak in a vertical section of pipe. The stain is most likely below the actual leak; you'll probably need to remove an entire vertical section of the wall (see page 63) to find it.

If you don't hear running water or see any telltale drips or stains, the leak is likely to be under the house in the crawl space or the basement; use a flashlight to check the pipes there.

FIXING A LEAKING PIPE: If the leak is major, turn off the water immediately, either at the fixture shutoff valve or the main house shutoff (see page 152). You'll probably have to replace the leaky section of pipe (see the facing page).

If the leak is small, you may install a simple, temporary solution until you have time for the replacement job. Sleeve clamps (see photo at left) should stop most leaks for some months, or even years; it's a good idea always to have some on hand. Sleeve clamps are usually sold with a built-in gasket. A clamp that fits the pipe diameter exactly works best. Another quick fix, an adjustable hose clamp in size #12 or #16, will stop a pinhole leak on an average-size pipe. Be sure to use a piece of rubber, such as part of a bicycle inner tube or electrician's rubber tape, along with the clamp. In a pinch, you could use a household C-clamp, a small block of wood, and rubber or tape.

If you don't have a clamp, you can still stop a pinhole leak temporarily by plugging it with a pencil point—just put the point in the hole and break it off. Then, wrap several layers of pipe-wrap tape so it extends 3 inches on either side of the leak. Overlap each wrap of tape by half.

Epoxy putty will often stop leaks around joints where clamps won't, but it doesn't hold as long. The pipe must be clean and dry for the putty to adhere; turn off the water supply to the leak to let the area dry.

REPLACING A PIPE: The ultimate solution for any leak is to replace the pipe. The method you choose depends on whether your damaged pipe is copper, plastic, or galvanized steel. Be sure to brace the pipe run with your hand or with pipe hangers while you cut.

Epoxy putty

Hose clamps

Pipe-wrap tape

Sleeve clamp

If your leaky pipe is rigid copper tubing and the leak is small, you may be able simply to cut out the leaky spot, pull the pipes away from each other, slip on a repair coupling (shown at right), and solder it in place. If the damage is more extensive—or if you can't get enough slack for the coupling—you'll need to cut out the damaged section of pipe and add a new piece of pipe and two slip (no-shoulder) couplings, as shown on page 72.

If your pipe is rigid plastic and the leak is small, try cutting out the leaky spot and slipping on a repair union, as shown at center right. Otherwise, you'll need to cut out a section and patch in a new pipe, as discussed on page 75.

For galvanized steel pipes, you'll have to cut through the leaky pipe run, follow it back to the nearest fittings on both sides, and unscrew the pipe sections from each fitting (see page 73). You'll need to replace the entire run with two new pipe lengths and a galvanized union, as shown at right.

And what if your DWV system springs a leak? You'll find a selection of flexible repair fittings, like the elbow shown below, at plumbing supply stores and home centers. These fittings, available in common DWV sizes, are designed to clamp onto existing cast-iron, plastic, and galvanized drainpipes just like no-hub couplings (see page 59).

Flexible DWV elbow
Copper repair coupling
Galvanized union
Plastic repair union

REPLACING LEAKY PIPES

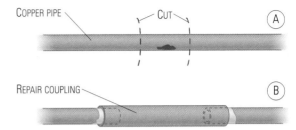

To replace a leaky copper pipe, first cut out a small section (A); then solder on a repair coupling (B).

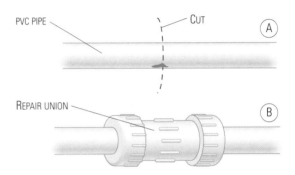

For a small leak in PVC plastic, saw through the center of the leak (A) and pull the pipes apart; then slip on a repair union (B) and tighten down its compression nuts.

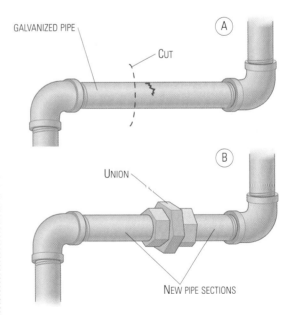

To fix a leaky galvanized pipe, you'll need to saw through the run (A) and remove the cut pieces back to the nearest fitting on each side. Then install two new pipe lengths and join them with a union (B).

How Do I Close Down My Plumbing For the Winter?

First, turn off the main house shutoff or have the water company turn off service to the house. Starting at the top floor, open all faucets, inside and out. When the last of the water has dripped from the taps, open the drain plug at the main house shutoff valve (you may have to contact the water company) and let it drain.

Turn off the electricity or gas to the water heater and open its drain valve.

Empty water from the traps under sinks, tubs, and showers by opening cleanout plugs or, if necessary, by removing, emptying, and reinstalling the traps (page 165). Empty toilet bowls and tanks, then pour a 50-50 solution of automotive antifreeze and water into each toilet bowl and fixture.

If your home has a basement floor drain and/or a main house trap (see page 173), fill each with full-strength automotive antifreeze.

FOUR WAYS TO WARM YOUR PIPES

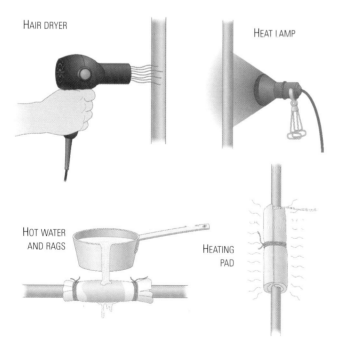

HAIR DRYER

HEAT LAMP

HOT WATER AND RAGS

HEATING PAD

THAWING FROZEN PIPES

A faucet that won't produce water is the first sign of frozen pipes. In a severe cold snap, prevent freezing and subsequent bursting of pipes by following the suggestions below. In the event pipes do freeze, you can thaw them before they burst if you act quickly.

TO PREVENT PIPES FROM FREEZING: Keep a trickle of water running from faucets throughout the house. Aim a small lamp or heater at exposed pipes. Wrap uninsulated pipes with foam insulation (see page 183) and install heat tapes according to the manufacturer's instructions. (Insulation helps heat tapes operate more efficiently; by itself, though, insulation won't prevent pipes from freezing.) The best heat tapes have built-in thermostats that turn off

Heat tape

when the outdoor temperature rises above freezing; this type should be used with plastic pipes. Finally, leave doors ajar between heated and unheated rooms to distribute heat evenly.

WARMING FROZEN PIPES: If a pipe freezes, first shut off the main water supply (page 152) and open the faucet nearest the frozen pipe. Cover the area with waterproof drop cloths, then use one of the following methods to warm the frozen pipe, working from the faucet back toward the iced-up area. When using an electrical device to thaw a pipe, make sure it is plugged into a GFCI receptacle or GFCI-protected extension cord to avoid the possibility of shock. Wear rubber gloves as backup protection, and avoid contact with water.

Use a hair dryer (shown at left) turned on low to defrost a pipe. A heating pad is a more gradual but effective method. For freezes that are concealed behind walls, floors, or ceilings, beam a heat lamp 8 inches or more from the wall surface. (Be careful not to let water splash onto the hot glass or the glass may shatter.) If no other method is available, wrap the pipe in rags and pour boiling water on it; this method has the advantage of not involving electricity.

NOISY PIPES

Pipe noises run up and down a nonmusical scale, ranging from loud banging to high-pitched squeaking, irritating chatter, and resonant hammering. Listen carefully to your pipes; the noise, plus the information below, will tell you what measures to take to quiet the plumbing.

See page 70 for information on getting at pipes hidden in walls and ceilings.

STOPPING WATER HAMMER: The most common pipe noise—water hammer—occurs when you quickly turn off the water at a faucet or an appliance. The water flowing through the pipes slams to a stop, causing and a hammering noise.

Many water systems have short sections of straight or coiled pipe rising above each faucet or appliance called air chambers (or water-hammer arresters), which act as shock absorbers. When a valve is closed abruptly, the moving water rises in one of these air-filled pipes instead of banging to a stop. Over time, however, air chambers have a tendency to get completely filled with water and lose their effectiveness as cushions. To restore air chambers, take these steps: Check the toilet tank to make sure it is full, then close off the supply shutoff valve just below the tank. Close the main house shutoff. Open the highest and lowest faucets in the house to drain all water. Then, close the two faucets and reopen the main house shutoff and the shut-

AIR CHAMBER

off valve below the toilet tank. Normal water flow will re-establish itself for each faucet when you turn it on. (You can expect a few grumbles from the pipes before the first water arrives.)

ELIMINATING BANGING, SQUEAKING, OR FAUCET CHATTER: If you hear a banging noise whenever you turn on the water and it's not a water hammer problem, check the way the pipes are anchored. You may find that a vibration-causing section of pipe is inadequately supported. See page 77 for pipe-hanging guidelines. If the noise continues, slit a piece of old hose or cut a patch of rubber and insert it in the hanger or strap as a cushion. For masonry walls, attach a block of wood to the wall with masonry fasteners, then anchor the pipe to it with a pipe hanger. Be careful not to anchor a pipe—especially a plastic one—too securely; leave room for expansion with temperature changes.

Pipes that squeak are always hot water pipes. As the pipe expands, it moves in the support, and friction causes the squeak. To silence it, insert a piece of rubber between the pipe and supports, as you would to eliminate banging.

Faucet chatter is the noise you hear when you partially open a compression faucet. To correct the problem, tighten or replace the seat washer on the bottom of the faucet stem (page 155).

THREE WAYS TO STOP BANGING PIPES

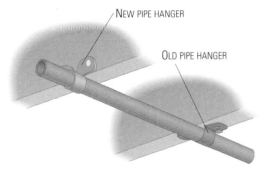

Nail additional pipe supports to joists to stop horizontal pipes from banging.

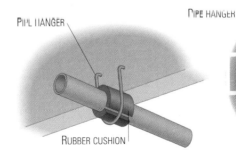

Wrap a rubber blanket or hose around a noisy pipe to cushion it in its strap.

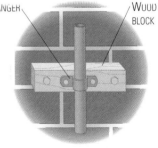

Fasten a wood block to a masonry wall; strap on the pipe.

FIXING FAULTY SPRINKLERS

Sprinklers may clog, jam, leak, or spray improperly in the course of normal operation. They can also be damaged by a lawn mower or car. Faulty sprinklers can not only harm plants, but they can also waste huge amounts of water. That's why it's important to inspect them at least once a month during the watering season.

Fixing or replacing broken or damaged parts is usually easy: few special tools are required, and replacement parts are readily available at home centers and stores that specialize in irrigation equipment. Because many different manufacturers make sprinklers, take the part with you so you can get a correct replacement. For instructions on fixing leaking pipes, see page 185.

INSPECTING AND ADJUSTING SPRINKLERS: Because water pressure varies during the day, it's important to inspect your system at the time it's normally in use, even if you have to get up early to do it. Turn each circuit on in sequence and look at the sprinkler heads.

First, note whether the spray from any head is blocked. If this is the case with lawn sprinkler heads, keep the grass clipped low around the heads and dethatch—over time, a lawn may gain several inches of height from built-up thatch. In new shrub and ground cover plantings, sprinklers often are installed too low to spray over the plants once they mature. Solve that problem by replacing each riser with a longer one or adding a coupling and a new riser extension (see below).

THREE SPRINKLER REPAIRS

T-FITTING   BROKEN RISER

To replace a broken riser, carefully dig down to the T-fitting or elbow. Clear soil from around the fitting, then unscrew the riser and thread on a replacement.

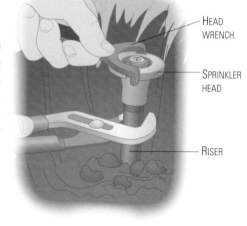

To remove a damaged brass lawn head, dig down until you can access the riser and hold it with slip-joint pliers; use a head wrench or a second pair of pliers to turn the head.

HEAD WRENCH

SPRINKLER HEAD

RISER

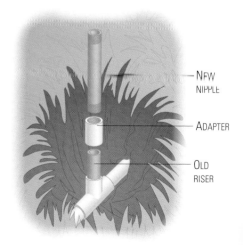

If a broken riser was cemented to the T fitting or elbow, cut the riser off cleanly, then add a threaded adapter and a new nipple above it. This trick also helps you raise a sprinkler head that's too low.

NEW NIPPLE

ADAPTER

OLD RISER

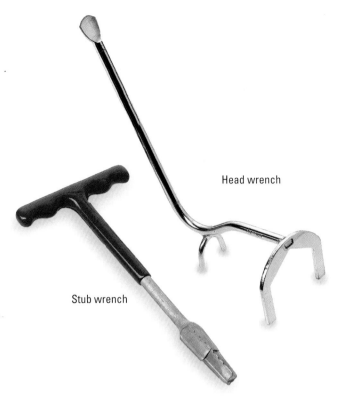

Head wrench

Stub wrench

Scrutinize any part-circle sprinklers, especially those along the perimeter of the lawn and planting beds. If any one is spraying off center, gently turn the head or nozzle, or adjust the rotor's arc—following the manufacturer's directions—until it covers the desired area.

UNCLOGGING SPRINKLER HEADS: Several times during the season, check heads for uneven spray patterns while the system is on. Clean the slits or holes of any affected spray head with a knife or a piece of thin, stiff wire. If that doesn't work, remove the entire head (see below) and clear it of debris.

With pop-up brass heads, debris may collect around the wiper seal on the stem, preventing the head from sealing; water will then squirt or bubble out from the base, and the spray will be weak. Clean around the seal.

REPAIRING DAMAGED HEADS: To replace a broken head, you'll need to unscrew it and replace it with another of the same kind. Most heads are easily removed by hand or with a wrench by just unscrewing the head counterclockwise. To remove brass lawn heads, which sit flush with the ground, you may need a head wrench. Purchase one that's the same brand as your sprinklers or buy an adjustable universal head wrench. Old brass heads are sometimes difficult to remove; for extra lever-

age, slip a length of pipe over the handle of the head wrench to make a longer fulcrum.

When you unscrew the head, try not to remove the threaded nipple riser that sits underground between the head and the supply line. If you feel the riser turning as you unscrew the head, remove enough soil so you can hold the riser with pliers or a pipe wrench. If the head has rusted onto the riser and you can't separate them, you'll have to replace both parts.

FIXING BROKEN RISERS: If a threaded riser is difficult to extract, carefully dig down to the threaded T or elbow into which it's screwed, clearing away the surrounding soil. Unscrew the broken riser from the line. Wrap the threads of a replacement riser with pipe-thread tape and screw it in place. If solvent cement was used to install the riser, cut the riser pipe off cleanly and attach a new one, using an adapter fitting (see the facing page).

Sometimes, a plastic riser will break off inside the T or elbow in the water pipe, leaving a piece that's difficult to remove. Use a stub wrench to remove the riser piece, or try to unscrew the piece with an old chisel, wedging it against one edge of the piece and twisting in a counterclockwise direction. Be careful not to damage the threads of the T or elbow. Then, attach a new riser.

If you suspect that some dirt may have fallen into the pipe while you were working, remove all the heads on the circuit and flush the system until the water runs clear.

Winterizing Your Watering System

If you live in a cold-winter climate, you must drain your irrigation system prior to the first freeze, before water freezing and expanding in pipes causes the pipes to burst. First, close the system's shutoff valve. Opening the drain valves at the low points in the system will extract most of the water in the pipes. The best way to remove any remaining water from the system is to blow compressed air through it—this is usually a job for a professional.

In milder regions where occasional freezes occur, wrap any aboveground pipes or valves that will contain water in winter.

GLOSSARY

ABS: Acrylonitrile-butadiene-styrene; rigid plastic drainpipe.

ADAPTER: Connects one type of pipe to another.

ANTISIPHON VALVE: Device installed on a supply line to prevent siphoning of contaminated water back into potable water supply system.

BACK VENTING: Vent looping up from a fixture and connecting to main soil stack or a secondary vent at a higher level.

BRANCH: Horizontal run of supply pipe that distributes hot and cold water to risers, which in turn feed individual fixtures and appliances.

BRANCH DRAIN: Horizontal pipe that carries waste from a fixture or fixture group to the vertical soil stack.

CAP: Fitting with a solid end used for closing off a pipe.

CENTER-TO-CENTER: In mounting faucets: Distance between centers of holes on a sink deck. In pipefitting: Distance between centers of two consecutive pipes.

CLEANOUT: Opening providing access to a drain line or trap; closed with a threaded cleanout plug.

CODE: Legal requirements for a plumbing installation.

COMPRESSION FITTING: Easy-to-use fitting for copper or plastic tube. Pushed in and hand-tightened.

COUPLING: Fitting used to connect two lengths of pipe in a straight run. Also a ring or nut that secures a trap to a tailpiece or drainpipe, or that holds a supply tube to a faucet or toilet inlet valve.

CPVC: Chlorinated polyvinyl chloride; rigid plastic pipe for hot and cold water.

CRITICAL DISTANCE: Maximum horizontal distance allowed between a fixture trap and a vent or soil stack.

CROSS CONNECTION: Plumbing connection that could mix contaminated water with potable water supply.

DWV: Drain-waste and vent; system that carries away waste water and solid waste, allows sewer gases to escape, and maintains atmospheric pressure in drainpipes.

ELBOW: Fitting used for making turns in pipe runs (for example, a 90° elbow makes a right-angle turn). Also called an ell fitting.

EMITTER: Water distribution device used in drip irrigation.

ESCUTCHEON: Decorative trim piece that fits over a faucet body or pipe extending from a wall.

FEMALE: Pipes, valves, or fittings with internal threads.

FITTING: Device used to join pipes.

FIXTURE: A non-powered water-using device such as a sink, bathtub, shower, or toilet.

FIXTURE UNIT: Equal to 7½ gallons or 1 cubic foot of waste water per minute. Used to rate fixture loads when sizing supply and DWV systems.

FLANGE: Flat fitting or integral edging with holes to permit bolting together (a toilet bowl is bolted to a floor flange) or fastening to another surface (a tub is fastened to wall through an integral flange).

FLARE FITTING: Threaded fitting used on copper and plastic pipe that requires enlarging one end of the pipe.

FLEXIBLE SUPPLY TUBE: Bendable piece of tubing that delivers water from a shutoff valve to a fixture or appliance.

FLUE: Large pipe through which fumes escape from a gas water heater.

GASKET: Device (usually rubber) used to make a joint between two parts watertight. Term is sometimes used interchangeably with washer.

GRAY WATER: Household waste water from showers, bathtubs, sinks, and washing machines; sometimes used to water landscaping.

HOSE BIBB: Valve with an external threaded outlet for accepting a hose fitting.

HOUSE TRAP: U-shaped fitting in some older homes that has two adjacent cleanout plugs; visible at floor level if main drain runs under floor.

JOIST: A horizontal wood framing member placed on edge, as a floor or ceiling joist.

LOCKNUT: Nut used to secure a part, such as a toilet water inlet valve, in place.

MAIN CLEANOUT: Fitting in shape of letter T near bottom of soil stack or where drain leaves house.

MAIN SUPPLY PIPE: Cold water pipe that brings water into the house from the water meter; runs to the water heater, where it divides into hot and cold branches.

MALE: Pipes, valves, or fittings with external threads.

NIPPLE: Short piece of pipe with male threads used to join two fittings.

NO-HUB: Modern cast-iron pipe joined with neoprene gaskets and stainless-steel clamps.

O-RING: Narrow rubber ring; used in some faucets as packing to prevent leaking around stem and in swivel-spout faucets to prevent leaking at base of spout.

PACKING: Material that stops leaking around the stem of a faucet or valve.

PB: Polybutylene; flexible plastic tubing for hot or cold water supply lines.

PE: Polyethylene; flexible plastic tubing for cold water supply outdoors.

PIPE-JOINT COMPOUND: Sealing compound used on threaded fittings (applied to external threads).

PIPE-THREAD TAPE: Special tape used as a joint sealer in place of pipe joint compound.

PLUG: Externally-threaded fitting for closing off a fitting that has internal threads.

PP: Polypropylene; rigid plastic pipe used for traps.

PRESSURE-REDUCING VALVE: Device installed in a water supply line to reduce water pressure.

PVC: Polyvinyl chloride; off-white, rigid plastic pipe for cold water outdoors. Larger sizes are used in some areas for DWV systems.

REDUCER: Fitting that connects pipe of one diameter with pipe of a smaller diameter.

RISER: Vertical run of supply pipe.

RUN: Horizontal or vertical series of pipes.

SADDLE TEE: T-fitting that is fastened onto side of pipe, eliminating cutting and threading or soldering; usually requires drilling into pipe.

SANITARY FITTING: A fitting with smooth bends and no inside shoulders to block flow of waste; used to join DWV pipe.

SECONDARY VENTING: Venting fixtures distant from main stack to roof through a second vent.

SHOULDER: The ridge or stop inside a fitting's outlet that controls the depth to which a pipe can be inserted.

SHUTOFF VALVE: A valve that controls water flow through supply pipes. A fixture shutoff stops water to an adjacent fixture; the main house shutoff controls the entire system.

SILICONE GREASE: A type of synthetic grease used to lubricate faucet parts; non-petroleum base won't break down rubber washers and other components.

SIPHONING: Action occurring when atmospheric pressure forces water into a vacuum in a pipe.

SLIP COUPLING: Used to join a new fitting into a run of copper or plastic tubing. Unthreaded, and without a center shoulder so it can slide along a tube. Also called a repair coupling.

SOIL STACK: Large DWV pipe that connects toilet and other drains to house drain and also extends up and out roof; upper portion serves as a vent.

SOLVENT CEMENT: Compound used to join rigid plastic pipes and fittings.

SPACER: Short piece of unthreaded plastic or copper pipe cut to size; used when repairing or extending pipe. Sometimes referred to as a nipple.

STANDPIPE: Special drainpipe for a washing machine.

STREET FITTING: A fitting that has one male and one female end. The male end slips directly into the shoulder of an adjacent fitting.

STUBOUT: End of a supply pipe or drainpipe that extends from a wall or floor.

STUD: A vertical wood framing member; also referred to as a wall stud. Attached to sole plate below and top plate above.

SUPPLY SYSTEM: Network of hot water and cold water pipes throughout the house. Runs from meter to water heater and on to individual fixtures and appliances.

SWEAT SOLDERING: A method of using heat to join copper tube and fittings.

T-FITTING: Or tee. T-shaped fitting with three openings.

TRANSITION FITTING: Adapter fitting that joins pipes of plastic and metal.

TRAP: Device (most often a curved section of pipe) that holds a water seal to prevent sewer gases from escaping into a home through a fixture drain.

UNION: Fitting that joins two lengths of pipe permitting assembly and disassembly without taking the entire section apart.

VALVE: Device that controls the flow of water.

WASHER: A flat thin ring of metal or rubber used to ensure a tight fit and prevent friction in joints and assemblies. Term is sometimes used interchangeably with gasket.

WASTE ARM: Elongated elbow fitting that connects a fixture's trap to the drainpipe.

WATER HAMMER: Sound of pipes shuddering and banging. Water-hammer arresters (also called air chambers) are designed to stop water hammer.

WET VENTING: Venting arrangement in which a fixture's drainpipe, tied directly to soil stack, vents fixture also.

Y-FITTING: Or wye; DWV fitting with three outlets in shape of letter Y.

INDEX